Finding Full Assurance of Faith

The New Covenant in Three Dimensions

R.W. ALDERSON

Copyright © 2023 R.W. Alderson.

All rights reserved. No part of this book may be reproduced, stored, or transmitted by any means—whether auditory, graphic, mechanical, or electronic—without written permission of both publisher and author, except in the case of brief excerpts used in critical articles and reviews. Unauthorized reproduction of any part of this work is illegal and is punishable by law.

New American Standard Bible®, Copyright © 1960, 1971, 1977, 1995, 2020 by The Lockman Foundation. All rights reserved.

ISBN: 979-8-89031-752-0 (sc)
ISBN: 979-8-89031-753-7 (hc)
ISBN: 979-8-89031-754-4 (e)

Because of the dynamic nature of the Internet, any web addresses or links contained in this book may have changed since publication and may no longer be valid. The views expressed in this work are solely those of the author and do not necessarily reflect the views of the publisher, and the publisher hereby disclaims any responsibility for them.

One Galleria Blvd., Suite 1900, Metairie, LA 70001
(504) 702-6708

To my readers,

I want to thank you for acquiring my book, "Finding Full Assurance of Faith." This effort has been a fifteen-year pregnancy as God has been revealing truths progressively about the new covenant without a clear picture of when the "delivery" would take place. These insights have come through a number of varied sources, including a Michael Card song and an amazing resource written by Alfred Edersheim, a nineteenth century scholar. This endeavor has created in me a deeper appreciation of the New Testament relationship with God, a spiritual relationship. And since it has been such a blessing for me, I am convinced many others will also benefit from these perspectives.

I was particularly encouraged by the commentary I received from the Editorial Assessment Department at AuthorHouse after its work was completed:

> "*Finding Full Assurance of Faith* is an insightful, biblically wise book that shares important material and context regarding God's new covenant to believers. It will help readers grow on their Christian journey. Thank you for bringing your work to AuthorHouse."

It would be a great blessing to further the expansion of these truths if you would consider leaving a review at amazon.com after reading at least a portion by signing into your account, click "Returns & Orders," locate the book, then click "Write a product review," and finally select an overall rating. Your efforts will help others looking at purchasing the book to gain a measure of comfort that the book addresses the subject thoughtfully and accurately.

If you wish, contact me at pastorbill@rwalderson.com or rwalderson.com. You will find my blogs posted as well as links to my weekly podcasts.

Many blessings,

R. W. (Pastor Bill) Alderson

Contents

Introduction		1
Chapter 1	Fully Assured	7
Chapter 2	The New Covenant	11
Chapter 3	The Church in Crisis	17

Revelations from the Gospel of John

Chapter 4	The Spiritual Gospel of John	25
Chapter 5	A Ministry of Excellence	31
Chapter 6	Born From Above	35
Chapter 7	A Covenant of Grace & Mercy	41
Chapter 8	Life in the Holy Spirit	48
Chapter 9	The Deity and Humanity of Jesus	54
Chapter 10	Believing in the Promises	60
Chapter 11	Hearing the Voice of God	66
Chapter 12	The Voice of Truth	71
Chapter 13	Sin and Blindness	74
Chapter 14	Forgiven-ness	81
Chapter 15	The Role of Confession	85
Chapter 16	The Way	91
Chapter 17	Resurrection Life	97
Chapter 18	Becoming A Follower	103
Chapter 19	Jesus Feeds His Church	109
Chapter 20	Being Taught by God	114
Chapter 21	The Temple	120
Chapter 22	Fruitful	126
Chapter 23	Devotion and Prayer	131

Chapter 24	Discipline of the Lord	137
Chapter 25	Life in the Body of Christ	143
Chapter 26	Spiritual Warfare	147
Chapter 27	The Kingdom of Heaven	153
Chapter 28	The Work is Finished	159
Chapter 29	Recognizing the Risen Lord	164
Chapter 30	Loving the Risen Lord	173

TRANSITION FROM OLD TO NEW

Chapter 31	Why the Law of Moses?	179
Chapter 32	From Law to Grace	185
Chapter 33	From Pentecost to Pentecost	188
Chapter 34	Blessings of the New Covenant	193
Chapter 35	The Law Fulfilled	197
Chapter 36	The Transformation of Saul to Paul	201
Chapter 37	Two Goats	205

CONCLUSION – FULLNESS OF FAITH

Chapter 38	Between His First & Second Comings	209
Chapter 39	Upper Room	215
Chapter 40	Learning How to Follow	220
Chapter 41	Lord of All	223
Chapter 42	The Blessings of Abraham	228
Chapter 43	The Eighth Day	233
Chapter 44	The Mantle of the Lord	237
Chapter 45	From Religious to Spiritual	240
Chapter 46	The Heart of the Matter	244

INTRODUCTION

Is the Bible truly the words of God? Does Scripture speak on a level deeper than just reporting historical facts or an individual's personal lamentations or a program for righteousness? Why are so many Christians struggling in their relationship with God, so that life is no longer simply mundane, but exhilarating? And is the church teaching what believers need to know to find real intimacy with God, to draw closer to him and be less distracted by the things of this world?

Ian Anderson of the rock band Jethro Tull wrote the following words in his song, "Skating Away (On the Thin Ice of the New Day)":

Cause you were bred for humanity and sold to society
One day you'll wake up in the present day
A million generations removed from expectations
Of being who you really want to be
Skating away, skating away, skating away,
On the thin ice of the new day.

The song suggests forces are controlling our lives, keeping us subject to those forces. "Bred for humanity" is a reference to our genetics, our physical and mental nature, while "sold to society" speaks to our environment and surroundings. The Bible tells us that part of our genetics is the sin nature that each one inherits as a descendant of Adam, the first man (Romans 5:12-14), while these powers that control the environment are the cosmos, not just the physical world we live in, but the organized system controlled by the god of this world (Satan, the devil). According to 2 Corinthians 4:4, he *has blinded the minds of the unbelieving so that they might not see the light of the gospel of the glory of Christ, who is the image of God.* The devil is the head of a hierarchy that represents principalities and powers, rulers of darkness, and spiritual forces of wickedness (Ephesians 6:12). The devil and his hierarchy hold major influence over human matters. These organized forces keep mankind from finding meaning and purpose in life and disrupt his relationship with God.

Our Wake-up Call

Reading and understanding the truths from God's Word is our wake-up call. Scripture defines these spiritual forces and the victories that the Lord provides so that a believer can become the unique person God intended him to be in authentic relationship with his Lord. What Jesus Christ accomplished on behalf of all humanity was to institute a new relationship with the Father through the Son (John 14:6) and to restore man to his intended position before the fall of Adam and Eve. The Bible defines this relationship with God in Christ as the new covenant, or a new promise made by God. It was first introduced through Jeremiah and brought to fruition in the completed work of Christ (John 19:30), intended for all and available to all who believe, who seek and find that relationship in response to God's Word and in acceptance of God's perfect love.

There are very few direct references to this new covenant in Scripture, but understanding its meaning and ability is a critical part of the deliverance the believer can access and experience in his relationship with Jesus Christ. This understanding helps him to comprehend and walk in the spiritual environment that makes his relationship with God more than a religious effort to honor a bunch of dos and dont's. This covenant relationship presents an opportunity to experience God on a three-dimensional level, in all its fullness.

As Christians, we are called to respond to this wake-up call by considering the Lord's desire to meet with us, to relate with us, to walk with us. Look back to one of the earliest examples of God's desire to meet with His people: the construction of the tabernacle in Exodus 25 and 26.

"THERE I WILL MEET WITH YOU"

The tabernacle as instructed by the Lord to Moses consists of three areas, the outer court (porch), the Holy Place, and the Holy of Holies. The outer court surrounded the other two areas and was available to all while the priests performed their religious duties in the Holy Place. The Holy of Holies contained the ark of the covenant, representing the presence of God. A curtain of badger skin called the veil separated the Holy of Holies from the Holy Place. Only the High Priest had access to the Holy of Holies and that only once a year, the Day of Atonement, to offer sacrifices for the sins of ignorance. On the top of the ark was the mercy seat made of gold and two cherubim facing each other. It was there that God told Moses, "***There I will meet with you***; *and from above the mercy seat, from between the two cherubim which are upon the ark of the testimony, I will speak to you about all that I will give you in commandment for the sons of Israel*" (Exodus 25:22).

In Exodus 26:31 (also Exodus 36:35 and 2 Chronicles 3:14), God instructed the craftsmen to embroider an image of the cherubim on the veil, to be visible to the priests in the Holy Place. It is a picture of the two-dimensional (religious) relationship that believers can have with God through the old covenant; the priests could only view the image of the cherubim. The Torah (the Law of Moses) and the tabernacle/temple represent these two dimensions. The Torah describes the standards by which a believer would live, and the completion of these standards would take place in the tabernacle/temple.

The role of the Son of Man was not evident in Old Testament Scripture, but a *mystery which has been hidden from the past ages and generations, but has now been manifested to His saints, to whom God willed to make known what is the riches of the glory of this mystery among the Gentiles, which is Christ in you, the hope of glory* (Colossians 1:26-27). The new covenant introduces a three-dimensional relationship with God, "in Christ," which is now available to us every day.

Jesus is our Mercy Seat

The moment Jesus died, Matthew 27:51 tells us that the veil was torn from top to bottom, signifying that the new covenant believer has access to the Holy of Holies and the presence of God. It means that through one's recognition of Jesus as Messiah, God in the flesh, he enters into a new covenant relationship, a three-dimensional relationship at the mercy seat, Jesus Christ being our advocate and mercy seat (1 John 2:1-2), *And if anyone sins, we have an Advocate with the Father, Jesus Christ the righteous; and* **He Himself is the propitiation** [mercy seat] ***for our sins**; and not for ours only, but also for those of the whole world.*

The following chapters provide texture to that new relationship with God, in His new covenant with us and all who believe. The Gospel of John was written many years after the other three gospels and contains many insights into that relationship, a spiritual connection to the Father through the Son and the Holy Spirit. Many of these writings come from a deeper examination of John's Gospel. Scripture has so much more to tell than what appears on the surface, two-dimensionally. When the Holy Spirit takes the believer into the depths of who God really is, he finds the richness of the new relationship in living color. It is the fullness of a relationship with the Father, the Son, and the Holy Spirit: three dimensions of genuine relationship which transcends the two-dimensional realities of religion found in the Torah and the tabernacle/temple.

Why?

I chose the picture of a hot balloon flying in a bright sky and over a textured landscape to be the background of the cover to signify that the new covenant can provide an amazing view from above and will bring the believer to new heights in his relationship with God. In John 3:8, Jesus spoke about the new life in the Holy Spirit in this way: *"The wind blows where it wishes and you hear the sound of it, but do not know where it comes from and where it is going; so is everyone who is born of the Spirit."* Putting one's trust in the vessel of the person and work of Jesus allows the wind of the Holy Spirit to take him to places unimaginable and to a new and living way.

The chapters are grouped into four separate sections: "Background," "Revelations from the Gospel of John," "Transition from Old to New," and "Conclusion - Fullness of Faith." "Background" begins with a discussion of what being fully assured in faith means and how it is intended for every new covenant believer. There is also a Biblical analysis of the basis for the new covenant and then a sobering review of the church and some of its failures in creating a spiritual environment in which believers can grow.

"Revelations from the Gospel of John" is the primary focus of this work since it was through John's Gospel that God revealed unique insights to me regarding the nature and ability of the new covenant, particularly in comparison to the old covenant. It begins with a discussion of the character and nature of the Gospel, itself, and then revelations from each of John's twenty-one chapters that provide definition and depth to this new relationship with God manifested through Jesus's public ministry. Is it any coincidence that there are twenty-seven chapters in this section and twenty-seven chapters in the New Testament?

When considering the question, "why the law of Moses," there has to be some eternal value to the Lord's plan to institute the Law of Moses as a solution to a problem that would not be fully resolved until the Messiah would be revealed. "Transition from Old to New" addresses particulars of the environment that created a receptivity to a new spiritual relationship with God. "Conclusion – Fullness of Faith" describes many of the critical conditions created by the new covenant to bring the believer into the deepest connection to his God, eternal life, and true fulfillment.

Except where noted, all scriptural references are from
the New American Standard Bible (NASB).

Chapter 1

FULLY ASSURED

For this reason it is by faith, in order that it may be in accordance with grace, so that the promise will be guaranteed to all the descendants, not only to those who are of the Law, but also to those who are of the faith of Abraham, who is the father of us all, (as it is written, "A FATHER OF MANY NATIONS HAVE I MADE YOU") in the presence of Him whom he believed, even God, who gives life to the dead and calls into being that which does not exist. In hope against hope he believed, so that he might become a father of many nations according to that which had been spoken, "SO SHALL YOUR DESCENDANTS BE." Without becoming weak in faith, he contemplated his own body, now as good as dead since he was about a hundred years old, and the deadness of Sarah's womb; yet, with respect to the promise of God, he did not waver in unbelief but grew strong in faith, giving glory to God, and being fully assured that what God had promised, He was able also to perform. Therefore, IT WAS ALSO CREDITED TO HIM AS RIGHTEOUSNESS. **Romans 4:16-22**

It is no surprise that Abraham is the father of the faith and therefore, father of us all as believers in Christ (Verse 16). Abraham showed amazing faith in God when he obeyed the command to, *"Go forth from your country, and from your relatives and from your father's house, to the land which I will show you"* (Genesis 12:1). His entire religious experience until that time had been the worship of pagan gods. Despite his willingness to step out in faith, it took many trials and tests of faith to bring him to the place where he would be fully assured that God could fulfill His promises. Paul quotes from Genesis 15:6 when he speaks about righteousness as coming to one by faith. At salvation, God credits (imputes) righteousness to the believer through his faith in the one who saves while to properly experience this (imparted) righteousness in the details of life, he learns to trust God in extreme situations and to believe the most incredible promises (see also Romans 1:17). In these times, we too can discover God Almighty in new and real ways.

El Shaddai

Paul begins this passage by saying that it must start with faith so that it can *"be in accordance with grace"* and makes the promises *"guaranteed to all descendants."* People with this kind of faith can believe in something that does not yet exist! This believer recognizes his total dependence on God doing it to fulfill His promises. In Verse 20, Paul says Abraham did not waver in unbelief (concerning God's promises) but grew strong in his faith in what God had promised. It was always about His promises. In Genesis 17:1-8, God Almighty (El Shaddai) spoke to Abram as a ninety-nine-year-old and told him to *"walk before Me and be blameless."* Abram's response was to fall on his face, and this was when God told Abram that His covenant was with Abram, and He was now changing Abram's name to Abraham. God was telling Abraham things he could not believe unless El Shaddai would do it. Faith places its complete confidence in the One who would fulfill it.

Since the new covenant is with every believer individually, it assures each one with that same confidence that Abraham possessed, once the believer follows in faith. Future generations will also enjoy full assurance as Hebrews 11:13-16 tells us:

All these died in faith, without receiving the promises, but having seen them and having welcomed them from a distance and having confessed that they were strangers and exiles on the earth. For those who say such things make it clear that they are seeking a country of their own. And indeed, if they had been thinking of that country from which they went out, they would have had opportunity to return. But as it is, they desire a better country, that is, a heavenly one. Therefore, God is not ashamed to be called their God; for He has prepared a city for them.

Real faith happens when each believer recognizes he is a stranger and an exile on the earth, not attaching himself to the material world, and seeks to rise above it. While the world changes, often so very quickly, God remains reliable and unchangeable.

God's Unchangeableness

In the same way God, desiring even more to show to the heirs of the promise the unchangeableness of His purpose, interposed with an oath, so that by two unchangeable things in which it is impossible for God to lie, we who have taken refuge would have strong encouragement to take hold of the hope set before us. This hope we have as an anchor of the soul, a hope both sure and steadfast and one which enters within the veil where Jesus has entered as a forerunner for us. **Hebrews 6:17-20**

The foundation for full assurance and complete confidence in God is His integrity (He cannot lie) and His purpose represented by His promises. These become an anchor for the soul, so we are more than willing to change our desired course for His unchangeable purpose that always leads us in triumph in Christ (2 Corinthians 2:14). Consider the following:

The Lighthouse

I once heard a story about a battleship at sea. The ship had come under severe weather, and the captain got a report that there was light up ahead. "Is it steady or moving?" the captain called out. The lookout replied, "Steady, Captain." This meant that the ship was on a collision course. The captain sent out a message to the vessel up ahead warning, "We are on a collision course; advise you change course twenty degrees." But the reply that came back said, "Advisable for you to change course twenty degrees." The captain was furious and retorted, "I'm a battleship! You change course twenty degrees." The reply flashed back, "I'm a lighthouse."

The unchangeableness of God is our lighthouse and our hope, and it brings the believer *"within the veil"* where he finds the presence of God and where Jesus, like Abraham, has become our forerunner in the faith. This kind of hope or confident expectation is the source for our salvation, as in Romans 8:24-25, *For in hope, we have been saved, but hope that is seen is not hope; for who hopes for what he already sees? But if we hope for what we do not see, with perseverance we wait eagerly for it.*

Like the lighthouse seen from a distance, we wait eagerly for the fulfillment of the promises of God and for the ultimate conclusion of all things. Within the veil of the new covenant, there is great security.

Chapter 2

THE NEW COVENANT

The God of the Bible is a covenant God and has established multiple covenants (legal agreements) with various men on behalf of God's people, including Noah, Abraham, Israel (through Moses), and David. These covenants with Noah, Abraham and David were unconditional, meaning that God promised to do something without man meeting conditions. The old covenant, God's covenant with Moses at Mount Sinai, was different since it required man to fulfill his part for God to complete His. Then in Jeremiah 31, God revealed the new covenant, another unconditional covenant with Israel and the church also benefits from this covenant in Hebrews 8:10-12.

> *But this is what I commanded them, saying, "Obey My voice, and I will be your God, and you will be My people; and you will walk in all the way which I command you, that it may be well with you." Yet they did not obey or incline their ear but walked in their own counsels and in the stubbornness of their evil heart and went backward and not forward. Since the day that your fathers came out of the land of Egypt until this day, I have sent you all My servants the prophets, daily rising early and sending them. Yet they did not listen to Me or incline their ear but stiffened their neck; they did more evil than their fathers."* **Jeremiah 7:23-26**

Throughout Old Testament times, it became clear that the conditional covenant God gave to Moses on Mount Sinai was not producing a faithful people, their unfaithfulness leading to the Northern and Southern Kingdoms being taken captive by heathen enemies. According to Jeremiah 7:23-26, the Lord commanded the Jews to obey, and He would be their God, but they became stubborn in their hearts and refused to listen to God. Because the old covenant is a conditional covenant and therefore depends on man to fulfill his end of the agreement, it does not bring the believer into full fellowship with God. Can man be relied upon to be completely consistent in any human endeavor? Is man reliable like an unchanging God? According to the Apostle Paul, in Romans 7, we can conclude that the answer is "no". The things that Paul did not wish to do, he did and the things he wished to do he did not. *Oh, wretched man that I am* (Romans 7:24); there must be a provision for his failure whenever man has a choice. Though the Hebrews saw the miracles of God on their behalf throughout Old Testament history, it was their evil hearts (Jeremiah 17:9) that caused them to rely on the counsel of man rather than their God. In this way, man proved his own unfaithfulness and failure, as God had expected all along (Galatians 3:23-24). Man's failure to keep his side of the bargain in the conditional old covenant had become the necessary experience that led him to Christ.

Man's Heart is the Real Problem

Circumcise yourselves to the Lord and remove the foreskins of your heart, men of Judah and inhabitants of Jerusalem, or else My wrath will go forth like fire and burn with none to quench it, because of the evil of your deeds. **Jeremiah 4:4**

The real difficulty with the old covenant is related to man's heart. Man's heart requires a circumcision, if you will, but man could avoid it since Jewish leaders administered the covenant externally. When the administration of the law is from without, man's nature is to look for the minimum requirements and shortcuts so he can get by without the heart getting involved, thus preserving his own life. He can get by on natural ability, concealing the failures, and just going through the motions.

The only way this covenant works is if man chooses to surrender to its authority and be subject to its consequences. Yet we see only a small number, the remnant referred to in Romans 11:4 (quoting from 1 Kings 19:18) as, *"I have kept for Myself seven thousand men who have not bowed the knee to Baal"*. Scripture says in Zephaniah 3:12-13 regarding the remnant, *"...a humble and lowly people,"* who *"... will take refuge in the name of the Lord"*, and *"... will do no wrong and tell no lies, nor will a deceitful tongue be found in their mouths."* This covenant requires going beyond natural ability and goodness; it requires the power of God to fulfill. And that is possible only with one who will be humble and lowly and *take refuge in the name of the Lord* and that willingness to approach God can only happen when one is willing to surrender self into obedience to Christ!

I Will Remember Their Sins No More

In Jeremiah 31:31-34, God reveals the new covenant through the prophet Jeremiah at a time when the nation of Israel was heading for punishment for its failures to keep the old covenant. This new covenant is based on what God would do for man and not conditioned on what people would or could do. We find the basis of this covenant in Hebrews 8:12: *"For I will be merciful to their iniquities, and I will remember their sins no more."* God was going to provide a merciful way for forgiveness of their sins without the old covenant system of sacrifices.

The writer of Hebrews quotes Jeremiah 31:31-34 in two separate places (Hebrews 8:10-12 and Hebrews 10:16-17) as a means of introducing this covenant, originally intended for the House of Israel (fulfilled in the Millennial Kingdom), now as a new covenant with the church, Jesus being the mediator of this covenant of mercy (Hebrews 9:15). Although Jesus only mentioned the new covenant directly on one occasion, at the last supper, His entire public ministry was a demonstration of what the dynamics of the covenant would look like.

A New Administration

In comparing the new covenant to the old, there is a complete change in the administration. In the Mosaic Law, Jewish leaders administered God's laws and enforced them externally, sometimes arbitrarily or without mercy, while this new covenant is the responsibility of the Holy Spirit from within the believer. In John 8, the Pharisees brought a charge against the woman caught in the act of adultery and asked Jesus if the law of Moses should convict her. This is a picture of how the leadership could arbitrarily enforce the law (where is the adulterer). The new covenant picture is found later in the account, when Jesus says to the woman, *"I do not condemn you, either. Go. From now on sin no more"* (John 8:11). If God forgives our sins (Hebrews 8:12) as in this new covenant, then the emphasis is that we do not do it again!

In Exodus 31:18, the Scripture tells us that the finger of God wrote the tablets of stone. In the new covenant, the Holy Spirit writes God's laws deep within each believer, in their hearts and minds and not on stone. God wishes to change our hearts from stone (self-centered) to flesh so that we can experience the presence and power of God (Ezekiel 36:26). If we are to have this dynamic relationship with the living God, it can only happen because of God's work in changing our hearts. The old covenant demands change from the outside; the new covenant works its changes from the inside when the heart is given over to God.

Facing God with Weaknesses and Failures

If I am to become one of God's people, it will require learning how to love God's laws so that I will desire to obey them on the basis of honor for the relationship instead of duty or fear of retribution. It is like a child who desires to honor his parents' wishes on the basis of love. The one who loves the laws of God is the one who has adopted the standards of God, His righteousness, as the standards which will lead to the highest quality of life. This one is willing to face God with his weaknesses and failures, recognizing that God is a God of mercy, but at the same time willing to face the consequences. Proverbs 24:16

teaches us that the righteous man does fall, even seven times, and rises again. The new covenant relationship with God provides a perfect environment to fall since there is a provision to get back up. And if discipline is necessary, it is meant to be for the purpose of training and not punishment.

The heart is the place where man decides what things he is to value or treasure. Growing up in this world, this cosmos in which the devil has much authority, causes most of us to embrace the material over the eternal and the devil is constantly enticing our senses, our lusts, and weaknesses, to get us to make wrong choices. To overcome this condition, God has ordained that He must work these value changes within the heart, typically through trials and other challenges. He is always revealing His eternal value system and wants us to choose that system over the temporal. This is a process defined by the believer allowing God to do the things internally that he would not choose for himself. He experiences the faithfulness of God as the Lord gently coaxes (and sometimes not so gently) man to make the right decisions. This process teaches the believer to trust, which is the essence of faith.

Taught by the Grace of God

In this new covenant, the Holy Spirit is the real teacher, who combines *"spiritual thoughts with spiritual words"* (1 Corinthians 2:13) to illuminate the mind to the things of God. Although one may be listening to a pastor or other teacher of the Scriptures, the Holy Spirit accomplishes the real work of teaching from within, and this gives him a deeper understanding of God's heart and mind. Even in the old covenant, God is the ultimate teacher as Isaiah 54:13 says, *All your sons will be taught of the Lord.* In this way, the believer is getting to know the Person of God, not just things about Him. And anyone who has the Spirit of God within (i.e., born again) is capable of understanding the deepest things of God while the unbeliever (natural man) is never able to comprehend, since the Spirit is the one who illuminates the mind and heart to these truths. To know God in a personal way is to agree with what He stands for.

In the new covenant relationship with God, Jesus brings salvation to all men by His grace (unearned), and it is this grace that teaches us how *to live sensibly, righteously, and godly in the present age* (Titus 2:11-12). Our greatest enemies against this quality of life are the flesh, the world, and the devil. The devil, who knows our weaknesses by observation, energizes the lusts of our flesh through outside stimulus from the world and inside through human weaknesses. But the divine solution is our consistent gaze (*looking for the blessed hope*) at the coming glory of the risen Lord in His second coming that purifies the believer to do *good deeds* (Titus 2:13-14).

Once for All

Hebrews 10 declares the shortcomings of the old covenant exposed as it emphasizes the need for a perfect sacrifice, one that will be *once for all* (Verse 10). In Verse 3, the daily sacrifices serve as a *reminder of sins year by year.* Instead of these constant reminders, the new covenant, through the blood of Christ, will *cleanse your conscience from dead works to serve the living God* (Hebrews 9:14). The new covenant remains forever and does not need any improvements since is also known as an everlasting (eternal) covenant (Isaiah 55:3, Hebrews 13:20). This is why He is making the old covenant obsolete (Hebrews 8:13).

It is clear from the Scriptures that the new covenant provides the environment necessary for the believer in Jesus as Messiah to experience the deepest relationship with God through the death, burial, and resurrection of Christ. Man can never attain this highest quality of life apart from God's work on his behalf and his willingness to receive and accept the free gift of salvation.

Chapter 3

THE CHURCH IN CRISIS

There is a relationship with God available in the new covenant, but there is a big crisis in the Church! According to a study of one thousand adults from 2020, only 33 percent say they attend church nearly every week. On the other end of the spectrum, 54 percent never or seldom attend church. The churches of today are not attracting people who have recognized a need for God and God's family, the body of Christ. Churches are not teaching a spiritual relationship with God, but commonly a relationship with church. I call it churchianity. The church is attracting and producing churched, not spiritual people.

Spirituality is the result of something God does in humanity by His Spirit; it is not what humanity is able to do for God (John 3:6). True spirituality manifests itself in a surrendered life and submitted to God. It is measured by one's willingness to deny self (the natural desire to elevate self over everything else), take up one's cross, a willingness to do things against natural desire, and follow Christ (Luke 9:23). It results in believers having the confidence to hear from God when God speaks to them, thus becoming true disciples. Most Christians today do not have this confidence. The church is not teaching spirituality. There is a crisis in the church!

> *To the angel of the church in Laodicea write: The Amen, the faithful and true Witness, the Beginning of the creation of God, says this:*

"I know your deeds, that you are neither hot nor cold; I wish you were cold or hot. "So, because you are lukewarm, and neither hot nor cold, I will spit you out of My mouth. "Because you say, "I am rich, and have become wealthy, and have need of nothing," and you do not know that you are wretched and miserable and poor and blind and naked, I advise you to buy from Me gold refined by fire so that you may become rich, and white garments so that you may clothe yourself, and that the shame of your nakedness will not be revealed; and eye salve to anoint your eyes so that you may see. Those whom I love, I reprove and discipline; therefore, be zealous and repent. "Behold, I stand at the door and knock; if anyone hears My voice and opens the door, I will come in to him and will dine with him, and he with Me. He who overcomes, I will grant to him to sit down with Me on My throne, as I also overcame and sat down with my Father on His throne. He who has an ear, let him hear what the Spirit says to the churches." **Revelation 3:14-22**

BE ZEALOUS & REPENT

In Revelations 2 and 3, we find seven letters written by Jesus Christ to seven first century churches, identifying various characteristics of each church that were either commendable or deserving of reprimand. These seven letters not only refer to seven actual churches in history, but many scholars believe that they are representative of the general conditions of a typical church in different ages of the church since the time of Acts 2. For instance, Laodicea, the last church mentioned in Revelations 3 references churches in the current age. These churches are typically rich and wealthy and have need of nothing (Revelation 3:17). Looking closely at this letter in Revelations 3:14-22 can give us insight into many churches of today.

As the text reveals, the Laodicean church had many issues that caused Jesus to say that this church was so distasteful that He will *"spit [them] out of [His] mouth."* We find these conditions in Verses 17 & 18 where they are rich, having become wealthy, and do not recognize a need for anything. Rather, He tells them that they are wretched and miserable and poor and blind and naked. How could this be that they were so rich and yet so poor? The riches attained by the church and its people had caused them to be unaware of the underlying depravity of mankind, as illustrated by the Apostle Paul in Romans 3:10-18.

These people were deceived into believing that their participation in the church was all they needed to be spiritual; they could continue enjoying the riches and treasures of the world, contrary to what Jesus prayed in John 17:15-16, that they were not to be of this world. The Word of God sanctifies the believer (John 17:17) and means separation from the world for God's purposes (which is the very definition of the Greek word, "*hagiozo*"). Jesus told them that they needed to be zealous and repent (change your direction), that they needed to buy gold refined by fire (gold refers to true riches of God – Zodhiates), white garments for clothing (white garments speaks of holiness and sanctification), and eye salve to anoint your eyes (eye salve meaning a need for healing of spiritual understanding). The people of God were not relating to God or experiencing Him!

THE NEW TESTAMENT CHURCH

God initiated the church as a gathering place for Gentiles and converted Jews, the entire community of believers, to seek the Lord, as spoken by James, the half-brother of Jesus in Acts 15. The Greek word "*ekklesia* " means ones who are "called out" and can refer to the universal body of believers worldwide and to local churches or denominations. We must understand that multiple New Testament references to the church speak about the universal group of believers rather than a particular local assembly. Why is this so important? Because the teaching of the New Testament church is as a collection of believers individually connected to Christ rather than an institution or organization (see illustration below). The priority of the church as an institution is to encourage the deeper connection of each believer to Christ instead of to itself. When the teaching of the church organization does not accomplish this, it does a disservice to all its believers. Instead, churchgoers have great difficulty discerning the difference between the church leadership and God, Himself. In Exodus 20:18-19, the Jewish leadership told Moses to go up and meet God on Mount Sinai because they were afraid to go themselves. The teaching of the church must help the believer distinguish between God and the giftedness of the church leadership. Otherwise, believers will be afraid of God!

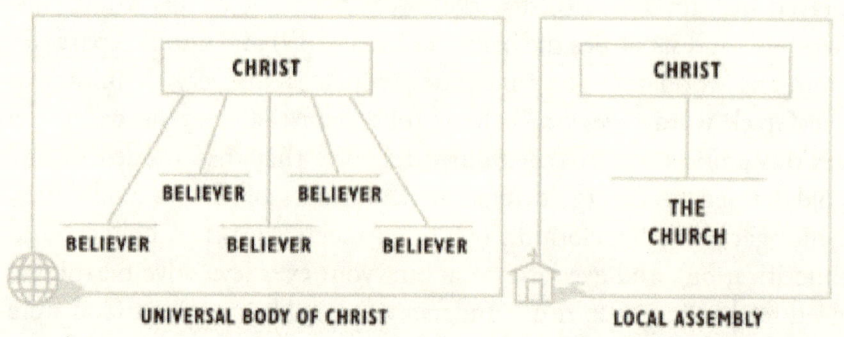

Jesus taught us in Matthew 16:15-18 that the testimony of Peter is the church's foundation, that, *"you are the Christ, the Son of the Living God."* Membership in the church is determined by a relationship with Christ and not a local organization or institution. And that relationship with Christ is the primary issue in a believer's life (Colossians 1:18). Therefore, the church's greatest responsibility is to define, promote, and encourage that relationship in each believer's life. The problem with the Laodicean church was that its attachment to worldly benefits was causing its spiritual temperature to be "lukewarm," neither hot nor cold. Both the cold water from Colossae and the hot water from Hierapolis would be lukewarm by the time it arrives from Laodicea. In the same way, the burning heart caused by the fire of God's Spirit (Isaiah 4:4) becomes extinguished by the church's effort to allow the corruption of the world system to infiltrate the believer's relationship with God. This condition was so distasteful to God that Jesus says He would rather the believer be cold than lukewarm (Verse 15).

MEGA-CHURCH MOVEMENT

The last forty years has seen the emergence of the mega-church movement in America with the growth of many local assemblies of at least two thousand or more participants in weekly services and some as large as thirty thousand or more. According to Scott Thumma, PhD in his, "Exploring the Mega-Church Phenomena: Their characteristics and cultural context," mega-churches typically fall into three expressions – evangelical, charismatic, or fundamental – within a functionally non-denominational framework. Because these churches are non-traditional, they must establish a specific vision that provides for a unique identity, usually relating to the intended audience to which the church wishes to cater (i.e., seekers as exemplified by Willow Creek Community Church and others). They provide an environment for "one stop shopping," focusing not only on the religious interests of the members, but also the physical and temporal needs, like a spiritual shopping mall. This gives participants multiple options for becoming involved in the core activities that define the church's existence. There is also typically great attention paid to the production of the worship events. Accomplished speakers who draw audiences because of their own appeal and charisma deliver culturally relevant messages. Major resources are devoted to sophisticated audio and video equipment and contemporary mega-church chapels looking more like theaters entertaining churchgoers each church service, many times without mentioning Jesus or God's Word.

But relationships are not completely ignored. More recently, the emphasis on the small group dynamic of establishing personal connections to a large member base has become a popular approach by many mega and other large churches. Since much of the discipling (spiritual training) of believers is best in more intimate settings, it is important that churches of any size have mature leaders that can personally invest in an individual's life. Accomplishing that feat in a church with hundreds or thousands in a church service cannot happen without smaller group gatherings. Spiritual growth is most often the byproduct of personal investment and imparted wisdom. The difficulty with the small groups model in any church is in the limited number of mature and trained teachers to go around. This can mean that social relationships within the church begin to overshadow the importance of each believer's maturing in their individual relationship with God.

Jesus was speaking to small and large groups (there may have been fifteen thousand or more when He spoke the Sermon on the Mount), but He was always teaching twelve, most often in small group sessions, discussing the issues at hand. Discipleship does not happen by just attending weekly services; it requires personal investment on the part of both the participant and leader/teacher, with the relationship between them submitted to each one's relationship with God under the new covenant.

Intimacy in Discipleship

Once He came into His public ministry, Jesus spent His time with either His Father or His disciples. The impartation of His character cannot take place listening to sermons, but in the relational intimacy of personal time and practical teaching. Jesus took three of the disciples with Him to the Mount of Transfiguration in Matthew 17 and showed them things that are not teachable through a sermon. Peter writes about the impact of this event in 2 Peter 1:16-21 where he says, *"we were eyewitnesses of His majesty"*. Therefore, he says in Verse 19, *"We have the prophetic word made more sure...."* The Word of God comes alive to us because of our unique, individual experiences with Him.

The Greek word for disciple, *"mathetes,"* means a learner or pupil in its basic form. According to Spiros Zodhiates, it is more than a pupil since this pupil accepts the instruction given as his rule of conduct. This pupil recognizes the ultimate authority of the teacher and the subject taught. Growing up spiritually into a disciple requires a process of recognizing the Word of God as absolute truth! Any compromise of this reality undermines the transformation process that the Word of God and His will intends (Romans 12:2).

Continuing

So, Jesus was saying to those Jews who had believed Him, "If you continue in My word, then you are truly disciples of Mine; and you will know the truth, and the truth will make you free." They answered Him, "We are Abraham's descendants and have never yet been enslaved to anyone; how is it that You say, 'You will become free?" Jesus answered them, "Truly, truly, I say to you, everyone who commits sin is the slave of sin. "The slave does not remain in the house forever; the son does remain forever. "So, if the Son makes you free, you will be free indeed." **John 8:31-36**

The Greek word for "continue" is "*meno*" and has the extended meaning, "to be and remain united with the Word, one with the Word in heart, mind, and will." Being a true *disciple* only can become a reality with a *continuing* and vital relationship with the Word of God as it sets him free! These two Greek words complement each other in that to be a disciple, one must see the understanding of Scripture as more than an academic pursuit, but it must involve the heart, where the value system of man is determined. When the heart finally comes into full agreement with the Scriptures, the believer finds his relationship with God, and his life-transforming freedom!

Spirit Taught

The Holy Spirit is the real teacher of the Word of God to the heart, through whom one is able to receive and understand the meaning of the Word of God in practical application. In 1 Corinthians 2:10, the Bible tells us that the Holy Spirit is qualified to teach man's heart since He can search *"even the depths of God"*. This passage identifies that the spirit of man, which comes alive at the moment of salvation, knows the thoughts of man, but only the Holy Spirit knows the thoughts of God. The Holy Spirit teaches the human spirit by combining spiritual thoughts with spiritual words and gives the believer understanding that the unbeliever (natural man) is not capable of comprehending since his spirit is not yet alive (see Verse 14). This process defines how we receive the mind of Christ (Verse 16).

We can conclude that the church as an organization will not be able to fulfill its obligation to raise up disciples to all nations (Matthew 28:19) as Jesus charged his disciples (before His ascension) until the church becomes less concerned about its numbers and more about its spirituality. One of the five theological beliefs of the Protestant reformers is known as "Solus Christus," Latin for "Christ Alone." It rejects the need for believers to have access to God and His grace through a priest or other church official but recognizes the believer as a member of the priesthood (1 Peter 2:5, 9). As a priest in God's eyes, the believer's relationship directly with Christ as the mediator of the new covenant is sacred and no church official should circumvent that relationship. Only Jesus Christ, through His Spirit (Romans 8:9) has the right to speak to His sheep, according to John 10. Anyone else is only a hireling. Recognizing and applying the dynamics of the new covenant is the only means by which believers in the New Testament age can find true spirituality.

Chapter 4

THE SPIRITUAL GOSPEL OF JOHN

For countless Christians, the Gospel of John is the most precious book of the Bible. It is dramatically different than the other three gospels on numerous levels; an examination of the circumstances and motivations of its writing make it especially unique. Much of this perspective of the Gospel of John comes from William Barclay's, "The Gospel According to John, Volume 1." It provides an in-depth analysis of many historical facts and background that most other commentaries on John's Gospel never address.

There seems to be no real consensus about the year each of the gospels was written, but it is fairly clear that the synoptic gospels of Matthew, Mark and Luke were written prior to A.D. 65 while John's Gospel was not written until somewhere between A.D. 90 – 100. The Christian world at the end of the first century consisted of mostly Gentiles while the early gospels appeared during a time dominated by Jewish Christians. In addition, the more than thirty-year time difference represented a maturing of the Christian community in terms of its understanding of doctrine since the lion's share of New Testament letters had been circulating among the churches for many years. It also meant that doctrinal deviations and heresies were appearing, and John's Gospel and his letters addressed some of these heresies, including Gnosticism and Docetism which challenged the humanity of Christ and the value of the material realm. John accepted and acknowledged to others his agreement with the facts presented in the first three gospels, but there were new concerns that needed to be addressed.

The Mind of God

The early church had spread into a Gentile world which was largely influenced by Greek philosophy and ideas, including the principle of *Logos*. It means *word* or *reason* in Greek and the mind of the typical Greek saw life through the lens of the world as a place of order and reason. The *Logos* created and managed this order, understood as the mind of God. It was this same mind of God dwelling inside man that allows him to think rationally. John took this mindset and addressed it by defining that mind as Jesus Christ (see John 1:1 and John 1:14) and that this mind has become a man. Also, the Greek mind (as defined by Plato) conceived of two worlds, the material world in which we live and the immaterial and unseen world. It was the unseen world which was the real world while the material realm consists of shadows and copies and not real. Jesus is the incarnation of not only the mind of God, but also reality! The life of Jesus is a window into the mind of God and His priorities and realities. One of these priorities is the revelation of God's glory.

John's treatment of various miracles is a fitting example of this priority. Instead of emphasizing the compassion (which was surely present as mentioned in MML) that motivated Jesus to heal a particular individual, John also reveals that the miracles (signs) he was performing were meant to reveal the glory of God. In John 11:4, *But when Jesus heard this, He said, "This sickness is not to end in death,* **but for the glory of God***, so that the Son of God may be glorified by it."* In dealing with the man born blind in John 9, He said, *"It was neither that this man sinned, nor his parents; but it was* **so that the works of God might be displayed in him***"* (Verse 3). And to put a bow on the miracle of changing the water into wine at the wedding at Cana, John says in John 2:11, *This* *beginning of His signs Jesus did in Cana of Galilee, and **manifested His glory**, and His disciples believed in Him.* The glory of God is a central theme in John's Gospel.

Uniqueness of John's Gospel

There are many dramatic differences in not only the events covered by the three synoptics as compared to John's Gospel, but even more importantly the depth of the coverage of the actual events and particular conclusions. Here are some important observable differences:

1. The synoptics conclude that the beginning of Jesus's public ministry was the imprisonment of John the Baptist while John begins earlier, including the events covered in John 2, 3, and 4.
2. The emphasis of Matthew, Mark, & Luke (MML) were the events that took place in Galilee while the main scene of John's coverage is Jerusalem and Judea.
3. John covers all three years of His ministry as evidenced by the facts that his gospel included three Passovers: John 2:13, John 6:4, and then the Last Supper while MML deals with one or two.
4. Many events covered by John are unique to his gospel, including the wedding at Cana (John 2:1-11), Jesus's meeting with Nicodemus in John 3, the meeting with the Samaritan woman at Jacob's well in John 4, and the raising of Lazarus in John 11.
5. John covers a variety of personal details about individuals that provide texture to their lives. John 20:24-29 contains a notable example of this where there is a rich exchange with Thomas. In fact, John's Gospel has the only references to Thomas speaking at all.
6. In the same way, John provides many more details when MML remains silent, for instance, the fact that the bread used in the feeding of the 5,000 was barley loaves (John 6:9). This suggests that John had a great interest and memory for details, even as an elderly man.

Quote from William Barclay's Commentary on John's Gospel

"It was with this in mind that that great scholar Clement of Alexandria (about A.D. 230) arrived at one of the most famous and true of all verdicts about the origin and aim of the Fourth Gospel. It was his view that the gospels containing the genealogies had been written first, that is *Luke* and *Matthew*; that then *Mark* at the request of many who had heard Peter preach composed his gospel, which embodied the preaching material of Peter and that then *'last of all, John, perceiving that what had reference to the bodily things of Jesus's ministry had been sufficiently related, and encouraged by friends, and inspired by the Holy Spirit, wrote a spiritual gospel'* (quoted in Eusebius, *The Ecclesiastical History*). What Clement meant was that John was not much interested in the mere facts as in the meaning of the facts, that it was not facts he was after but truth. John did not see the events of Jesus's life simply as events in time; he saw them as windows looking into eternity, and he pressed towards the spiritual meaning of the events and the words of Jesus's life in a way that the other three gospels did not attempt."

John 6 is one splendid example of his disclosure of spiritual realties beyond the historical facts. John takes the account of the feeding of the 5,000, covered by all four writers and brings the event to a spiritual conclusion, not only quoting Jesus as, *"I am the bread of life"*, but further explains its meaning in a way that illustrates *"the will of My Father"* as the ultimate reality of spiritual life.

Quotes Attributable to Clement of Alexandria

"This gospel is intended to reveal the one person who possesses reality instead of shadows to lead men to reality." It was not just John's idea to write his gospel; he had been teaching it orally for many years, but he now recognized, with the encouragement of others, "the rest of the story," as Paul Harvey might say. When all is said and done, it is the Holy Spirit's account!

Again, another passage from William Barclay's commentary gives us further insight into the matter:

> "Papias, who loved to collect all that he could find about the history of the New Testament and the story of Jesus, gives us some interesting information. He was Bishop of Hierapolis, which is quite near Ephesus [where John wrote his gospel], and his dates are from A.D. 70 to about A.D. 145. That is to say, he was actually a contemporary of John. He writes how he tried to find out 'what Andrew said or what Peter said, or what was said by Philip, by Thomas, or by James, or by John, or by Matthew, or by any other of the disciples of the Lord; and what things Aristion and *the elder* John, the disciples of the Lord say.' In Ephesus, there was the *apostle* John, and the *elder* John; and the *elder* John was so well-loved a figure that he was actually known as *The Elder*. He clearly had a unique place in the church. Both Eusebius and Dionysius the Great tell us that even to their own days in Ephesus there were two famous tombs, the one of John the apostle, and the other of John the elder."

It is interesting to note that the first verses in John's second and third letters begin as follows: 2 John 1, *The elder to the chosen lady and her children, whom I love in truth*; and 3 John 1, *The elder to the beloved Gaius, whom I love in truth*. It seems clear that much of the apostle John's work from Ephesus was not just his own, but a spiritual support group contributed to make them as spiritual as they could be. John's intention in writing his gospel was to provide a spiritual framework for understanding the life and work of Christ as the God/man and encourage the Christian's spiritual roots and heritage.

The Spiritual Man

There is a vast difference between the moral man and the spiritual man. The moral man defines his life by whatever moral code he values and derives his self-image and identity from his ability to live up to that code. God's standards do not drive the spiritual man, but instead His love! Paul discovered that the strength and power (ability) of God becomes real in his life through the connection of the human spirit (inner man) to the Holy Spirit. In Ephesians 3:16-19,

> *that He would grant you, according to the riches of His glory, to be strengthened with power through His Spirit in the inner man, so that Christ may dwell in your hearts through faith; and that you, being rooted and grounded in love, may be able to comprehend with all the saints what is the breadth and length and height and depth, and to know the love of Christ which surpasses knowledge, that you may be filled up to all the fullness of God.*

Understanding the framework of the new covenant provides the believer the greatest opportunity to find the structure of the spiritual life in Christ. The new covenant defines the boundaries of the spiritual man since it identifies God's love and how to function within that love. The spiritual man is *able to comprehend with all the saints what is the breadth and length and height and depth and to know the love of Christ*. To be *filled up to all the fullness of God* is the end result of being rooted and grounded in love, preoccupied with the love of Christ. This rooting in love takes us deep and this grounding establishes a solid foundation in that love. Since God is love (1 John 4:8, 16), that love defines everything He does; He cannot do anything outside of that love. Once the believer sees the details of his life as the ultimate byproduct of God's love, he discovers the spiritual man.

Chapter 5

A MINISTRY OF EXCELLENCE

One of the most important statements Jesus made at the Sermon on the Mount dealt with the people's concerns about who He was in relationship to the Old Testament, defined by the Law and the Prophets. In Matthew 5:17, He said that He did not come to abolish (do away with) the Law or the Prophets, but to fulfill them. He further said that it is a sure thing in Verse 18. Jesus was telling them that He came to complete the required relationship with God as revealed in the Law of Moses so that He could introduce a new one. This new relationship would be better than the old since He would become the strength of it as its mediator. He was introducing a better ministry, the best ministry by introducing the new covenant. Hebrews 8:6 says, *but now He has obtained a more excellent ministry, by as much as He is also the mediator of a better covenant, which has been enacted on better promises.*

From Old Covenant to New

On the third day there was a wedding in Cana of Galilee, and the mother of Jesus was there; and both Jesus and His disciples were invited to the wedding. When the wine ran out, the mother of Jesus said to Him, "They have no wine." And Jesus said to her, "Woman, what does that have to do with us? My hour has not yet come." His mother said to the servants, "Whatever He says to you, do it." Now there were six stone waterpots set there for the Jewish custom of purification, containing twenty or thirty gallons each. Jesus said to them, "Fill the waterpots with water." So, they filled them up to the brim. And He said to them, "Draw some out now and take it to the headwaiter." So, they took it to him. When the headwaiter tasted the water which had become wine and did not know where it came from (but the servants who had drawn the water knew), the headwaiter called the bridegroom, and said to him, "Every man serves the good wine first, and when the people have drunk freely, then he serves the poorer wine; but you have kept the good wine until now." **John 2:1-10**

It is significant that Jesus's first miracle in His public ministry took place at a wedding in Cana (celebrating a new covenant between a man and a woman) and showed that He came to introduce a new covenant. It will be at a wedding, the marriage supper of the Lamb (Revelations 19:7-9) where the bride (believers in the new covenant) will adorn fine linen, representing the righteous acts of the saints. Also take note of the waterpots, *set there for the Jewish custom of purification* as required by the old covenant laws. Jesus instructed the servants to fill them with water and then draw some and bring them to the headwaiter. It was determined that it was not just wine, but *"the good [kalos –* choice, excellent] *wine."* Wine reminds us of the cup Jesus offered in Luke 22:20, *"This cup which is poured out for you is the new covenant in My blood."* By changing the water into wine, Jesus symbolized the introduction of a more excellent ministry, replacing the old covenant rites of purification with Jesus's life through His blood.

Take note that wine speaks of the coming kingdom age and the new covenant. In Isaiah 25:6, *The Lord of hosts will prepare a lavish banquet for all peoples on this mountain; a banquet of aged wine, choice pieces with marrow, and refined, aged wine.* In Genesis 49, Jacob prophesied over each of his sons. Regarding Judah in Verses 10-11, he said, *The scepter shall not depart from Judah, nor the ruler's staff from between his feet, until Shiloh comes, and to him shall be the obedience of the peoples. He ties his foal to the vine, and his donkey's colt to the choice vine; He washes his garments in wine, and his robes in the blood of grapes.* This is a clear reference to the coming Messiah, the Lion of Judah, who would rule with a scepter over the world in the Kingdom Age.

Better Promises

What makes the new covenant excellent? As Hebrews 8:6 states, it is based on better promises. Those better promises include, but are not limited to:

- The promise of God's grace – the new covenant is dependent on what God has done, according to grace.
- The promise of internal change – the new covenant promises God will create a new heart and spirit.
- The promise of forgiveness for all – the new covenant depends on the blood of Christ paying the price.
- The promise of eternal blessing – the new covenant promises eternal life to all who receive it by faith.

We notice from these promises that the things that make the ministry excellent is that God does something for us that we could not do for ourselves; this is the very definition of grace. When the ministry depends on God and not just angels or other created beings, it has a good chance of being excellent. Jesus taught His disciples in Matthew 9:17, "*Nor do people put new wine into old wineskins; otherwise, the wineskins burst, and the wine pours out and the wineskins are ruined: but they put new wine into fresh [new] wineskins, and both are preserved.*" The old wineskin represents the law and all its requirements; you cannot be a successful new covenant believer living under all those legal demands.

In Hebrews 1:4 in reference to angels, Jesus *has inherited a more excellent name than they*. This ministry is excellent because Jesus has become not only its mediator, but also its guarantor (Hebrews 7:22).

The Excellence of Agape Love

And I show you a still more excellent way.
1 Corinthians 12:31

The last Verse of 1 Corinthians 12 is an introduction to chapter 13, the "love" chapter. The still more excellent way is love, *agape* love, sometimes translated charity. It is greater than any spiritual gift. The foundation of the new covenant is *agape*, God's love, unconditional love. In Romans 5:8, *But God demonstrates His own love toward us, in that while we were yet sinners, Christ died for us.* The proof of the excellence of the new covenant is that it is based on God's love. This love is the greatest love since it willingly lays down its life for others. It starts with Jesus, but it does not end there. This love becomes the evidence of the new covenant in the believer's life. In 1 John 3:14 and 16, *We know that we have passed out of death into life, because we love the brethren. We know love by this, that He laid down His life for us; and we ought to lay down our lives for the brethren.* This love confirms that the believer has passed from death into life (*zoe* – God's life).

This *zoe* life, God's life, a laid down life, is rooted in love and in our response to God's love. Paul teaches in Romans 13 that the true believer owes others only love (Verse 8). This kind of love, expressed as loving your neighbor as yourself, leading to the fulfillment of the old covenant law. It is the royal law! To receive God's love personally opens the door to be able to love others in this way. Excellence flows from this kind of love.

Chapter 6

BORN FROM ABOVE

In John 3, Jesus introduces the concept of being born from above with a Pharisee named Nicodemus. Most modern English translations of the Bible translate John 3:7 as, *"you must be born again"* in reference to the new birth of a believer. The Greek word translated "again" is *"anoethen"* and its basic meaning is from above or from a higher place. Of the thirteen times it appears in Scripture, John 3:3 and 7 are the only times when the word is translated "again" rather than "from above". It is my conviction that Jesus was referring to a birth that only could come from heaven and not earth and His intention was to emphasize this fact. The new birth is the result of the Spirit of God coming into a person's life and establishing a spiritual life in the midst of the natural life.

Nicodemus' question to Jesus in Verse 4 indicates that he did not understand what Jesus was saying, so Jesus explained it further. In Verse 5, Jesus clarifies the issue for Nicodemus by qualifying that the natural birth is of water while the spiritual birth is of the Spirit. Then in Verse 6, He makes a profound statement that reveals a new understanding of the natural birth and natural life in comparison to the spiritual birth and the spiritual life. The natural birth and life are derived from the flesh, of the earthly, while the spiritual birth comes from the Spirit of God, from above and the spiritual life allows the Spirit to direct our lives just as the wind blows where it wishes (see Verse 8).

The Battle for Control

Man is made up of three parts, body, soul, and spirit. The body is the physical, material part, while the soul and spirit are immaterial. The soul consists of the mind, heart, emotions, conscience, and self-consciousness (awareness of self). The human spirit is the place in man that can commune with the Holy Spirit. The human spirit died in Genesis 3 when Adam and Eve fell and it remains dead in each person until the moment of the new birth, the moment that one decides to accept Jesus as God and believe (trust) in Him for his future.

Galatians 5:17-18 illustrates this battle, *For the flesh sets its desire against the Spirit, and the Spirit against the flesh; for these are in opposition to one another, so that you may not do the things that you please. But if you are led by the Spirit, you are not under the Law.* This "war" between the flesh (meaning the soul) and the Holy Spirit is about control. The soul wishes to be in charge and make all the important decisions while the Holy Spirit is looking for the human spirit to reign. The soul can be religious by doing what it can to live up to the Ten Commandments (the Law) and its religious requirements, but the Holy Spirit looks to lead the believer apart from the Law. This puts God in charge.

The Spirit of Man

This battle between soul and spirit centers on the Word of God. In Hebrews 4:12, the Bible tells us that the Word of God is like a two-edged sword and is able to divide that which is of the soul from that which is of the spirit and is a judge ("*kritikos*" – critic) of the thoughts and intentions of the heart. The Word defines for us where our thoughts and intentions come from – the soul (natural man) or the spirit (from the Holy Spirit).

In the New Testament, there are three particular verses that speak to the human spirit, using the term, "inner man." In Ephesians 3:16, *that He would grant you, according to the riches of His glory, to be strengthened with power through His Spirit in the **inner man**.* The power of God moves from the Holy Spirit into the human spirit to give the believer a life of abundance. In 2 Corinthians 4:16, *Therefore we do not lose heart, but though our outer man is decaying, yet our **inner man** is being renewed day by day.* This renewal is the work of the Holy Spirit within the believer as one agrees with His Word and His work. And in Romans 7:22-23, *For I joyfully concur with* [delight in] *the law of God in the **inner man**, but I see a different law in the members of my body, waging war against the law of my mind and making me a prisoner of the law of sin which is in my members.* In this Verse, the warfare centers on *the law of God* verses *the law of my mind,* making Paul *a prisoner of the law of sin*. The victorious life comes from the law of the Spirit of life in Christ Jesus who has set the believer free from the law of sin and death (Romans 8:2).

TOWER OF BABEL

In John 3:13, Jesus tells us that *"no one has ascended into heaven, but He who descended from heaven, the Son of Man."* The spiritual life is the result of God coming to us and not man reaching God. This is the exact mistake that the people of Babel in Genesis 11, led by Nimrod, made in trying to *"make for ourselves a name."* The tower of Babel was man's attempt, through human effort to bridge the gap between earth and heaven. Man always tries to accomplish things, even religious matters, by human effort, without God's help. In this way, man can take credit for his work. This is why salvation is a work of God alone and it is the Son of God that delivers salvation to man by grace from heaven to earth. No matter how good man's efforts may be, they can never measure up to the standard God's justice demands (Isaiah 64:6).

The old covenant provided an opening for the religious man to make himself righteous through adherence to less important laws to make them appear spiritual to the masses. Jesus exposed this condition in Matthew 23:23, *"Woe to you, scribes and Pharisees, hypocrites! For you tithe mint and dill and cummin and have neglected the weightier provisions of the law: justice and mercy and faithfulness; but these are the things you should have done without neglecting the others."* The weightier provisions of the law represent His heart: justice and mercy and faithfulness and the Pharisees were not after His heart. The religious Jew misses the mark when he wishes to establish his own righteousness (Romans 10:3). The new covenant provides no room for self-righteousness.

Justified Apart from the Law

In Romans 3:20-21, *because* **by the works of the Law no flesh will be justified in His sight**; *for through the Law comes the knowledge of sin. But now apart from the Law the righteousness of God has been manifested, being witnessed by the Law and the Prophets.* The works of the Law, human effort to maintain the laws of God apart from God, cannot satisfy God's standards of justice. Righteousness, representing the standards of God, comes to man apart from human effort to maintain His standards. It comes by faith (*pistis* – being persuaded, having a conviction, trusting) in the person and the work of Christ who already completed, on our behalf, both the fulfillment of the Law and the penalty of death for our breaking of the Law. And this same opportunity for righteousness is not restricted to any particular group of people, but is offered to all in the same way, without distinction. The old covenant provides promises of God to respond to human effort, while the new covenant depends completely on the work of God, in Christ, to fulfill His just demands. He invites those who become tired of their efforts apart from God to trust in God's work alone, receiving the fullness of the relationship strictly on the basis of faith.

According to John 1:12, God's offer to us is to become children of God as a right or privilege reserved for those who receive or accept Him strictly on the basis of faith in what God has done and not any effort associated with the will or the flesh. Being born of God means accepting the free gift of salvation on God's terms. In 1 John 5:1-4, John writes again about this experience of being born of God and the effect it has on a believer to transform from the inside. Our faith in who Jesus is provides the vehicle God uses to bring one into the beloved (Ephesians 1:6), the place where I love and receive love, and this faith also gives one the victory to overcome all the obstacles that the world throws his way.

A New Heart and Spirit

The prophet Ezekiel received a vision of what the new covenant relationship with God would look like in the Kingdom Age. In Ezekiel 36:25-27,

> *"Then I will sprinkle clean water on you, and you will be clean; I will cleanse you from all your filthiness and from all your idols. "Moreover, I will give you a new heart and put a new spirit within you; and I will remove the heart of stone from your flesh and give you a heart of flesh. "I will put My Spirit within you and cause you to walk in My statutes, and you will be careful to observe My ordinances."*

Since Jeremiah's original promise of the new covenant addressed the Jews during this same period, this passage in Ezekiel also applies to believers in the Church age. It tells us that God is the one who makes our hearts clean and gives us a new spirit so that we will be able to walk in His statutes and be careful to observe His ordinances.

In Genesis 28, Jacob leaves his father, Isaac's house to go back to Haran to find a wife for himself with his uncle Laban. This event is the beginning of God's focus on Jacob as the patriarch instead of Isaac, who is elderly now. After leaving Beersheba, he travels the entire day and needs to find a place to stay for the night. This is Bethel meaning "house of God" since Jacob had a profound experience with God. God gives him a vision of a ladder going between earth and heaven, giving Jacob encouragement that God would honor him as the new patriarch in spite of his shortcomings.

Spiritual Riches

This ladder, with angels ascending and descending on it is a picture of this new relationship with God that the new covenant provides. Man is weak and continues with his sin nature after salvation, yet God is still with him in his humanity. In 2 Corinthians 4:7, Paul tells us that *we have a treasure within the earthen vessel, so that the surpassing greatness will be of God and not from ourselves.* This ladder speaks of the riches of the life that we can have with God within the earthen vessel (human weakness) so that we recognize His power and ability and rely on that instead of our own strength. Being born from above allows us to experience life in the Holy Spirit and all the benefits it provides.

Chapter 7

A COVENANT OF GRACE & MERCY

After these things there was a feast of the Jews, and Jesus went up to Jerusalem. Now there is in Jerusalem by the sheep gate a pool, which is called in Hebrew Bethesda [House of Mercy], *having **five** porticoes. In these lay a multitude of those who were sick, blind, lame, and withered, [waiting for the moving of the waters; for an angel of the Lord went down at certain seasons into the pool and stirred up the water; whoever then first, after the stirring up of the water, stepped in was made well from whatever disease with which he was afflicted.] A man was there who had been ill for thirty-eight years. When Jesus saw him lying there, and knew that he had already been a long time in that condition, He said to him, "Do you wish to get well?" The sick man answered Him, "Sir, I have no man to put me into the pool when the water is stirred up, but while I am coming, another steps down before me." Jesus said to him, "Get up, pick up your pallet and walk." Immediately the man became well and picked up his pallet and began to walk. Now it was the Sabbath on that day. So, the Jews were saying to the man who was cured, "It is the Sabbath, and it is not permissible for you to carry your pallet." But he answered them, "He who made me well was the one who said to me, 'Pick up your pallet* *and walk.'" They asked him, "Who is the man who said to you, 'Pick up your pallet and walk'?" But the man who was healed did not know who it was, for Jesus had slipped away while there was a crowd in that place. Afterward Jesus found him in the temple and said to him, "Behold, you have become well; do not sin anymore, so that nothing worse happens to you." The man went away and told the Jews that it was Jesus who had made him well. For this reason, the Jews were persecuting Jesus, because He was doing these things on the Sabbath. But He answered them, "My Father is working until now, and I Myself am working."* **John 5:1-17**

In Ephesians 2:8, the Word of God tells us that salvation (the new covenant) is by grace, through faith, not man's work, but God's work alone. Grace (Greek word *"charis"*) means that God gives it to us as a free gift, not according to effort. The passage from John 5 above illustrates this principle in the man afflicted 38 years and yet healed by Jesus.

Pick up your Pallet

In this passage there was a feast of the Jews (we are not sure which one) that required Jewish men living within fifteen miles of Jerusalem to be there. Jesus appears at this pool called Bethesda, Hebrew for House of Mercy, and a man afflicted 38 years with a disease that left him lame. This gate has five porticoes and five is the Biblical number for grace. This pool was a place that required the person to enter the pool at the right time and healing would take place. Of course, this man's problem was that he could not climb into the pool on his own when the bubbles appeared, and he complained that others would step into the pool before him so he would not benefit from the pool. Jesus decided to heal the man immediately instead of requiring the man to enter the pool. And when healing was acknowledged, Jesus told him to get up and *"pick up your pallet,"* which he did.

Looking under the surface of what is actually taking place, we get a picture of the new covenant as one that is a work of God and not man, that God is not requiring any "work" by man to enter into this covenant. The fact that this man could not walk prior to his healing is a picture of the impact that this covenant can have on one's "walk" or lifestyle. Salvation provides an opportunity to change the way he lives since God empowers this relationship with Him. Here is the Messiah as prophesied by Scripture in Isaiah 61:1 anointed by the Father to bring good news to the afflicted! This afflicted man received good news when Jesus said to him, *"Get up, pick up your pallet and walk."*

GOD IS RICH IN MERCY

Later in this John 5 account, Jesus spoke to this man and said, *"Behold, you have become well, do not sin anymore, so that nothing worse happens to you"* in Verse 14. What a picture of the saved man! Salvation provides forgiveness for sins, but committing sin has a negative effect on a man's walk. This is why the believer needs confession. Our position from God is perfect, but our experience requires cleansing. In 1 John 1:9, when we confess our sins, He is faithful to forgive and to cleanse from all unrighteousness. Because sins have an inherent energy to repeat themselves, the cleansing process deals with the proclivity to repeat, namely the effects of sin.

The signature Verse of the Bible is John 3:16 which tells us that God so loved us that He sent His son to die to provide eternal life. Paul says in Ephesians 2 that we were all in the same condition, *dead in your trespasses and sins* in Verse 1 and *we too all formerly lived in the lusts of our flesh, indulging the desires of the flesh and of the mind* in Verse 3. This demonstration of love occurred while we were still sinners and enemies (Romans 5:8). But why? Because God is rich in mercy! Because of His great love with which He loved us! (Verse 4). The greatest expression of God's love is His grace and mercy. In John 1:14, Jesus came to earth as a man full of grace and truth and we realized this grace and truth through the new covenant (John 1:16). The foundational principle of the new covenant as stated in Hebrews 8:12 is that He *will be merciful to their iniquities and remember their sins no more*. The greatest expression of God's grace and mercy is forgiveness!

Grace is our Instructor

For the grace of God has appeared, bringing salvation to all men, instructing us to deny ungodliness and worldly desires and to live sensibly, righteously, and godly in the present age, looking for the blessed hope and the appearing of the glory of our great God and Savior, Christ Jesus, who gave Himself for us to redeem us from every lawless deed, and to purify for Himself a people for His own possession, zealous for good deeds. **Titus 2:11-14**

In this passage in Titus, grace, in the form of Christ, has appeared bringing the new covenant to all men. This grace not only saves us, but it also instructs us how to live godly lives, by denying ungodliness and worldly desires (taking up the cross). Grace is the avenue not only of salvation, but sanctification as well. Grace is the avenue that He uses to purify us to be His possession (Verse 14), where we will desire greatly good deeds. And this godliness causes us to be looking forward, toward our future of hope and His reappearing.

It is important that a believer knows forgiveness. A conviction that he has received forgiveness produces a heart that is grateful to God and capable of expressing love to God and to others. When Jesus healed ten lepers in Luke 17:12-19, only one came back to express gratitude to Him for this great gift of healing. Yet, He was still willing to heal all ten. When God's grace and mercy confront him, they bring the believer to a deeper appreciation for God's love and that love promotes Christian service.

Noah Found Grace

Then the Lord saw that the wickedness of man was great on the earth, and that every intent of the thoughts of his heart was only evil continually. The Lord was sorry that He had made man on the earth, and He was grieved in His heart. The Lord said, "I will blot out man whom I have created from the face of the land, from man to animals to creeping things and to birds of the sky; for I am sorry

that I have made them." But Noah found grace in the eyes of the Lord. These are the records of the generations of Noah. Noah was a righteous man, blameless in his time; Noah walked with God.
Genesis 6:5-9

Most Christians see grace as a New Testament concept, but the fact is grace is an Old Testament principle as well. In Genesis 6, we find a man named Noah, a good man, whom God favored by having him build a big boat! The Bible tells us that he was faithful to complete the project in spite of the people mocking him. God chose Noah and his family to be the ones delivered from this evil world. Looking closely at this "big boat", we see profound parallels with the dynamics of salvation as revealed in the New Testament.

The ark was built with cypress wood which was employed in shipbuilding by the Phoenicians due to its lightness and durability. It used bitumen, a pitch-like substance on both the inside and outside to make it watertight. There were three decks with a multitude of small compartments to house Noah's family and all the animals.

SALVATION AND NOAH'S ARK

In addition, it was three hundred cubits long, fifty wide, and thirty high and constructed more like a big chest, with a flat bottom and flat or slightly sloping roof. The intention of this type of construction was that it was meant to float with no ability to move on its own. There was one window at the top to provide light and air and one door on the side. The purpose, as stated by M. R. Unger in his Bible Dictionary, *"was to preserve certain persons and animals from the deluge with which God intended to overwhelm the land, in punishment for man's iniquities."* There was one pair of all "unclean" animals and seven pairs of all that were clean.

Now let us take a look at what this all means:

1. Cypress wood is light and durable. Salvation is able to weather any storm (John 10:30).

2. Bitumen provided a watertight environment to stand up to the waters. In Ephesians 1:13, *you were sealed in Him by the Holy Spirit of promise* which gives believers a safe environment.
3. The three decks speak to the fact that all three members of the Trinity play an important part in salvation (Ephesians 1:3-14).
4. Noah constructed the ark more like a chest than a boat, with no ability to move on its own. Salvation is a movement of God by the Holy Spirit who leads the believer (John 3:8).
5. The one window on the top is representative of the fact that our light and air (spiritually) come from God above (Romans 8:5-6).
6. God would close the one door on the side (Genesis 7:16) which speaks of Jesus as the door (John 10:9).

Just as the ark delivered the inhabitants to a new land and a new life, salvation provides the believer a brand-new life (2 Corinthians 5:17) and a new way to relate to the world around. The ark was safe and built specifically to fulfill its purpose. The grace of God that provides the environment for salvation to be possible to all believers (Ephesians 2:8) is abundant for all circumstances and situations (Romans 5:20-21). It is our job to learn to trust its provisions by standing in it in spite of the obstacles we face so that we can grow up to be the persons God has ordained (Romans 5:2).

"**Grace** *keeps giving me things I don't deserve;* **mercy** *keeps withholding things I do.*" – Wayne Watson

These words come from Wayne Watson's song, "Grace" and tell us that because of grace, I get things I do not deserve and because of mercy, I do not get what I deserve. That covers much ground and reminds us that He blesses us, despite our shortcomings.

An Illustration

Billy Graham tells the story about being pulled over by the police for traveling ten miles per hour over the speed limit. Upon appearing in court, the judge did not immediately recognize Dr. Graham, he read the charges to him, and told him that the fine would be $10. $1 for each mph over the limit. When Dr. Graham spoke and accepted a guilty plea, the judge finally recognized who he was. He reached into his pocket and took out a $10 bill, told Billy that he would pay the fine and told him he wanted to treat him to a steak dinner. You see, the $10 bill represents mercy, not getting what we deserve, and the steak dinner is His grace, getting what we do not deserve.

Chapter 8

LIFE IN THE HOLY SPIRIT

There came a woman of Samaria to draw water. Jesus said to her, "Give Me a drink." For His disciples had gone away into the city to buy food. Therefore, the Samaritan woman said to Him, "How is it that You, being a Jew, ask me for a drink since I am a Samaritan woman?" (For Jews have no dealings with Samaritans.) Jesus answered and said to her, "If you knew the gift of God, and who it is who says to you, 'Give Me a drink,' you would have asked Him, and He would have given you living water." She said to Him, "Sir, You have nothing to draw with and the well is deep; where then do You get that living water? "You are not greater than our father Jacob, are You, who gave us the well, and drank of it himself and his sons and his cattle?" Jesus answered and said to her, "Everyone who drinks of this water will thirst again; but whoever drinks of the water that I will give him shall never thirst; but the water that I will give him will become in him a well of water springing up to eternal life." **John 4:7-14**

It was the practice of the Jews to avoid the area known as Samaria when traveling between northern and southern Israel and use an eastern route along the Jordan River rather than come in contact with any Samaritan (*for Jews have no dealings with Samaritans*). But in John 4, Jesus and the disciples purposely went through Samaria on their way to Galilee and stopped at the place called Jacob's well. The woman at the well was a Samaritan and a wonderful conversation took place between Jesus and her. This exchange is rich in symbolism.

THE HOLY SPIRIT IS A GIFT

In Verse 10, Jesus refers to knowing the gift of God and *"the one it is who says to you, 'Give Me a drink.'"* This is a clear reference to salvation in Ephesians 2:8-9: *For by grace you have been saved through faith; and that not of yourselves,* **it is the gift of God**; *not as a result of works, so that no one may boast.* Scripture further reveals that this gift also manifests itself in the form of the Holy Spirit (Acts 2:38). In John 7:38-39, *"He who believes in Me, as the Scripture said, 'From his innermost being will flow rivers of living water.'"* **But this He spoke of the Spirit**, *whom those who believed in Him were to receive; for the Spirit was not yet given, because Jesus was not yet glorified.* The Holy Spirit is the very life source of a living relationship with God in the new covenant age.

The central issue of salvation is knowing who Jesus is, as the exchange in Matthew 16 between Jesus and Peter about who do *"you say that I am"*. Jesus told Peter and the disciples in Matthew 16:18, *"I also say to you that you are Peter, and upon this rock I will build My church; and the gates of Hades will not overpower it."* The rock that Jesus refers to is Peter's confession of faith in Verse 16, *"you are the Christ, the Son of the living God."* An individual's confession of who Jesus is builds the church and the Holy Spirit, the Spirit of Christ bears witness to who Jesus is (Romans 8:9-11).

FOUNTAIN OF LIVING WATER

There are many other references to water in the Scriptures that speak to the living water as the Holy Spirit. Psalm 1:3, Ezekiel 47:5, Proverbs 11:25, Isaiah 58:11, and Jeremiah 2:13 are also passages dealing with the life of the Holy Spirit expressed in terms of water. In Jeremiah 17:13, *O Lord, the hope of Israel, all who forsake You will be put to shame. Those who turn away on earth will be written down, because* **they have forsaken the fountain of living water,** *even the Lord.* This living water is the very life force of God in each believer. Jesus was introducing a new concept in that the Spirit would reside within each believer instead of "on" certain ones in the old covenant (see Isaiah 61:1). The life of the Spirit is the eternal life that God promises all believers in Christ.

Having this new life of the Spirit within, the believer has the ability to overcome the power of the sin nature which attaches itself to the flesh. The law of the Spirit of life in Christ Jesus which has set us free from the law of sin and death (Romans 8:2) provides the victory. This Holy Spirit is the source of the spiritual life and manifests Himself in the things that occupy one's mind. In Romans 8:5-8,

> *For those who are according to the flesh set their minds on the things of the flesh, but those who are according to the Spirit, the things of the Spirit. For the mind set on the flesh is death, but the mind set on the Spirit is life and peace, because the mind set on the flesh is hostile toward God; for it does not subject itself to the law of God, for it is not even able to do so, and those who are in the flesh cannot please God.*

The Holy Spirit gives us the option of walking with God by our mindset, our thought life. Colossians 3:2 instructs us to set our minds on things above, not on things of the earth.

SONS OF GOD

> *for if you are living according to the flesh, you must die; but if by the Spirit you are putting to death the deeds of the body, you will live.* **For all who are being led by the Spirit of God, these are sons of God.** *For you have not received a spirit of slavery leading to fear again, but you have received a spirit of adoption as sons by which we cry out, "Abba! Father!" The Spirit Himself testifies with our spirit that we are children of God.* **Romans 8:13-16**

As Romans 8 further illuminates in the passage above, the maturity barrier for the believer is a willingness for the leading of the Spirit of God (Verse 14) and when we do, we become sons (*huios*), not just children (*teknon*). One's willingness to die to the flesh (the part of me that wants to be in control, independent from God), comes through this leading of the Spirit. Putting to death the deeds of the body mean he does not allow the needs of the flesh to place lifestyle demands on him. He learns to trust that the Holy Spirit provides the divine ability to stand up against the lusts of the sin nature. It may require suffering, but it will be worth it, for we will be glorified with Him! The spirit of adoption as sons in Christ has given us victory over the spirit of slavery.

THE WORK OF THE HOLY SPIRIT

The Holy Spirit is an integral part of the successful life of the believer in Christ. Without the Holy Spirit, we have no ability to discern (appraise – examine evidence so as to understand) the things that are spiritual. Jesus refers to the Holy Spirit as the "*Spirit of truth* " and that "*He will guide you into all the truth* " in John 16:13. When Jesus challenged the Samaritan woman at the well with knowledge that He could not know except supernaturally, he was referring to this ability that the Holy Spirit gives. This ability to speak the truth caused her to recognize Jesus as Messiah (the Christ) and this is how the work of salvation reveals itself in a new believer's life. It is a supernatural work of the Holy Spirit, identifying Jesus as the Christ to anyone who seeks to know the truth.

In Genesis 24, the Scriptures tell us about Abraham getting elderly and desiring to find a wife for his son Isaac, but not from the Canaanites in the land where they lived, but from the place where Abraham grew up, Ur of the Chaldeans. This is symbolic of the work of the Holy Spirit in the new covenant age to find the bride for the Son. Abraham represents the Father, Isaac the Son, the servant is the Holy Spirit, and the wife is the church, the bride of Christ. The Father sends the Holy Spirit from the place where the Father and Son reside (heaven) to earth to find the bride for the bridegroom. The servant arrives at another well and is waiting for the right woman to respond to him, *"Drink and I will water your camels also."* The Holy Spirit is on the earth now that the Son no longer resides here, to find those who will believe in Christ and thus become his bride (Revelations 19:9). Salvation is a work of the Holy Spirit in the new covenant age and believers are willing participants in the process. In Proverbs 11:30, *The fruit of the righteous is a tree of life, and he who is wise wins souls.* We see the Samaritan woman used by the Holy Spirit to reveal the identity of the Messiah to other Samaritans (gentiles).

The Wise Win Souls

From that city **many of the Samaritans believed in Him because of the word of the woman who testified, "He told me all the things that I have done."** *So, when the Samaritans came to Jesus, they were asking Him to stay with them; and He stayed there two days. Many more believed because of His word; and they were saying to the woman, "It is no longer because of what you said that we believe, for we have heard for ourselves and know that this One is indeed the Savior of the world."* **John 4:39-42**

The story of the Samaritan woman continues with many Samaritans coming to Jesus to find out for themselves who He really was. They needed to find out for themselves that He is *"indeed the Savior of the world."* God uses us to encourage others to consider who Jesus really is, but it is the Spirit of God that confirms it in a new believer's life. Jesus's last words to His disciples in Matthew 28:19 and Acts 1:8 was for them to go into all the world and be witnesses of Jesus; it is the Spirit's job to make believers. We are workers in His field, and He is the Lord of the harvest (Matthew 9:37-38).

THAT WHICH IS BORN OF THE SPIRIT IS SPIRITUAL

The Holy Spirit is an integral part of the Christian's life, and we cannot overlook His importance. In Isaiah 58:11, *And the Lord will continually guide you, and satisfy your desire in scorched places, and give strength to your bones; and you will be like a watered garden, and **like a spring of water whose waters do not fail***. The work of the Holy Spirit brings us to new heights in our walk with God as we learn to experience all of God's blessings in the midst of scorched places, times when life challenges as in a desert. This personal experience with the Spirit of Christ will bring immense joy as *we joyously draw water from the springs of salvation* (Isaiah 12:3).

The Holy Spirit brings spiritual life and human effort, even good works cannot create it. In John 3:6, Jesus says, *"That which is born of the flesh is flesh, and that which is born of the Spirit is spirit* [spiritual].*"*

Chapter 9

THE DEITY AND HUMANITY OF JESUS

*In the beginning was the Word, and the Word was with God, and **the Word was God**. He was in the beginning with God. All things came into being through Him, and apart from Him nothing came into being that has come into being. In Him was life, and the life was the Light of men. The Light shines in the darkness, and the darkness did not comprehend it. There came a man sent from God, whose name was John. He came as a witness, to testify about the Light, so that all might believe through him. He was not the Light, but he came to testify about the Light. There was the true Light which, coming into the world, enlightens every man. He was in the world, and the world was made through Him, and the world did not know Him. He came to His own, and those who were His own did not receive Him. But as many as received Him, to them He gave the right to become children of God, even to those who believe in His name, who were born, not of blood nor of the will of the flesh nor of the will of man, but of God. **And the Word became flesh, and dwelt among us, and we saw His glory**, glory as of the only begotten from the Father, full of grace and truth. John testified about Him and cried out, saying, "This was He of whom I said, 'He who comes after me has a higher rank than I, **for He*** *existed before me." For of His fullness, we have all received, and grace upon grace. For the Law was given through Moses; grace and truth were realized through Jesus Christ. No one has seen God at any time; the only begotten God who is in the bosom of the Father, He has explained Him.* **John 1:1-18**

For many Christians, the gospel of John is their favorite book of the Bible. It is so different than the other gospels on many levels, not the least of which is its unique perspective, focusing its attention to the events in Jesus's life on the "why" rather than the "what happened." This is one reason Clement of Alexandria around 230 A.D. wrote: *"Last of all, John, perceiving that the bodily facts had been made plain in the gospel, being urged by his friends, composed a spiritual gospel."*

After nearly a century of life experiences and challenges against the central events of his life (namely the three years or so spent with the Savior of the world), John had a unique approach to telling the story after it had been told already by others qualified to tell it so many years before. He could choose particular events to relate that would agree with his Spirit-inspired narrative. His emphasis was the beginning of Jesus's ministry and its ending. Many of these events are not mentioned by the other writers, including the marriage feast at Cana (chapter 2), the coming of Nicodemus to Jesus (chapter 3), the Samaritan woman at the well (chapter 4), the raising of Lazarus (chapter 11), the washing of the disciples' feet (chapter 13), and the many references to the Holy Spirit, the Comforter in chapters 14-17. And it is also interesting to note that John does not reference any parables in his work!

GNOSTICISM

Written more than 30 years after the other three gospels, John wrote it most likely from Ephesus at the end of the first century when he was in his nineties and at the urging of friends and colleagues. The times were vastly different, with heresies perpetrated by an enemy that was still trying to destroy Christianity in its infancy. Two in particular that were gaining momentum at the time needed addressing. Gnosticism, a movement that saw matter as evil and spiritual as good, argued that God had nothing to do directly with creation, but through a series of emanations until the creator would come forth, far removed from God. The other heresy recognized John the Baptist as someone more than a prophet and therefore did not allow Jesus's acknowledgement as Messiah.

Not only did John wish to specifically address these heresies, but he also wanted to address the Greek (Hellenistic) and Jewish minds of the day through the concept of the "*logos*." To the Greeks, "*logos*" meant not only *word*, but more importantly *reason*, organized thought, and in reference to God, His *mind*. They believed in two worlds, the one we live in where realities are unclear and the spiritual realm representing the real world. They saw the material world as full of unrealities while the immaterial as fully real!

THE WORD

Unlike the Greeks, the Jews saw words as more than mere sounds, but things with power of their own. This concept of the word still exists today in the East, people seeing the word as having power and doing things. According to William Barclay's "The Gospel of John, Volume 1", it is told that Sir George Adam Smith was traveling in the desert in the East and a group of Moslems gave his party the customary greeting: "Peace be upon you." They discovered later that he was a Christian and hurried back to try to take back the words of blessing from the infidel. They believed the blessing of words had a life of its own.

The Jews also view words of God as having creative power, consistent with Genesis 1 and Psalm 33:6 – *By the word of the Lord the heavens were made.* The wisdom books of the Old Testament also use the word "*wisdom*" as having power unto itself.

It was with these issues in mind that John, under inspiration, addressed these various realities through the first eighteen Verses of his gospel. In this passage, John confirms that the Word, the very mind of God, existed before creation and was God. This Word also was responsible for all of creation (also see Colossians. 1:16). In vss. 6-8,

John addresses John the Baptist and his position in relation to Jesus. In Verse 14, *the Word became flesh, and dwelt among us*. It is clear from these Scriptures that Jesus Christ is fully God and fully man. Then in Verse 17, he contrasts Moses and the old covenant (the Law) to Jesus and the new covenant, a covenant defined by grace and truth.

CARDINAL DOCTRINES

To enter the new covenant, one must believe in the deity and incarnation (humanity) of Jesus; these are cardinal doctrines, meaning they are requirements. The gospel of John begins with these truths because they are foundational to a relationship with Him. There are religious systems that refer to themselves as Christian, but they do not recognize the full deity of Jesus. Yet the Scriptures are clear on this subject. In fact, Jesus went out of His way to make that point to many, including the Jewish leadership. They could recognize His humanity, but not His deity. As a result, Jesus spoke to His disciples and His enemies in a multitude of ways that He was the Messiah and therefore, fully God (see John 4:25-26). John 1:1 is one of many testimonies in Scripture to His deity. However, many over the years have raised real questions about His humanity.

In 1 John 4:2-3, *By this you know the Spirit of God:* **every spirit that confesses that Jesus Christ has come in the flesh is from God; and every spirit that does not confess Jesus is not from God;** *this is the spirit of the antichrist, of which you have heard that it is coming, and now it is already in the world.* John was making it clear that confessing the incarnation, the fulfillment of Isaiah 7:14 and other Old Testament verses, was one barometer of a legitimate salvation. This matter also becomes a point of contention for those who have embraced a spirit of antichrist. In 2 John 7, *For many deceivers have gone out into the world who do not confess Jesus Christ as coming in the flesh. This is a deceiver and an antichrist.* Like the Gnostics at the time John wrote these words, they operate with the same deceitful methods as the god of this world.

Heresies

There are heresies that are the result of a lack of acceptance of the deity and humanity of Christ. These include not only Gnosticism, but also Ebionism, Sabellianism, Arianism, and Apollinarianism, to name a few. In each case, there is not a full acceptance of both the deity and humanity of Christ which causes some doctrinal error or heresy. Plenty of non-Christan movements are rooted in some of these philosophies, including the Jehovah's Witnesses. But why are both doctrines of critical importance?

When Jesus, the second person of the Trinity, who was and is God became a man, He revealed that man now had a means of experiencing the full blessings of a relationship with God, Himself. In fact, He said as much in John 14:6, when He told Thomas, *"I am the way, the truth, and the life"*. He was teaching that through Him, the mediator of a new covenant, man could experience the supernatural privileges of being "in Christ," who was both God and man. *For there is one God, and one mediator also between God and men,* **the man Christ Jesus** – 1 Timothy 2:5. It is through identification with our humanity that the new covenant would surpass the old covenant. In 2 Corinthians 3:7-11,

> *But if the ministry of death, in letters engraved on stones, came with glory, so that the sons of Israel could not look intently at the face of Moses because of the glory of his face, fading as it was, how will the ministry of the Spirit fail to be even more with glory? For if the ministry of condemnation has glory, much more does the ministry of righteousness abound in glory. For indeed what had glory, in this case has no glory* **because of the glory that surpasses it**. *For if that which fades away was with glory, much more that which remains is in glory.*

Triumph over Death and Sin

Another accomplishment requiring His full humanity was His triumph over death. In Hebrews 2:14, *Therefore, since the children share in flesh and blood, He Himself likewise also partook of the same, that through death He might render powerless him who had the power of death, that is, the devil.* By overcoming death, Jesus not only conquered death, but also provided a victory over the fear of death that subjects people to slavery (Verse 15). In addition, Romans 8:3 testifies that *He condemned sin in the flesh* since Jesus was *an offering for sin* by His Father. This could only be accomplished in the flesh.

Finally, Paul summarized the mystery of godliness (*eusebeia* – well-directed reverence, externalized piety, or devotion) this way in 1 Timothy 3:16, **He who was revealed [made incarnate] *in the flesh*,** *was vindicated* [justified] *in the Spirit, seen by angels, proclaimed among the nations, believed on in the world, taken up in glory.* It is divine power confirmed through the true knowledge of Christ's deity and humanity that *has granted to us everything pertaining to life and godliness* (2 Peter 1:3).

Chapter 10

BELIEVING IN THE PROMISES

Therefore, He came again to Cana of Galilee where He had made the water wine. And there was a royal official whose son was sick at Capernaum. When he heard that Jesus had come out of Judea into Galilee, he went to Him and was imploring Him to come down and heal his son; for he was at the point of death. So, Jesus said to him, "Unless you people see signs and wonders, you simply will not believe." The royal official said to Him, "Sir, come down before my child dies." Jesus said to him, "Go; your son lives." The man believed the word that Jesus spoke to him and started off. As he was now going down, his slaves met him, saying that his son was living. So, he inquired of them the hour when he began to get better. Then they said to him, "Yesterday at the seventh hour the fever left him." So, the father knew that it was at that hour in which Jesus said to him, "Your son lives;" and he himself believed and his whole household. This is again a second sign that Jesus performed when He had come out of Judea into Galilee. **John 4:46-54**

We can understand God's plan for humanity within seven different dispensations that God has provided in sequence covering the entire gamut of human history: Innocence, Conscience,

Human Government, Promise, Law, Grace, and The Kingdom. Dispensations are ages of history when God uniquely deals with His people. For example, in Genesis 2, in the age of Innocence, God has a unique relationship with Adam and Eve in the Garden of Eden. Then in Genesis 3, things changed because of the failure of Adam and Eve and God removed them from the Garden and the Age of Conscience began. The fourth of these, Promise, centers on Abraham and the unconditional promises God made to him. Because many of these promises have not yet been fulfilled, it is still relevant today. Paul spoke extensively of Abraham and God's promises to him as part of the new covenant age in Romans and Galatians. During the old covenant age, the requirements of the Law of Moses directed the Jews, and the promises of God were not the priority.

Learning how to believe in the promises of God is not an easy task. It requires believing that the promised event is possible and that the one promising it can and will accomplish it. That is what makes the event in John 4 so remarkable. Here we have a gentile, a royal official asking Jesus to come to heal his son from a deadly condition. The account tells us that he came himself rather than sending a servant which suggests the level of concern for his son as well as his confidence that Jesus was the answer. He originally asked Jesus to come to the place where his son was, but Jesus told him, "*Go, your son lives.*" This gentile believed it immediately and resumed his plans as if the deed was a reality. As a fact, he found out later from his slaves that the healing of his son took place the very moment that Jesus pronounced it. Jesus became Messiah to him and his whole household.

HE IS BOTH WILLING AND ABLE

A similar event occurs in Matthew 8:5-13 with the healing of the servant of a Roman centurion in Capernaum. In this instance, Jesus offered to come, but the centurion made his famous statement, "*Lord, I am not worthy for You to come under my roof, but just say the word, and my servant will be healed.*" He continued by recognizing what authority is and acknowledged that Jesus had the authority to heal simply by speaking the word and it would be done. And Jesus commended his statement by saying *"Truly I say to you, I have not found such great faith with anyone in Israel."* Here is another non-Jew, demonstrating more faith than a Jew.

And then there was the leper in Matthew 8:1-3, approaching Jesus with this statement, *"Lord, if You are willing, You can make me clean."* He acknowledged that Jesus was able and the only question in the leper's mind was His willingness to do it. Of course, we know that Jesus responded, *"I am willing; be cleansed"* and healed the man. Believing in the promises means believing that He is both willing and able. It means that the believer acknowledges that Jesus is God, fully capable to fulfill His promises and that it would happen if He promised it.

God will Provide

There is a no more notable example of this kind of faith than that of Abraham in Genesis 22, when God tells him to offer His promised son, Isaac on an altar on Mount Moriah to the Lord. The account suggests no wavering on Abraham's part, but he got up early the next morning and brought Isaac, servants, and split wood for the offering and traveled more than two days to get there. As the two of them walked together, Isaac asked his father where the sacrifice of the lamb would take place? Abraham's response is profound: *"God will provide for Himself the lamb for the burnt offering, my son"* (Verse 8). But where did this kind of faith come from?

In the book of Hebrews, we get a chance to go behind the scenes, "the rest of the story" as Paul Harvey would say and see what was on his mind when he chose to believe God. Hebrews 11:19 says, *He considered that God is able to raise people even from the dead, from which he also received him back as a type.* Abraham actually believed that, because the fulfillment of these promises would happen through Isaac, God would have to raise him from the dead. Of course, we know that God did not require Isaac's sacrifice, but was testing Abraham's faith in the promises of God. In fact, the Lord says that *"I now know that you fear God."* God was demonstrating to Abraham and to all of us the depth of Abraham's willingness to trust Him. Believing in the promises means we are all in and are holding nothing back!

We also see in this account a picture of the Father and the Son and the Father's willingness to offer His Son for us (John 3:16). It testifies to us that He is willing.

BLESSINGS OF ABRAHAM

God made some amazing promises to Abram in Genesis 12, when He told him to leave Haran and go to a land Abram knew nothing of. And it is there that Abram, later to be Abraham, would come and begin to receive the blessings. God made many promises to Abram and Abraham, as expressed by M. F. Unger in his Bible Dictionary, including the following fourfold blessing: *"(1) increase into a numerous people; (2) material and spiritual prosperity-"I will bless you"; (3) the exaltation of Abraham's name-"make your name great"; (4) Abraham was not only to be blessed by God, but to be a blessing to others, implicitly by the coming of the Messiah through his descendants (Genesis 12:1-3)."*

Paul refers specifically to these promises in both Galatians and Romans and their impact on new covenant believers. His perspective is that the promises God made to Abraham occurred hundreds of years before the Law of Moses and the Law does not invalidate all those promises He made to Abraham. He speaks of inheritance as the means by which the believer receives the blessings of the covenant God made to Abraham more than four thousand years ago. In fact, according to Galatians 3:16, *Now the promises were spoken to Abraham and to his seed. He does not say, 'And to seeds,' as referring to many, but rather to one, 'And to your seed,' that is, Christ.* So then, the agency of receiving these promises is faith in Jesus Christ, as part of our inheritance, as it says in Verse 22, *so that the promise by faith in Jesus Christ might be given to those who believe.*

Believing the Unbelievable

Paul emphasizes in Romans 4 that because it is by faith, it must also be in accordance with grace in Verse 16 as the means by which believers in Christ receive the benefits of these promises. For it was Abraham who pioneered the way for all believers in Christ to live by faith, as if God's promises would come true. His faith did not waver because he held on to the promise that he and Sarah would have a child of their own, even though it was physically impossible. It would happen because God said it would happen. The only unanswered question was when! Verse 21 tells us that Abraham became fully assured or persuaded that when God promises something, it undoubtedly will happen. His faith becomes our faith by believing that Jesus, the seed is the Christ, that He accomplished full payment for our sins (speaks of worthiness), and that He is coming back to set things straight for the church and the Jews.

In Hebrews 11:1, *Now faith is the assurance of things hoped for, the conviction of things not seen*. It tells us that God's unanswered promises will come true and that He is not lying about what He says He has already accomplished. The Greek word for conviction is *"elegchos"* and it means certain persuasion. Just like Abraham, believers in Christ become *fully assured that what God had promised, He was able also to perform* (Romans 4:21). This quality of faith can only happen once one believes that the promised event is possible and that the One promising it can and will accomplish it. He must believe in the character of the One making the promises, that He will be faithful even when the believer is not (2 Timothy 2:13).

Children of the Promise

Paul tells us in Galatians 4:28 that, like Isaac, we are children of promise. He tells us that we must not become offspring of the standards of righteousness achieved by human effort, but only by putting our full confidence in the righteousness of Jesus Christ can we receive our promised inheritance. Works programs do not afford us any benefits with God. In fact, Romans 9:6-8 tells us that not all Israel are children of God, but only those who are children of the promise. We must learn not to allow those who hold onto the works of the Law as a means of righteousness to influence us, but *"cast out"* those who would negatively influence our walk of faith by grace.

One of the most important lessons a believer in Christ must learn is how to wait. When God does not act as quickly as we would like, we get anxious and want to take matters into our own hands. But 2 Peter 3:9 says, *The Lord is not slow about His promise, as some count slowness, but is patient toward you, not wishing for any to perish but for all to come to repentance.* He wants us to exercise patience and he will reward that patience as James 1:12 says, *Blessed is a man who perseveres under trial.* We are to look for the *blessed hope and the appearing of the glory of our great God and Savior* (Titus 2:13) and *walk by faith and not by sight* (2 Corinthians 5:7).

Chapter 11

HEARING THE VOICE OF GOD

A critical part of spiritual maturity is developing the ability to hear the voice of God. Without it, the believer becomes part of the herd, following others who are following others. The uniqueness of each relationship with God requires the Christian to hear the gentle whisper (still small voice – 1 Kings 19:12) as He leads, directs, guides, teaches, encourages, corrects, and convicts each one who desires to know God intimately. This ability does not happen by accident but begins with the believer recognizing that hearing the quietness of His whispers is the byproduct of knowing one's identity as a child of God. In Psalm 46:10, *Be still, and know that I am God; I will be exalted among the nations, I will be exalted in the earth!*

In John 6:45, *It is written in the prophets, "AND THEY SHALL ALL BE TAUGHT OF GOD." Everyone who has heard and learned from the Father, comes to Me.* Jesus was teaching His disciples that to be a learner, the very meaning of being a disciple, requires the ability to hear from God, and that this is the avenue for a deeper relationship with Him. God wanted the Jews to understand that they must be taught His ways, the avenue that allows each to walk in His paths. In reference to the future kingdom age, Isaiah said, *And many peoples will come and say, "Come, let us go up to the mountain of the Lord, to the house of the God of Jacob; that He may teach us concerning His ways and that we may walk in His paths." For the law will go forth from Zion and the word of the Lord from Jerusalem* (Isaiah 2:3). To hear the voice of God in the new covenant ages, both church age and kingdom age, the believer must listen to the Messiah, Jesus Christ. In Matthew 17:5, the Father spoke to Peter, James & John on the Mount of Transfiguration, *"This is My beloved Son, with whom I am well-pleased; listen to Him!"*

FALSE TEACHERS

In John 10:1, Jesus speaks of a door through which the shepherd must enter into the sheepfold; the thief or robber uses another door. The reference is to false teachers, who set themselves up to the Jewish people as rabbis and prophets but cannot hear from God and are not the true teachers. The Lord warned about these false teachers in Jeremiah 23: 1-2, *"Woe to the shepherds who are destroying and scattering the sheep of My pasture!" declares the Lord. Therefore, thus says the Lord God of Israel concerning the shepherds who are tending My people: "You have scattered My flock and driven them away, and have not attended to them; behold, I am about to attend to you for the evil of your deeds," declares the Lord.* The greatest enemy of the believer comes from within the church and not from without. Jesus is identifying the scribes and Pharisees as false teachers, having attained their positions through means other than recognition of, faith in, and reliance upon Messiah (John 10:26). The door of the sheepfold is a door of mercy and not just the occupation of high ecclesiastical office. It is the result of a heavenly commission, like the prophet in Jeremiah 1:5, *Before I formed you in the womb I knew you, and before you were born, I consecrated you; I have appointed you a prophet to the nations.* The new covenant commentary on this appears in Ephesians 4:11, where Paul identifies those whom God has gifted for ministry.

Like the Pharisees within the Jewish faith, Paul identifies this same phenomenon within the church as a work of Satan to destroy its foundation through false teaching and human accomplishment as opposed to the work of God in and through the believer. They make themselves look and sound like apostles of Christ, but they are really wolves in sheep's clothing (Matthew 7:15). This has always been Satan's strategy, to counterfeit the goodness of God in order to destroy the work of God from within. In John 10:10, *"The thief comes only to steal and kill and destroy."* These servants of the devil disguise themselves as *"servants of righteousness,"* yet they rely on man's work and are judged by that work (Revelation 20:12). The fullness of this work of Satan manifests itself in the anti-Christ, the lawless one, who is prophesied to come in the near future in Paul's second letter to the Thessalonians.

THE GOOD SHEPHERD

The ability of the believer to hear and respond to the voice of God defines his ability to be led by God. According to John 10, the shepherd speaks, and the sheep recognizes the voice. It is the voice of the Good Shepherd, speaking to each believer and through the pastor with the heart of God (Jeremiah 3:15), feeding the people of God on knowledge and understanding. As Elijah arrived at Mount Horeb, the same area Moses had heard from God on Mount Sinai many years earlier, scriptures reveal in 1 Kings 19:11-12 that God would not speak with him through wind, an earthquake, or a fire (the signs of God's judgment), but the sound of a gentle whisper (still small voice in KJV). He was instructing the people of God that He will speak in quiet whispers and not an audible voice that all can hear. God wishes His people to develop an ability to hear His voice as He speaks in the quietness of the details of life and not by the fire and brimstone through which He had been known.

To hear the voice of the Good Shepherd, the believer must recognize His authority just as the sheep recognizes the authority of the shepherd. The shepherd has demonstrated His willingness to lay His life down for the sheep and therefore found trustworthy in everything. His voice is dependable and is able to fulfill every promise He makes. In Psalm 29:4-5, **The voice of the Lord** *is powerful,* **the voice of the Lord** *is majestic.* **The voice of the Lord** *breaks the cedars; yes, the Lord breaks in pieces the cedars of Lebanon.* The new covenant believer learns to trust

His voice since He always speaks the truth and wishes to lead the flock in safe places.

THE SHEPHERD & THE SHEEP

The 23rd Psalm may be the most recognizable passage of Scripture. It speaks of the relationship between the shepherd and the sheep (believer) and the work of the shepherd in the believer's life. It is undeniable that Jesus had this passage in mind when He spoke of the shepherd and sheep in John 10. The Psalm gives the believer great insight into the profound relationship that exists between shepherd and believer creating the confidence of the believer that, when the Lord is my shepherd, I shall not want (I shall want of nothing). It speaks of the commitment that the Lord has to the believer in all points of life, including the very face of death. Recognizing the full commitment that the Lord has in the believer's life is foundational to listening and hearing the Lord as He leads the believer through the details and challenges of life. When the Lord speaks, He speaks with full authority and the believer can expect that what He promises, He is also able to do and will do (Ephesians 3:20).

A DOER

"Why do you call Me, 'Lord, Lord,' and do not do what I say? Everyone who comes to Me and hears My words and acts on them, I will show you whom he is like: he is like a man building a house, who dug deep and laid a foundation on the rock; and when a flood occurred, the torrent burst against that house and could not shake it, because it had been well built. But the one who has heard and has not acted accordingly, is like a man who built a house on the ground without any foundation; and the torrent burst against it and immediately it collapsed, and the ruin of that house was great." **Luke 6:46-49**

Once the voice of God has been heard, it becomes necessary for the believer to act on that voice. Jesus's brother, James warns us that faith without works is dead (James 2:17). The very foundation of faith is a willingness to act, to do what God has commanded. In James 1:22-24, *But prove yourselves doers of the word, and not merely hearers who delude themselves. For if anyone is a hearer of the word and not a doer, he is like a man who looks at his natural face in a mirror, for once he has looked at himself and gone away, he has immediately forgotten what kind of person he was.* The measure of the confidence the believer has in his own faith in who Jesus is and what He accomplished is related to his conviction to act on what he has heard.

Chapter 12

THE VOICE OF TRUTH

There is a battle going on in the world for the control of the minds and hearts of man. This is a spiritual battle and centers on the issue of truth versus the lie. The Greek word translated truth is *aletheia* and it means that which is true or real, "the unveiled reality lying at the basis of and agreeing with an appearance" (Zodhiates Complete Word Study). Truth is a matter that rests on authentic facts to reveal that which is real. Truth originates with a person, Jesus Christ (John 14:6) and then testified to by the Holy Spirit (John 16:13). Truth is also the language He uses in speaking to His followers, the voice of truth. When Pilate was interrogating Jesus in John 18:37, Jesus told him, "*for this I have come into the world, to testify to the truth.* **Everyone who is of the truth hears My voice**." In John 10:27, "*My sheep hear My voice, and I know them, and they follow Me.*"

There is another voice which is contrary to the truth. Its intention is to distort the truth or modify it, thereby removing its distinct sound. Jesus tells us that this other voice comes from the devil in John 8:44, "*You are of your father the devil, and you want to do the desires of your father. He was a murderer from the beginning and does not stand in the truth because there is no truth in him. Whenever he speaks a lie, he speaks from his own nature,* **for he is a liar and the father of lies**." Jesus teaches that all lies originate with the devil who "*does not stand in the truth because there is no truth in him.*" His agenda is to lead people away from the truth. When Jesus spoke these words, He was addressing the Pharisees, who did not believe Him because they were not of the truth (Verses 45-47).

What is Truth?

There are so many examples of the devil twisting the truth to lead people astray. In fact, it happened at the very beginning of man's existence when he deceived Eve and then Adam to their fall from the garden of Eden in Genesis 3. He also tried to deceive Jesus in Matthew 4 by twisting Scripture, but Jesus clearly understood what the evil one was doing. Jesus's response was to quote Scripture accurately. The devil continues to represent the lie as truth, illustrated by the story below.

> A story is told about a man who was walking through a forest when he saw a tree with an arrow embedded in the exact center of a target. Impressed, the man took note but continued his walk only to find another tree a few yards away, again with an arrow exactly in the center of the target. As he continued on, he saw another tree with a perfect hit, and then another, and still another. After about ten trees the man decided that he must find the talented archer and recruit him for the king's army. After searching, he found a man shooting arrows. "Are you the man who has shot the arrows at all the trees in this forest?" asked the traveler. "Indeed, I am," replied the archer. "How did you become such an expert archer?" inquired the man. The archer explained, "It was easy. I simply shot arrows at the trees. Then I drew the targets around the spot that I had hit!"

The devil redefines truth according to his own agenda; he disguises himself as an angel of light (2 Corinthians 11:14) by making his lie appear to be truth. Truth is eternal and immutable. God will reprove anyone who adds to His Word and proven to be a liar (Proverbs 30:6).

THE WORD OF GOD AND THE TRUTH

The primary vehicle that God employs to deliver the truth to His people is His Word. In John 8:31-32, *So Jesus was saying to those Jews who had believed Him, "If you continue in My word, then you are truly disciples of Mine; and you will know the truth, and the truth will make you free."* The Word of God is the truth (John 17:17) and should not be treated casually. To continue in His Word is to dwell there, to remain there, to live richly there. The true believer is not just passing through the Word of God, he is taking up residence there.

Truth is not just something one agrees with, but it defines the way he lives. It is the avenue by which the believer fellowships with God, hears His voice, and testifies to others. In 1 John 1:6, *If we say that we have fellowship with Him and yet walk in the darkness, we lie and do not practice the truth.* Practicing the truth means that it defines one's lifestyle and proves his motives, that *his deeds may be manifested as having been wrought in God* (John 3:21). He hears the voice of truth clearly.

BUY TRUTH

The psalmist prays to the Lord to, *Lead me in Your truth and teach me, for You are the God of my salvation* (Psalm 25:5). The Holy Spirit is our guide into the truth by the Word of God and we are enabled to discern the lie because of the richness of the truth resident in us. When the FBI trains its people to identify counterfeit currency, it emphasizes all aspects of the characteristics of a legitimate bill. The best way to identify a lie is to be an expert in the truth. Solomon writes in Proverbs 23:23 to buy, acquire, possess truth, and do not give it away or sell it since it brings wisdom, instruction, and understanding. Truth has a voice.

> *For I was very glad when brethren came and testified to your truth, that is, how you are walking in truth. I have no greater joy than this, to hear of my children walking in the truth.* **3 John 3**

Chapter 13

SIN AND BLINDNESS

To most, the passage in John 9 deals with a blind man healed by Jesus on the Sabbath, but it is much more about the healing from sin that Jesus accomplished at Calvary. The new covenant is the means by which every believer can find the victorious life and deliverance from the effects of sin which places believers in its bondage. Jesus uses this miracle, the only one in the gospels in which the one healed was **afflicted before birth**, to clear up many of the myths that the Jewish mindset embraced regarding the impact of sins on future generations. He also was illustrating the power of the cross in opening the eyes of believers to the mysteries of the kingdom of heaven which God has reserved for new covenant saints (Matthew 13:11).

The Jewish mindset of Jesus's day recognized a direct link between sin and suffering and was the reason for the disciples' question when passing this blind man in John 9. Their question was asking who was to blame for the man's blindness, as if every human affliction can be traced to some active failure by someone. Jesus's answer to the question was telling, *"It was neither that this man sinned, nor his parents; but it was so that the works of God might be displayed in him"* (Verse 3). He was saying that human affliction can have more to do with revealing God's glory than identifying someone to blame.

The Jewish Mindset

The Jewish thought at this time relating to sin and suffering can be summarized as follows:

1. The merits or demerits of the parents appear in the children. Certain special sins in the parents would result in particular diseases in the offspring.
2. The child up to age 13 was considered to be living in the effects of his father's sins, suffering for his guilt.
3. The thoughts of a mother might affect the moral state of her unborn offspring.
4. The terrible apostacy of one of the greatest Rabbis was caused by the sinful delight his mother had taken when passing through an idol grove.
5. They also adopted the idea from Plato and the Greeks that souls preexist creation in some heavenly place, waiting entry into the body. Although the Greeks saw all souls as good and contamination occurred when entering the body, the Jews believed that some souls were good and some bad.

This mindset is proliferated in the account of Job and his trial. Although God allowed Satan to attack Job physically, materially, and personally, Job's "friends" kept telling him that Job must have done something terribly wrong to have to go through what he did. Job did not believe it, but it left him with significant questions about God's justice – the answer to the question "why." It was not until after the trial was over and God had restored all that he had lost that we can now understand that his trial was to glorify God, God's work displayed in him.

Imputed Sin

Therefore, just as through one man sin entered into the world, and death through sin, and so death spread to all men, because all sinned — for until the Law sin was in the world, but sin is not imputed when there is no law. Nevertheless, death reigned from Adam until Moses, even over those who had not sinned in the likeness of the offense of Adam, who is a type of Him who was to come. **Romans 5:12-14**

The Greek word translated "sin" is "*hamartia*" and it means "*an offense in relation to God with emphasis on guilt, to miss the true end and scope of our lives, which is God,*" according to Spiros Zodhiates. As Paul relates in Romans 5, the sin nature is a condition of humanity that began with Adam in Genesis 3 (original sin) and has been imputed (transmitted) to each succeeding generation. Each human is born with a sin nature and therefore, sins (Romans 3:10-18). Even during the period before the Law of Moses, the sin nature was producing death in each person, because all sinned. The ultimate conclusion of this matter is that man is a sinner because of his sin nature and because of the sins he commits and no one other than Jesus is exempt.

In John 9:6-7, Jesus healed the man (on the Sabbath) by spitting on dirt to create clay, which he rubbed on the man's eyes. He then told the man to go to the pool of Siloam, the only freshwater basin in the immediate neighborhood in Jerusalem, to wash it off and he *came back seeing*. (This reminds us of Naaman's healing of leprosy through Elisha by washing in the Jordan River in 2 Kings 5:10-14). Just as Jesus had healed the man of his blindness, He also heals the sinner of the sin condition by offering a provision for that condition, namely His blood.

Sabbath Requirements

Jesus went out of His way to perform this miracle on the Sabbath to confront the foolishness of many once again of the man-made laws (Mishnah) that governed work on the Sabbath. To understand this issue, consider the following beliefs of the Jews during this time:

1. Saliva was commonly regarded as a remedy for diseases of the eye, but not a cure for blindness.

2. This healing is a manifold breach of the Mishnah since Jesus made clay.
3. There was a question about whether any remedy could be applied on the holy day. It could only be done to diseases of the organ (from the throat down) except when danger to life or the loss of an organ was involved.
4. It was lawful to apply wine to the outside of the eyelid on the grounds that it was considered washing, but unlawful to apply it to the inside of the eye. Use of saliva on the Sabbath was always considered unlawful.

Jesus was exposing not only the failure of the Mishnah to make a man righteous, but also revealing that He was able to heal without restriction. The healing of a man born blind was Messianic (see Verse 23) since it would require the ability to recreate, and no one but God, Himself could do it. Much of the rest of the account is a lame attempt by the Pharisees to in some way disprove that it really did happen or that Jesus was not from God. They finally got so frustrated with the healed man that they accused him of being "*born entirely in sins*" (Verse and then excommunicated him from the temple.

SPIRITUAL BLINDNESS

The account concludes in Verses 35-41 with Jesus finding the healed man after hearing about the excommunication and getting the man to recognize Him as the Son of Man, another term for Messiah. The man's confession of faith, "*Lord, I believe*" resulted in the man worshiping Jesus and then Jesus spoke of the relationship between blindness and sin. He said to the Pharisees, "*If you were blind, you would have no sin; but since you say, 'We see,' your sin remains.*" Jesus had referred earlier in Matthew 15:14, "*Let them alone; they are blind guides of the blind. And if a blind man guides a blind man, both will fall into a pit.*" Jesus was teaching that the unconverted sin nature causes man to be blind, blind to the sin condition that has plagued the human race since Adam.

Not only is the god of this world, the devil, blinding the minds of all unbelievers to be against Jesus and the gospel, there is a hardening of the heart that burdens all unconverted Jews during the new covenant age, resulting in a veil over their hearts (2 Corinthians 3:14-16). Whenever the Jew recognizes Jesus as Messiah, *the veil is taken away* and therefore his blindness is resolved in Christ. This warfare centers itself on man not seeing *the glory of God in the face of Christ* (2 Corinthians 4:6). When the Light begins to shine in their hearts, meaning the enlightenment of God illuminates the minds of those who seek him with sincerity of heart, there is a new understanding of the God who leads one to salvation. A notable example of this process reveals itself in the salvation of the apostle Paul in Acts 9:3-6, when a light shone, and he was able to hear the Lord speaking directly to his heart in the midst of his blindness.

The Effects of Idolatry

I will lead the blind by a way they do not know, in paths they do not know I will guide them. I will make darkness into light before them and rugged places into plains. These are the things I will do, and I will not leave them undone. They will be turned back and be utterly put to shame, who trust in idols, who say to molten images, "You are our gods." Hear, you deaf! And look, you blind, that you may see. Who is blind but My servant, or so deaf as My messenger whom I send? Who is so blind as he that is at peace with Me, or so blind as the servant of the Lord? You have seen many things, but you do not observe them; your ears are open, but none hears.
Isaiah 42:16-20

The context of the above passage in Isaiah 42 is a reference to the coming Messiah, *"My Servant"* in Verse 1. The new covenant provides sight to the blind through a living faith in Jesus as Messiah. This passage reveals that the cause of the blindness and deafness of Israel was their idolatry, creating these idols as *molten images*. When the Lord used *"My servant"* in Verse 19 as being blind and deaf, He was speaking about Israel. When Jesus is not Lord, other lords are adopted, and the result will be blindness and deafness. James 1:14-15 tells us that the process of sin is to be *carried away and enticed by his own lust. Then when lust has conceived, it gives birth to sin; and when sin is accomplished, it brings forth death.* Human lust patterns are empowered when Jesus is not Lord and the temptation to entertain and act upon those lustful desires becomes overpowering, resulting in sin and unconfessed sin leads to *"death,"* separation from God (no fellowship).

SON OF DAVID, HAVE MERCY ON ME

As Jesus was approaching Jericho, a blind man was sitting by the road begging. Now hearing a crowd going by, he began to inquire what this was. They told him that Jesus of Nazareth was passing by. And he called out, saying, "Jesus, Son of David, have mercy on me!" Those who led the way were sternly telling him to be quiet; but he kept crying out all the more, "Son of David, have mercy on me!" And Jesus stopped and commanded that he be brought to Him; and when he came near, He questioned him, "What do you want Me to do for you?" And he said, "Lord, I want to regain my sight!" And Jesus said to him, "Receive your sight; your faith has made you well." Immediately he regained his sight and began following Him, glorifying God; and when all the people saw it, they gave praise to God. **Luke 18:35-43**

Luke's Gospel covers two fitting examples of this process as Jesus and the disciples are approaching Jericho (Luke 18:35-43) and then after entering Jericho (Zaccheus - Luke 19:1-10). This first man, unnamed, was told by the crowd that Jesus was passing by, so he cried out, *"Jesus, Son of David, have mercy on me!"* This man recognized that Jesus of Nazareth was Messiah and that He was capable of healing him. In Verse 42, Jesus acknowledged his faith when He said, *"Receive your sight; your faith has made you well."* This man immediately became a follower.

Man's problem with sin is entirely resolved in the work of Christ on the cross. Spiritual blindness is no longer sin's curse once the believer declares Jesus as Messiah, God in the flesh, and accepts His righteousness in the heart (Romans 10:9-10).

Chapter 14

FORGIVEN-NESS

C. S. Lewis once said, "*To be a Christian means to forgive the inexcusable because God has forgiven the inexcusable in you.*" To fully appreciate the quality of the Christian life, the believer must appreciate the quality of forgiveness and be willing to pass it on. Making this connection real begins with an acceptance that the new covenant offers the believer total forgiveness for all sins, past, present, and future. In Hebrews 8:12, "*FOR I WILL BE MERCIFUL TO THEIR INIQUITIES, AND I WILL REMEMBER THEIR SINS NO MORE.*" Like many Biblical realities, the Scriptures contain illustrations that make the principle more acceptable. In John 8:1-11, Jesus purposely demonstrates the principle to His disciples and then, to us.

The scene takes place in the temple, where Jesus would instruct the people. The scribes and Pharisees bring a woman to Him, caught in the act of adultery to test Jesus regarding the Law of Moses. He is asked what the Law should do to the woman. In Leviticus 20:10, the Law says, *If there is a man who commits adultery with another man's wife, one who commits adultery with his friend's wife, the adulterer and the adulteress shall surely be put to death.* The Jewish leaders ask him if the woman should be stoned to death. Jesus's response is to bend down and write on the ground with His finger. Their persistence results in Jesus challenging them with this statement, "*He who is without sin among you, let him be the first to throw a stone at her.*" You know the story; as Jesus writes again on the ground, each accuser walking away, beginning with the oldest.

THE NEED FOR A WITNESS

The legal issues surrounding this event require a closer examination. First, Leviticus 20:10 says that both the adulterer and adulteress should die. The leaders were only accusing the adulteress, where is the adulterer? Secondly, it is interesting to note that the Law of Moses (Deuteronomy 17:7) requires that in cases of capital punishment, a witness should throw the first stone. But the Law also says in Deuteronomy 17:6-7 that capital punishment requires that there be two or three witnesses. Where are the witnesses? None met these requirements. Jesus was challenging the administration of the Law of Moses, that it should be completely lawful, and the Pharisees were being selective in its application.

Looking closer at the events, we see a deeper meaning. In James 4:12, *There is only one Lawgiver and Judge, the One who is able to save and to destroy.* Compare that to Exodus 31:18 which says that the finger of God wrote the two tablets of stone, and you begin to see that Jesus, the Lawgiver wrote the old covenant with his finger, and He is now writing with His finger on the ground. The Lawgiver is writing a new covenant. He is not only writing it, but also demonstrating it.

SIN NO MORE

Back to John 8, Jesus is now alone with the accused woman. Jesus asks her if there is anyone left to condemn her, and she responds no. Now Jesus reveals the truth of the new covenant, found in Romans 8:1, that, *Therefore there is now no condemnation for those who are in Christ Jesus.* Jesus tells her He does not condemn her either. Then He makes this amazing statement which is the purpose of the new covenant, "*Go. From now on sin no more.*" The old covenant condemns, the new covenant does not; the old covenant is concerned with punishment while the new covenant centers its efforts on sinning no more. Living in the reality of forgiveness of all sin because of what Jesus did enables the believer to live in victory. This passage in the Gospel of John is graphically illustrating that the new covenant provides full forgiveness.

The Old Testament account of Joshua the high priest (Zechariah 3:1-5) foretells the total forgiveness of sins through the Messiah. It tells that Joshua was standing before *the angel of the Lord,* a reference to Jesus Christ and Satan was accusing Joshua, as evidenced by his filthy garments. The Lord rebukes Satan and in Verse 4, Jesus says, *"Remove the filthy garments from him,"* and then, *"See, I have taken your iniquity away from you and will clothe you with festal robes."* Jesus then commanded *"Let them put a clean turban on his head."* signifying the restoration of Joshua's priesthood. In 1 Peter 2:5 and 9, Peter recognizes the new covenant believer as a part of a holy and royal priesthood.

Man's ability to walk in the new covenant is related to his understanding and acceptance that the work of Jesus on the cross of Calvary paid for all of his failures, mistakes, rebellion against authority, immorality, broken promises, lies, etc... The more one comes to appreciate the depth of his depravity, the more he will recognize the quality of the payment Jesus made for him. It becomes motivation to acknowledge the holiness of God and live with an eye toward that holiness.

HE WHO HAS BEEN FORGIVEN MUCH

Turning toward the woman, He said to Simon, "Do you see this woman? I entered your house; you gave Me no water for My feet, but she has wet My feet with her tears and wiped them with her hair. "You gave Me no kiss; but she, since the time I came in, has not ceased to kiss My feet. "You did not anoint My head with oil, but she anointed My feet with perfume. "For this reason, I say to you, her sins, which are many, have been forgiven, for she loved much; but he who is forgiven little, loves little." Then He said to her, "Your sins have been forgiven." Those who were reclining at the table with Him began to say to themselves, "Who is this man who even forgives sins?" And He said to the woman, 'Your faith has saved you; go in peace." **Luke 7:44-50**

The woman in this passage was expressly described as a sinner (perhaps a prostitute) who had found forgiveness in Jesus and was expressing her "forgiven-ness" by demonstrating devotion to Jesus when she kissed his feet and poured perfume on His feet. She was willing to accept His forgiveness and it became a great teaching lesson for His disciples. Until His disciples could see themselves as sinners in need of forgiveness, like this woman, they would not be able to fulfill the divine call God had on their lives to bring the Gospel to the world after Jesus's ascension. As Jesus says in Verse 50, *"Your faith has saved you; go in peace."* Like the woman caught in the act of adultery, she was encouraged to go, living in the reality of her salvation. Forgiveness is a work of God; living in "forgiven-ness" is part of living in the new covenant. It is the result of the acceptance of man's fallenness and the incredible provision of God for that fallenness by His grace.

Chapter 15

THE ROLE OF CONFESSION

Jesus, knowing that the Father had given all things into His hands, and that He had come forth from God and was going back to God, got up from supper, and laid aside His garments; and taking a towel, He girded Himself. Then He poured water into the basin and began to wash the disciples' feet and to wipe them with the towel with which He was girded. So, He came to Simon Peter. He said to Him, "Lord, do You wash my feet?" Jesus answered and said to him, "What I do you do not realize now, but you will understand hereafter." Peter said to Him, "Never shall You wash my feet!" Jesus answered him, "If I do not wash you, you have no part with Me." Simon Peter said to Him, "Lord, then wash not only my feet, but also my hands and my head." Jesus said to him, "He who has bathed needs only to wash his feet, but is completely clean; and you are clean, but not all of you." For He knew the one who was betraying Him; for this reason, He said, "Not all of you are clean." So, when He had washed their feet, and taken His garments and reclined at the table again, He said to them, "Do you know what I have done to you? "You call Me Teacher and Lord; and you are right, for so I am. "If I then, the Lord and the Teacher, washed your feet, you also ought to wash one another's feet. "For I gave you an example that you also should do as I did to you." **John 13:3-15**

The Greek word translated sin is *"hamartia"* and is defined as a *"falling away from or missing the right path."* In the context of the Scriptures, God's standards as revealed in the Word of God determines the right path. When man operates outside the will of God, willfully or not, he is living in a state of sin. In Romans 14:23b, the Bible says, *whatever is not from faith is sin.* This means that when the believer is not believing (trusting) God, he is sinning. This speaks about our ongoing fellowship with God and the only solution to this problem for the believer is confession.

Breaking the Bondage

To understand the role of confession in a believer's life, we need to be convinced that our position "in Christ" is perfect and is not improvable, that Jesus did pay for all our sins. My experience as a human being living in a corrupt and fallen world is not so perfect because I am subject to all of my human weaknesses. Galatians 5:17 says, *For the flesh sets its desire against the Spirit, and the Spirit against the flesh; for these are in opposition to one another, so that you may not do the things that you please.* But if Jesus paid the price for all my sins, why do I need to confess them? Because these sins have an energy, a power unto themselves and can keep me in bondage to the failures and not allow me to experience the victorious life. Confession breaks this bondage by expressing to God a desire to change, agreeing with God's assessment of the failures. According to Frederick Buechner, *"To confess your sins to God is not to tell God anything God doesn't already know. Until you confess them, however, they are the abyss between you. When you confess them, they become the Golden Gate Bridge."*

In Mark 10:45, Jesus says, *For even the Son of Man did not come to be served, but to serve, and to give His life a ransom for many.* It was the role of a servant to wash the feet of guests since most traveled without shoes, but Jesus is again challenging the disciples' understanding of His expectations of them and what Jesus was willing to do in honoring His Father. In John 13, He becomes a servant to illustrate the importance of confession to each believer. He accomplishes this by washing each of the disciples' feet. An informative exchange unfolds when He gets to Peter, who questions this whole exercise.

Agreement with God

His first response to Jesus was, "*Lord, do you wash my feet?*" (Verse 6). He is asking the Lord why He should wash the feet of a sinner like Peter. Jesus tells Peter to wait, and you will understand later, but Peter responds to Jesus that this can never happen. Jesus tells Peter that if He does not do it, Peter will "*have no part with Me.*" Jesus was telling Peter that everyone needs the forgiveness and cleansing that only Jesus can give. Impetuous Peter then tells Jesus to wash not only his feet, but his hands and head also. Jesus' response is very telling, "*He who has bathed needs only to wash his feet, but is completely clean; and you are clean, but not all of you.*" Jesus is teaching Peter the principles of confession, found in 1 John 1:9, "*If we confess our sins, He is faithful and righteous to forgive us our sins and to cleanse us from all unrighteousness.*" He is also referencing Judas Iscariot when He said, "*but not all of you.*" Salvation deals with the sin condition and confession deals with our walk.

The Greek word translated confession is "*homologeo*" and is the combination of 2 Greek words, "*homo*" meaning same and "*logoe*" meaning to say. It means to say the same thing and contains the idea of agreement, consent, or admission. Confession is the process of the believer agreeing with God's assessment that what he did was wrong. By agreeing with God in this regard, we receive cleansing from God for the thing that we did wrong. The sin was paid for, but the effect of that sin has not yet been addressed. When Jesus spoke of those who have been bathed only needing their feet washed, He was teaching that a believer's faith makes him clean in his position, but his feet, speaking of his experience, his behavior, still needs cleansing from unrighteousness. In John 15:3, "*You are already clean because of the word which I have spoken to you.*" Confession is the cleansing of the soul from the power that a sin can have over a believer's life.

Put Him in Charge

The illustration of confession in John 13 is a powerful one because Jesus has become our servant, to cleanse our feet every time we confess. It reminds me of another passage in Genesis 39 dealing with Joseph, son of Jacob, a type of Christ in this passage. It takes place after Potiphar, an Egyptian officer buys Joseph as a slave, and becomes Potiphar's favored personal servant. In Verse 2, Scripture says, *The Lord was with Joseph, so he became a successful man* and in Verse 4, Potiphar saw that the Lord was with Joseph and put him in charge of everything he owned. Jesus wants us to allow Him to become our servant so that we will put Him in charge of everything. When we seek first the kingdom of God and His righteousness, He adds all things to us, so we do not have to be anxious about tomorrow (Matthew 6:33-34).

David is our Example

King David wrote Psalm 51 and Psalm 32 in response to his failures with Bathsheba and her husband. He asks the Lord to wash him thoroughly from the effects of these sins (Psalm 51:7), knowing that the guilt associated with these sins would destroy him. In Psalm 32:5, *I acknowledged my sin to You, and my iniquity I did not hide; I said, "I will confess my transgressions to the Lord;" and You forgave the guilt of my sin. Selah*. It was the guilt of the sin that David was addressing with his confession. He had already addressed his sin in Verses 1-2 when he acknowledged that the one whose sins are covered God will bless, he was referring to himself. This Hebrew word used for guilt is *awon* and it used to reference either the sin or the effect of that sin, namely guilt. The consequence of sin in the new covenant is guilt or conviction from the Holy Spirit within each believer. David recognizes that his sins have harmed his relationship with God (*Against You, You only, I have sinned and done what is evil in Your sight* – Verse 4) and acknowledges God's right to judge him.

Hyssop is mentioned in Verse 7 as an instrument of purification. In the ceremonial law, hyssop was used as a means by which the virtue of the sacrifice was transferred to the transgressor. This principle is a clear reference to the believer's forgiveness coming from the shed blood of another. In 1 Peter 2:24, *and He Himself bore our sins in His body on the cross, so that we might die to sin and live to righteousness; for by His wounds, you were healed.*

In Psalm 51:10, David asks God for a clean heart and a steadfast spirit. So much of our ability to continue in the path God has established for each believer is to maintain a clean or pure heart. In fact, Jesus said God will bless the one who has a pure heart, and he will see God (Matthew 5:8). Augustine once said, *"The confession of evil works is the first beginning of good works."* Confession leads to a life that produces the fruit of God's goodness, namely good works.

RECONCILIATION

The quality of confession is determined by the condition of the heart. A sincere heart is a heart that is transparent, not holding anything back, willing to admit all. It means drawing near (Hebrews 10:22) to God regularly, just as we need our feet washed often, and being confident that our willing heart will result in an internal change, *our hearts sprinkled clean from an evil conscience.* An evil conscience is one filled with guilt, either conscious or unconscious guilt. The blood of Christ can do so much more than the blood of goats and bulls to *cleanse your conscience from dead works to serve the living God* (Hebrews 9:13-14).

Getting back to our passage from John 13, we find Jesus commending the disciples to do to others as I have done to you (Verses 14-15). Paul captured the essence of what Jesus was teaching in 2 Corinthians 5:17-21 when he spoke about the ministry of reconciliation. First, as believers we are new creatures (Verse 17), having a new life and a new future. In Colossians 1:21-22, *And although you were formerly **alienated** and **hostile** in mind, engaged in evil deeds, yet He has now **reconciled you** in His fleshly body through death, in order to present you before Him holy and blameless and beyond reproach.* Reconciliation means I was once alienated and hostile in my mind toward God, but a transformation took place and my fellowship with God has been restored. My response to this supernatural work of God is to accept this ministry of reconciliation (Verse 18) as defined in Verse 19, that it is *reconciling the world to Himself* through the word of reconciliation. As a result, we become *ambassadors for Christ* and we *beg you on behalf of Christ, be reconciled to God.*

Max Lucado once said, "*We will never be cleansed until we confess, we are dirty. And we will never be able to wash the feet of those who have hurt us until we allow Jesus, the one we have hurt, to wash ours.*" By accepting the reconciliation offered to each believer at salvation, God calls us to draw near to Him to receive cleansing and empowerment to the ministry of reconciliation that allows believers to operate as ambassadors, in Christ's place, to become representatives of His heart and life for the world to witness.

Chapter 16

THE WAY

"And you know the way where I am going." Thomas said to Him, "Lord, we do not know where You are going, how do we know the way?" Jesus said to him, **"I am the way, and the truth, and the life**; *no one comes to the Father but through Me. "If you had known Me, you would have known My Father also; from now on you know Him and have seen Him." Philip said to Him, "Lord, show us the Father, and it is enough for us." Jesus said to him, "Have I been so long with you, and yet you have not come to know Me, Philip? He who has seen Me has seen the Father; how can you say, 'Show us the Father'? "Do you not believe that I am in the Father, and the Father is in Me? The words that I say to you I do not speak on My own initiative, but the Father abiding in Me does His works."* **John 14:4-10**

Jesus had a great deal to teach His disciples the night before His crucifixion, and many of those teachings are revealed by John in chapters 13-17. In John 14, Jesus's focus was on the way to heaven, the way to the believer's eternal future. He was trying to strike a contrast between the old covenant ways and a brand-new approach to God. The old covenant is based on a series of commandments required by Jews to follow or suffer consequences. In Deuteronomy 5:32-33, *So you shall observe to do just as the Lord your God has commanded you;*

you shall not turn aside to the right or to the left. You shall walk in all the way which the Lord your God has commanded you, that you may live and that it may be well with you, and that you may prolong your days in the land which you will possess. So, the old covenant commands the believer to follow a set of standards (commandments, precepts, statutes, etc.) that determine the quality of his future. On the other hand, the new covenant believer follows a man, the God-Man, the One who follows His Father.

THE SAME ESSENCE

Jesus begins this teaching with the guiding point of the entire chapter, that belief (trust) in Jesus is believing in the Father, that They consist of the same essence! He tells them in Verse 1 to believe in Jesus with the same substance of faith that you believe in God. The faith we place in Jesus as Messiah, as God Himself, is the personification of our faith in the Father.

No longer does a believer need the Law of Moses to have access to God, but the man Jesus Who is also God and Son of the Father. Jesus is the mediator of the new covenant and now the way, the avenue to finding and experiencing God the Father. In 1 Timothy 2:5, *For there is one God, and one mediator also between God and men, the man Christ Jesus*, Philip's question to Jesus in Verse 8 exposes his lack of understanding that Jesus and His Father were of the same essence (Hebrews 1:3) where Scripture says, *And He is the radiance of His glory and the exact representation of His nature.*

The apostle Paul is a splendid example of this principle. As Saul of Tarsus, he was one of the premier Pharisees of his day, having trained under Gamaliel and educated *strictly according to the law of our fathers, being zealous for God just as you all are today. I persecuted this Way to the death* (Acts 22: 3-4). His pursuit of God was through his intense zeal for the Law of Moses and the related man-made laws (Mishna) that Jesus referred to as *the traditions of the elders* (Matthew 15:2). Yet Paul tells the Galatians in Galatians 1:11-17 that the gospel he heard he did not receive from man, but it came right from *a revelation of Jesus Christ*.

Paul was able to recognize that the calling of God on his life came to him from his mother's womb and the revelation of His Son came within Paul and not the result of an academic pursuit. He tells the Galatians that he did not immediately seek out the other Christian leaders (Verse 16) to confirm or refine his understanding, but he needed to go away so that he would relearn the Scriptures in light of Jesus as Messiah.

A Circumcised Heart

Once Paul clearly understood his commission, he recognized the problem of his fellow Jews as being zealous for the Law and began to reach out to Gentiles to forsake the Law of Moses and the Jewish customs. He recognized that the true Jews (true circumcision) were those who *worship in the Spirit of God and glory in Christ Jesus and put no confidence in the flesh* (Philippians 3:3). Putting no confidence in one's own ability or effort flows out of his direct connection to Christ, Himself, through the Holy Spirit.

In Romans 2:28-29, the true Jew has had his heart circumcised, a spiritual work and not the result of applying the letter of the law in a person's life. Jeremiah 9:25-26 says the Lord will *punish all who are circumcised and yet uncircumcised* since *all the house of Israel are uncircumcised in heart*. This circumcision of the heart is a reference to one's personal devotion to the Lord, as revealed in Jeremiah 4:4, *Circumcise yourselves to the Lord and remove the foreskins of your heart, men of Judah and inhabitants of Jerusalem, or else My wrath will go forth like fire and burn with none to quench it, because of the evil of your deeds.* This consecration to the Lord was always His intention and understood in the context of the roller coaster relationship with God that Israel had since the introduction of the Law of Moses. In Deuteronomy 10:16, *So circumcise your heart and stiffen your neck no longer*, which speaks to the problem of stubbornness that works against a godly devotion. It is the Lord who circumcises the heart of Israel and descendants to love God with all the heart (Deuteronomy 30:6).

A New and Living Way

Therefore, brethren, since we have confidence to enter the holy place by the blood of Jesus, by a new and living way which He inaugurated for us through the veil, that is, His flesh, and since we have a great priest over the house of God, **let us draw near with a sincere heart in full assurance of faith***, having our hearts sprinkled clean from an evil conscience and our bodies washed with pure water.* **Hebrews 10:19-22**

The new covenant defines the environment in which the believer finds the confidence (boldness) to approach and draw near to God because this covenant is the direct result of the blood of Jesus and His priesthood. This *new and living way* is a relationship realized in the heart and the sincerity (Greek word *alethinos* meaning real or genuine, absence of lies) of that heart gives us the full assurance that we have received forgiveness, and our evil conscience is cleansed. In Proverbs 23:26, *Give me your heart, my son, and let your eyes delight in my ways.* This is the sentiment of a sincere heart, that we give it to God, that we are willing to be transparent with God. In so doing, His heart becomes our heart. In Psalm 73:28, *But as for me, the nearness of God is my good; I have made the Lord God my refuge, that I may tell of all Your works.* God is always interested in man's heart and wishes that man's search will bring him to God's heart. Jesus Christ is the manifestation of the Father's heart.

No Confidence in the Flesh

In Philippians 3:2-11, Paul writes to the church at Philippi about his background as a Pharisee and his deliverance from that life as he declares his conclusion in Verse 3, that to glory in (credit given to) Christ Jesus meant that he no longer needed to have any confidence in his own flesh. He resolved that every matter that exalted his own accomplishments or natural abilities was of no consequence when it came to getting to know (*ginosko* – knowledge through experience)

Christ. In fact, those things would oppose the process of knowing Him *and the power of His resurrection and the fellowship of His sufferings* (Verse 10) since he was being conformed to Christ's death. In Verse 9, Paul defines the ultimate victory as *not having a righteousness of my own derived from the Law, but that which comes from God on the basis of faith.*

The righteousness of God only comes to the believer on the basis of faith and not through any human effort or accomplishment (Romans 4:4-5). The real power of God demonstrates itself in the relationship with Christ, particularly through His resurrection. When the believer identifies with His resurrection, he enters into the deeper experience of that relationship. Colossians 3:1 says, *Therefore if you have been raised up with Christ, keep seeking the things above, where Christ is, seated at the right hand of God.*

THE WORKS OF GOD

The ending result of our faith in the deity of Christ and His substitutionary death on a cross is works; works are not the avenue to the relationship, but the byproduct of that relationship. This kind of faith is not simply acknowledging the existing of Jesus as the Son of God, but a trust and confidence in Him. As James 2:19 states, *the demons also believe, and shudder*! James uses Abraham's willingness to offer Isaac as a sacrifice in Genesis 22 as an example of the fruit of the relationship of faith in God. Faith cannot be perfected, brought to its ultimate conclusion without some guided action, real faith results in a call to action. James 2:17 is saying that a measurement of a real relationship with God is faith in action.

Romans 10:13, *"WHOEVER WILL CALL ON THE NAME OF THE LORD WILL BE SAVED."* is a quote of Joel 2:32 and addresses the issue of the *"Name of the Lord."* In Joel, it was referring to the Father, but Paul's implication is that it is a reference to Jesus, the Son of God. In our original passage from John 14:14, *If you ask Me anything in My name, I will do it.* When we see references to the name of God in Scripture, it is equivalent to His character and nature, His True Being. The new covenant acknowledges that the very character of the

Father manifests itself in His Son, Jesus. In Ephesians 5:20, Paul says, *always giving thanks for all things in the name of our Lord Jesus Christ to God, even the Father.* The Name of God is sacred because it references exactly who He is. Jesus promises that, *For where two or three have gathered together in My name, I am there in their midst.* (Matthew 18:20). Jesus has committed by His Name that He will be in the midst of those who gather and call on the His Name, even a gathering as small as two or three.

Resting from Works

As the believer's heart intertwines itself with the Lord's heart, he begins walking in the works and the ways of God (Ephesians 2:10). He knows that he no longer must perform to prove his spirituality or worthiness because he has found his rest in whatever God has prepared for him. What we are speaking about is the fact that the mature believer recognizes his need to be a servant of God. In John 12:26, Jesus says, *"If anyone serves Me,* **he must follow Me***; and where I am, there My servant will be also; if anyone serves Me, the Father will honor him."* Service in God's economy is the process of learning how to follow Christ and not requirements. In Psalm 37:5-6, *Commit your way to the Lord, trust also in Him, and He will do it. He will bring forth your righteousness as the light and your judgment as the noonday.* Service means the believer has nothing to prove because Jesus has accomplished the work on his behalf, and it is the righteousness of Christ that motivates him. Hebrews 4:10 says, *For the one who has entered His rest has himself also* **rested from his works***, as God did from His.* We learn how to serve by resting.

Chapter 17

RESURRECTION LIFE

The pivotal point of the account of the raising of Lazarus in John 11 is Jesus's words found in Verses 25-26, *"I am the resurrection and the life; he who believes in Me will live even if he dies, and everyone who lives and believes in Me will never die. Do you believe this?"* What point was he trying to make? To understand, we must look at the Jewish mindset of His day to fully appreciate the points He was making.

First, there was a split between the Pharisees and Sadducees regarding the existence of the resurrection of believers revealed through a confrontation by the Sadducees and scribes in Luke 20:27-40. The question posed to Jesus had to do with who a believer would be married to in the resurrection if he had more than one wife during his life. Jesus answered that marriage is for this age, but not for the age of the resurrection. In Revelation 19:7-10, all new covenant believers will be married to Jesus at the Marriage Supper of the Lamb.

Most Jews of Jesus's day believed in a bodily resurrection, but it was unclear what it looked like since there were few Scriptures to define it. In fact, Isaiah was one of the first to give any real definition in Isaiah 26:19, *Your dead will live; their corpses will rise. You who lie in the dust, awake and shout for joy, for your dew is as the dew of the dawn, and the earth will give birth to the departed spirits.* So much of the Old Testament references deal with Sheol, most often signifying the grave. Sheol is wrongly translated as "hell." According to William

Barclay, "*After death came the land of silence and of forgetfulness, where the shades of men were separated alike from men and from God.*" Both Old Testament and New Testament Jews live their religious lives without a clear sense of the here-after and any potential rewards, but only life with God as His people. Jesus was teaching that the new covenant believer has an eternal future with Him if he would only believe and that death does not end with the grave (2 Corinthians 5:8). But there is much more.

Love for Mary, Martha & Lazarus

The first thing we should note from the account is the quality of the relationship between Jesus, Mary, Martha, and Lazarus. In Verse 5, *Now Jesus loved Martha and her sister and Lazarus*. The strong friendship between them was evident from this and the account from Luke 10:38-42, but Jesus was saying more since He used the Greek word "*agape*" for love, indicating God's love which is more than friendship. This is the same love that God has for every one of his creations (John 3:16) and is the kind of love that motivates the believer to love others (1 John 4:19). The new covenant believer's future is secure because of this love.

The question comes up in this account why Jesus would stay away two extra days, a total of four days since Lazarus first became ill. In the Jewish mindset of the day, the spirit of the man remained with him three days after death. Jesus waited until the fourth day to make it clear that this was going to be a true work of God, a miracle that could only be attributable to God, Himself. This is why Jesus says in Verse 4, "*This sickness is not to end in death, but for the glory of God, so that the Son of Man may be glorified by it.*" Jesus was revealing His Messiahship! The resurrection of the body is a work of God.

The interactions with Martha and then Mary are also revealing. First, Martha challenged His lateness, that if He had been there on time, Lazarus would not have died. He assured Martha that Lazarus would rise from the dead, but Martha thought He was speaking of the resurrection of the dead on the last day. Later, Mary made the same statement to Jesus, and He became deeply moved in spirit. Both women were confessing the same concerns and Jesus wanted them to understand that whether He was there or not, physical death was not the end. This principle is a lesson to all new covenant believers to expect that all who are in Christ will be resurrected at the rapture, a future event representing the beginning of the Second Coming of Christ.

THE RAPTURE

> *For this we say to you by the word of the Lord, that we who are alive and remain until the coming of the Lord, will not precede those who have fallen asleep. For the Lord Himself will descend from heaven with a shout, with the voice of the archangel and with the trumpet of God, and the dead in Christ will rise first. Then we who are alive and remain will be* **caught up** *[Greek – harpazo, Latin - rapturo] together with them in the clouds to meet the Lord in the air, and so we shall always be with the Lord.* **1 Thessalonians 4:15-17**

The rapture (Latin - *rapturo* for "caught up") of the church, the next major event on the church calendar, is something believers should look forward to. The raising of Lazarus speaks to this event as something on all new covenant believers' calendar. When the trumpet sounds, the dead in Christ rise first, a bodily resurrection, followed by those who remain alive, being *"caught up"* together with the dead in the clouds to meet the Lord. Paul encourages the believers at Thessaloniki that they did not need to stop living and go to the mountaintops to wait for the Lord's coming, but could continue living for the Lord, knowing that Jesus was coming back for each of them. Jesus addressed this very issue in Matthew 24, defining the return of the Lord as a time when only the Father will know and life will continue with *"eating and drinking, marrying, and giving in marriage."* Two men will be working in the field and the unregenerate one will be left (Verse 40).

In the Meantime

In Matthew 24:36-42, Jesus taught the disciples to be on the alert, be ready by living with an expectation, knowing it could happen at any time. This is healthy Christian living because it keeps focus on Him and not on the natural life, which will end for each without notice. In Titus 2:13-14, ***looking for** the blessed hope and the appearing of the glory of our great God and Savior, Christ Jesus, who gave Himself for us to redeem us from every lawless deed, and to purify for Himself a people for His own possession, zealous for good deeds.* Living with an expectation of His imminent coming produces a purity that leads to a desire for good deeds.

Not only was Jesus's teaching of the bodily resurrection of every new covenant believer, but He was also referring to the quality of life that believers could have before death, in which Christians learn to live **through** the life of Christ. But how do we humans continue to live in our own fleshly bodies, yet live in the life of Christ? In Galatians 2:20, *I have been crucified with Christ; and it is no longer I who live, but Christ lives in me; and the life which I now live **in the flesh I live by faith in the Son of God**, who loved me and gave Himself up for me.* Faith in this verse references an active confidence in the saving work of Christ accomplished at calvary. It means I am no longer living to earn anything from God since my faith in Jesus provides everything I need for life and godliness (2 Peter 1:3). The practical reality of this reveals itself in the principle of resurrection life.

He Who Hates his Life Will Keep It

The resurrection of Lazarus in John 11 also speaks to a quality of life that a new covenant believer can have when he finds a new life in Christ. This quality of life occurs only when he decides that his own life (i.e., personal interests, agendas, priorities) is no longer supreme and that the life of another becomes preeminent (Colossians 1:18). Jesus refers to death being the doorway to becoming fruitful, meaning new life. When Jesus said in John 12:25, *"He who loves his life loses it, and he who hates his life in this world will keep it to life eternal,"* the paradoxical truth of this passage is that there is life when one devalues his life and the life of another takes on a higher value. This transition results in the believer becoming a servant. A willingness to die to self means one is open to embrace the life and priorities of Jesus and set aside his own priorities. This is not much different than what one goes through who enters the American military system and must first learn that his opinions no longer matter since the orders of superiors matter most!

This principle reveals itself in the Old Testament through a particular article placed within the ark of the covenant – Aaron's rod which budded (Hebrews 9:4). God chose the rod that sprouted (see Numbers 17:5) because it produced life - the sprout, from death - the rod. This teaches us that when the believer chooses to die to his priorities and becomes the vessel of God, He brings life, abundant life, as signified by the blossoms and the ripe almonds (Numbers 17:8). Almonds are the first fruit tree of the season to blossom, usually in late January or early February, before the leaves appear, *"so that the appearance of a tree in full bloom is striking"* (The New Unger's Bible Dictionary). When God does His work in and through man, it is unmistakably His work, and it is glorious. *With its oblong oval shape sharpened at one end and rounded at the other, the almond nut is remarkably graceful. This naturally led to its selection for ornamental carved work; and it was the pattern selected for the bowls of the golden lampstand (Ex 25:33-34; 37:19), symbolizing the speedy and powerful result of light.* Just as God chose the rod of Aaron because of its fruit, so the new covenant believer will walk in a fruitfulness derived from a willingness to surrender to His authority and will.

Death to the Self-Life

Therefore, we have been buried with Him through baptism into death, so that as Christ was raised from the dead through the glory of the Father, so we too might **walk in newness of life**. *For if we have become united with Him in the likeness of His death, certainly we shall also be in the likeness of His resurrection.* **Romans 6:4-5**

According to Romans 6, resurrection life also produces a higher quality of life since it provides the answer to the problem of sin and sin's control over mankind. Walking in newness of life (Verse 4) or resurrection life is the personal identification with Jesus's death and resurrection. Verse 5 tells us that becoming united with Him in His death is the doorway to identification with his resurrection. Resurrection life is the very life of Christ living within each new covenant believer. When one considers (Greek word "*logizomai*," meaning to reckon, to recognize as true) himself to be dead, it is death to the self-life, containing the sin nature and that death sets one free to live for God, since one is no longer trying to earn recognition or favor of self. Instead, walking in this newness of life is receiving the free gift of His righteousness and recognizing its value and priority.

Receive

Romans 5:17 teaches that the key to reigning in this life through Christ is learning how to receive (Greek word "*lambano*," meaning to take or accept, to receive what is given) the abundance of grace and the gift of righteousness. Believers put their faith in the life and work of another and no longer need to work to gain acceptance, recognizing that the work of Christ is more than sufficient. This type of faith creates in each believer an ability to *see the glory of God*, as Jesus commended Mary and Martha in John 11:40.

Chapter 18

BECOMING A FOLLOWER

Again, the next day John [the Baptist] *was standing with two of his disciples, and he looked at Jesus as He walked, and said, "Behold,* **the Lamb of God***!" The two disciples heard him speak, and* **they followed Jesus***. And Jesus turned and saw them following, and said to them, "What do you seek?" They said to Him, "Rabbi (which translated means Teacher), where are You staying?" He said to them,* **"Come, and you will see.***" So, they came and saw where He was staying; and they stayed with Him that day, for it was about the tenth hour. One of the two who heard John speak and followed Him, was Andrew, Simon Peter's brother. He found first his own brother Simon and said to him,* **"We have found the Messiah***" (which translated means Christ).* **John 1:35-41**

In John 1:11, *Jesus came to His own* [the Jews], *but those who were His own did not receive Him.* Very few had any interest in following Jesus. Yet right from the very beginning of His public ministry, He was looking for disciples, those who would be willing to learn from Him by accepting His instruction as truth, as rules to live by. God is always working through His disciples; in the Old Testament referred to as the remnant, those that refuse to bow their knee to Baal (1 Kings 19:18). The continuation of the new covenant requires ones who will continue the work after Jesus's time is gone and His followers would be an integral part of this new work of God.

The Apostle John reports in John 1:35-51 that the day after the baptism in the Jordan River, Jesus was looking to establish disciples, ones who would follow after Him and learn personally what it meant to be a true follower. John the Baptist identifies Him as the Lamb of God, a reference to his willingness to be the sacrifice for others (Mark 10:45) and a symbol that followers of Christ would have to suffer. Paul captured the essence of this reality in Romans 8:36, quoting from Psalm 44:22, which says, *for your sake we are being put to death all day long; we were considered as sheep to be slaughtered*. If you are looking for glory, this is not it!

COME AND SEE

As an ordained minister, I have grown up to understand that looking for glory, especially as a church leader is a trap and has only led to discouragement. Christ intended that none would glory in anything except the cross of our Lord Jesus Christ (Galatians 6:14), the place where I am willing to die to me and my private interests in order to experience Him (Galatians 2:20). John the Baptist understood this and expressed it in John 1:26-27, "*I baptize with water, but among you stands One whom you do not know. It is He who comes after me, the thong of whose sandal I am not worthy to untie.*"

Throughout this passage, Jesus is saying to the newfound followers, *come and you will see* (Verse 39). The key to becoming a follower of Christ is that you must come and see. Christianity is not a spectator sport, but it requires a willingness to act, taking steps of faith and in the process, you will see unexpected things that will strengthen your faith. You will see Him do things in your life that will prove His faithfulness. The disciples' three years with Jesus was a time to come and see. The same is true for us; we too must come and see.

A Direct Connection to Christ

In the passage, we also notice that two of the disciples belong to John the Baptist and they immediately became followers of Jesus. In John 3:29, John the Baptist acknowledged that he was not the bridegroom, but only a friend.

Unlike many religious systems, the new covenant is defined by a believer and his relationship to Christ and not to some other teacher or leader. Paul addressed this very issue in 1 Corinthians 1:12-13, *Now I mean this, that each one of you is saying, "I am of Paul," and "I of Apollos," and "I of Cephas," and "I of Christ." Has Christ been divided? Paul was not crucified for you, was he? Or were you baptized in the name of Paul?* This is a foundational principle of the new covenant, that each believer is related to Jesus and Jesus to each believer. In Hebrews 8:10, *I will be their God and they shall be my people.*

In Exodus 20:18-19, the Israelis gathered at Mount Sinai with God who was demonstrating His presence on the mountain top with fire and lightning and thunder and earthquakes, and the people were afraid. As a result, they told Moses to go up and hear from God and tell them what He said. This is a picture of many believers who are afraid to hear directly from God but will listen to others. Because of the work of Christ on the cross, we do not have to be afraid of God.

After Christianity introduces itself, the believer learns by following the example of others, including church leaders, and not connected to Christ. As he grows, he gleans all that he can from a mentor, but there comes a time when he recognizes that he needs more and is no longer satisfied with the status quo. The disciples of John the Baptist were now ready to become deeply connected to Christ. John had been pointing them to Messiah all along.

Abiding Fellowship

John 1:38 also tells us that Jesus's first words to the new disciples were "*What do you seek?*" Jesus was checking their motive for following. The Greek word for follow, "*akoloutheo,*" means more than coming behind, but it has a deeper sense of abiding fellowship with Him. If they are to become His disciples, they must come and see and stay with Him. They needed to get to see how He lived, how He responded to others, and how He dealt with many different situations. Our ability to follow Jesus is not just showing up at church on Sunday morning, but it involves the way we live our lives and Jesus has lessons for us through the Scriptures that can teach us how to face life's challenges. A disciple learns how to follow Jesus closely.

We also see that a true disciple has a tough time keeping quiet about his relationship with Christ. Andrew, one of those disciples of John the Baptist that now follows Jesus, immediately goes to tell his brother Simon that, "*We have found the Messiah* "(John 1:41) and in the presence of Jesus and He renames Simon as Peter, and he also becomes a follower. Then, Philip speaks to his friend, Nathanael and tells him the same basic message, that *"we have found Him of whom Moses in the Law and Prophets wrote…"* Once Jesus demonstrates His messiahship to Nathanael, he also follows. As one becomes a true follower, he will desire to share his faith with others.

Discipleship

In Luke 14:16-27, Jesus used a parable as an illustration of the more common excuses for not becoming a follower of Christ. The challenges that believers face relate to relationships with the details of life. When those details, including relationships with family members, job, pursuit of personal interests, etc. become more important than the pursuit of Jesus, then one cannot be a true follower (disciple). In Verses 26-27, *"If anyone comes to Me, and does not hate his own father and mother and wife and children and brothers and sisters, yes, and even his own life, he cannot be my disciple. Whoever does not carry his own cross and come after me **cannot be My disciple.**"* The big dinner that Jesus speaks of is the "Marriage Supper of the Lamb" found in Revelations 19:9 where all believers in Christ will become His bride. Our biggest priority will be our new relationship with Him, and He wants that to be our priority today as well. This is a process of growing in grace and the knowledge of our Lord (2 Peter 3:18).

A Walk of Faith

One major difference between the old and new covenants is that the Jews always needed a sign, some physical confirmation that they were hearing from God. In John 6:30, the Jews said to Jesus, *"what then do You do for a sign, so that we may see, and believe You? What work do You perform?"* Their faith limited itself by what they saw. These same limitations existed throughout the Old Testament times. This is why God used the cloud by day and the pillar of fire by night to move the nation of Israel throughout the wilderness. They learned to trust the outward sign of the cloud and pillar of fire to know that they were moving with God. But the new covenant disciple is one who must learn to walk by faith and not by sight (2 Corinthians 5:7). He learns not to rely on his eyes, but develops his sixth sense of faith, knowing that he has heard God and moves forward. God is faithful to lead every believer by His Spirit and believers must learn how to listen to His still small voice (sound of a gentle whisper) in the midst of the busyness of life. One notable example of this principle appears in the healing of the man born blind in John 9:35-41.

> *Jesus heard that they had put him out, and finding him, He said, "Do you believe in the Son of Man?" He answered, **"Who is He, Lord, that I may believe in Him?"** Jesus said to him, **"You have both seen Him**, and He is the one who is talking with you." And he said, "Lord, I believe." And he worshiped Him. And Jesus said, "For judgment I came into this world, so that **those who do not see may see**, and that those who see may become blind." Those of the Pharisees who were with Him heard these things and said to Him, "We are not blind too, are we?" Jesus said to them, "If you were blind, you would have no sin, but since you say, 'We see,' your sin remains."* **John 9:35-41**

Jesus is trying to illustrate a key point about the kind of sight we receive when we recognize Him as Messiah, as Savior, as Lord. For the one who does not believe, he will never be able to see, but faith in Christ gives us new sight, not physically, but spiritually, the sixth sense. According to Barnes Notes on this passage,

> *Hitherto he had understood little of the true character of Jesus. He believed that he had power to heal him, and he inferred that he must be a prophet in John 9:17. He believed according to the light he had, and he now showed that he was prepared to believe all that Jesus said. This is the nature of true faith. It believes all that God has made known, and it is premiered to receive all that he will teach. The phrase Son of God here is equivalent to the Messiah.*

The one who trusts in himself instead of Christ will die in his sins, but the true believer will learn to not be afraid to share his faith in Christ with others. In Matthew 5:8, *"Blessed are the pure in heart, for they shall see God."*

A Work of the Heart

The Pharisees made themselves look like followers of God on the outside (i.e., *"whitewashed tombs"*), but on the inside, full of *"dead men's bones"* (Matthew 23:27). Outward conformity to God's standards only deals with the outside, but God's work to make us true followers is a work of the heart and happens as we are willing to recognize the greatness of Jesus and what He accomplished on behalf of each one who believes.

Chapter 19

JESUS FEEDS HIS CHURCH

Old Testament prophecy speaks extensively about the coming kingdom age, the time when Messiah will reign for 1,000 years, but there are no direct references to the church. When I was growing up in the Boston area, my family and I did some hiking in the White Mountains of New Hampshire. From the top of one mountain, you can look out at other mountains with mountain peaks beyond, but you cannot judge between the peaks, neither the distance nor what exists between them. This is the principle in play with the Old Testament prophecies dealing with long distance, future events. Prophecy looks to the future, but only sees the mountain peaks. When the Old Testament prophesied about the coming Messiah (some like Isaiah 61:1-2 refers to both comings), it did not clearly discern the two comings and the distance in time between. Since the church age does not deal with Israel, the Old Testament is silent about it. In Ephesians 3:9-10, Paul refers to the church as a mystery, hidden in Old Testament times, yet revealed in the new covenant through the fellowship of Jews and Gentiles in one faith.

Importance of Receiving the Word

The account of Jesus feeding the five thousand is one of the few that all four gospels cover. If we look underneath the surface of this event, we have a picture of Jesus feeding His church in the new covenant age. Jesus had quoted from Deuteronomy 8:3 when the devil was tempting Him in the wilderness in Matthew 4:4 saying, *"It is written, 'MAN SHALL NOT LIVE ON BREAD ALONE, BUT ON EVERY WORD THAT PROCEEDS OUT OF THE MOUTH OF GOD.'"* The bread is a reference to *"every word that proceeds from the mouth of God"* and Jesus, the very Word of God in John 1:1 is delivering it to the pastors (disciples) who will in turn deliver it to the people, Mark's account tells us the people were divided into fifties and hundreds, just like churches. God's Word will feed the new covenant church, and it will satisfy every believer. In fact, there will be twelve baskets of leftovers. Twelve is a reference to the twelve tribes of Israel in the Old Testament and the twelve disciples in the New Testament. In Ephesians 2:20, the twelve apostles will be the foundation of the church and will continue to assist Jesus in feeding the new covenant church.

God's Nourishment

This picture of God feeding the church in the new covenant is different from the old covenant. The Law of Moses was a set of laws, categorized as civil, criminal, judicial, constitutional, ecclesiastical, and ceremonial, and all the Jews studied them not only to learn them, but follow them (see Deuteronomy 4). So much of this learning was academic and based on tradition, and the Lord rebuked the Jews in Isaiah 29:13 because they *"draw near with their words and honor Me with their lip service, but they remove their hearts far from Me, and their reverence for Me consists of tradition learned by rote."* The old covenant appetite for the Law produced people who were engaged with their minds, but not their hearts.

The Word of God was not meant to be tasted, but eaten like bread, the listener recognizing the need for its nourishing power. In John 6,

Jesus compared the bread that the multitude were eating to the manna of Jewish wilderness days. In Verses 32-33, Jesus said, *"Truly, truly, I say to you, it is not Moses who has given you the bread out of heaven, but it is My Father who gives you the true bread out of heaven. "For the bread of God is that which comes down out of heaven and gives life to the world."* This bread leaves the believer satisfied, not hungering or thirsting (Verse 35).

EXTRACTING PRECIOUS FROM WORTHLESS

In Jeremiah 15:16, *Your words were found, and I ate them, and Your words became for me a joy and the delight of my heart; for I have been called by Your name, O Lord God of hosts.* In the midst of Jeremiah's ministry of constant rejection of his words by God's people and God's refusal to bring swift judgment against the wicked, the Word of God became a sustenance for him and produced joy and delight in his heart. Jeremiah had separated himself from the evil surrounding him (John 17:17) but was questioning God's justice. God responded by challenging Jeremiah to return to trusting His plan and to *extract the precious from the worthless* so as to become His spokesman (Verse 19).

The Word of God has the ability to separate the precious from the worthless (Hebrews 4:12) by identifying in the listener's heart what is of the Spirit versus what is of the soul (flesh, natural man). In this way, we are sanctified to be His spokesman, His servants, His vessel of honor, prepared for every good work (2 Timothy 2:21). This commitment to hearing the Word of God is more than just listening but meditating on it and believing it. In Psalm 119:15-16, *I will meditate on Your precepts and regard Your ways. I shall delight in Your statutes; I shall not forget Your word.*

THE WORD OF LIFE

What was from the beginning, what we have heard, what we have seen with our eyes, what we have looked at and touched with our hands, concerning the Word of Life— and the life was manifested, and we have seen and testify and proclaim to you the eternal life, which was with the Father and was manifested to us— what we have seen and heard we proclaim to you also, so that you too may have fellowship with us; and indeed our fellowship is with the Father, and with His Son Jesus Christ. These things we write, so that our joy may be made complete. **1 John 1:1-4**

The new covenant revelation of the Word of God is that it is not just words on a page, but a person and the life of that person, eternal life, available to all who believe it and embrace it as truth (John 17:17). Faith in Jesus as His Son completes the believer's life, and the evidence of that finished work is real joy. Jesus came to manifest the Word of God in physical form for a season *so that you may believe that Jesus is the Christ, the Son of God; and that believing you may have life in His name* (John 20:31). The Word of God is not only the manifestation of His life, but also the avenue given for each believer to share in that life. The old covenant commanded the believer to follow closely the statutes, precepts, and requirements of the Torah without a person in view.

JESUS IS THE LIGHT OF THE WORLD

In 1 John 2:7-8, *Beloved, I am not writing a new commandment to you, but an old commandment which you have had from the beginning; the old commandment is the word which you have heard. On the other hand, I am writing a new commandment to you, which is true in Him and in you, because the darkness is passing away and the true Light is already shining.* The true Light is Jesus, who promised in John 8:12, "*he who follows Me will not walk in the darkness but will have the Light of life.*" The Word of God produces God's life through the person of Christ and revealed by the Holy Spirit.

The Word of God is the only place that reveals to man not only God's thoughts, but also His ways. These thoughts and ways are not man's and not compared to man's thoughts and ways since they are higher (Isaiah 55:8-9). This makes the Word so much more valuable and something to be desired. In fact, God says the Word will accomplish something extremely specific in each heart, in each life and will not return without accomplishing it. It is God's great agent in the church age because it represents the very thoughts of God. It will produce joy not only in believers, but in nature itself!

Chapter 20

BEING TAUGHT BY GOD

But when it was now the midst of the feast Jesus went up into the temple and began to teach. The Jews then were astonished, saying, "How has this man become learned, having never been educated?" So, Jesus answered them and said, ***"My teaching is not Mine****, but His who sent Me.* ***"If anyone is willing to do His will, he will know of the teaching****, whether it is of God or whether I speak from Myself. "He who speaks from himself seeks his own glory; but He who is seeking the glory of the One who sent Him, He is true, and there is no unrighteousness in Him."* **John 7:14-18**

In John 6:45, Jesus quoted from Isaiah 54:13 saying, *"And they shall be taught of God."* When the Jews asked Jesus where He got His learning, His response shocked them. Normally, religious learning came either from a traditional school or having been self-taught. But Jesus said the teaching (Greek word *"didache"* meaning the thing taught, precept, doctrine) came from God. In fact, in John 8:28, He said, *"I do nothing on My own initiative, but I speak these things as the Father taught Me."* Jesus is introducing a new concept that new covenant believers will be taught by God, just as Jeremiah 31:34 prophesied: *They will not teach again, each man his neighbor and each man his brother, saying, "Know the Lord," for they will all know Me, from the least of them to the greatest of them.*

He goes on to say that there is a direct link between knowing the teaching and a willingness to do it, to obey it. He is speaking of understanding from the heart. New covenant faith comes from believing the teaching from the heart, knowing that it comes from God and not some contrived notion or private interpretation of Scripture by man. Knowing God comes from teaching by God and this teaching requires humility (Psalm 25:9). In Psalm 25:4-5, *Make me know Your ways, O Lord; teach me Your paths. Lead me in Your truth and teach me, for You are the God of my salvation; for You I wait all the day.* David understood the need for God to do the teaching. David's heart to receive His teaching is an example to all new covenant believers.

CREATION OF THE MISHNAH

So much of learning is in the form of an academic pursuit of a subject, whether it be secular or sacred, and requires no heart to be engaged. Jesus cited this issue in Matthew 15 when quoting from Isaiah 29:13: *Then the Lord said, "Because this people draw near with their words and honor Me with their lip service, but they remove their hearts far from Me, and their reverence for Me consists of tradition learned by rote."* The idea communicated is that the Jews were interested in learning the traditions or precepts of man, by rote, meaning by repetition, mechanical, in a sense memorizing the rules that man has created rather than focusing on the priorities of God (see also Matthew 23:23). The precepts of man is a reference to the laws the rabbis and other Jewish leaders created to complement the 613 Laws of Moses given at Mount Sinai.

After the Jews returned to Jerusalem following the Babylonian captivity, Jewish leaders came together to come up with a strategy that would help the nation avoid breaking the Law of Moses and end up with similar or even worse punishment. They had also seen the number of Jews dwindle dramatically as a result of various uprisings. As a result of these concerns, Jewish leaders created the Mishnah, led by Rabbi Judah the Prince so as to record in written form the Oral Law, that is the laws that men of faith had created over the years to properly implement and administer the 613 Laws of Moses. In the process, Jewish leadership enforced more than five thousand laws as a "fence" around Moses' Laws, the strategy being that so long as the Mishnah was more stringent than God's Laws, breaking the Mishnah would not create the same response from God as previously. In the process, the Jews created a man-made system that took men's hearts away from God.

In Matthew 15:1-11, Jesus refers to the Mishnah (tradition of the elders) and its requirements that went far beyond the Law of Moses related to the laws of cleanliness and the commandments dealing with honor of father and mother in Exodus 20:12 and Exodus 21:17. Jesus was specifically addressing this problem created by literal and strong enforcement of the Mishnah on the Jewish people. The Mishnah had gone as far as to invalidate the Word of God (*"And by this you invalidated the word of God for the sake of your tradition"* - Verse 6), all in the name of making the Jews more holy! In Matthew 23, Jesus said that this man-made system, even in the name of God was *"because you travel around on sea and land to make one proselyte; and when he becomes one, you make him twice as much a son of hell as yourselves"* (Verse 15). Jesus was exposing the principle that altering the Word of God by adding to, taking away from, or privately interpreting Scripture is a grave mistake.

Revelations 22:18-19 says,

> *"I testify to everyone who hears the words of the prophecy of this book: if anyone adds to them, God will add to him the plagues which are written in this book; and if anyone takes away from the words of the book of this prophecy, God will take away his part from the tree of life and from the holy city, which are written in this book."*

And in 2 Peter 1:20, *But know this first of all, that no prophecy of Scripture is a matter of one's own interpretation.* The Word of God is pure unto itself (Psalm 119:140) and requires no alterations by man.

WILLING

Getting back to John 7, Jesus addresses an important principle in relation to receiving the teaching of God in Verse 17. *"If anyone is willing* [Greek word *"thelee"* meaning minded] *to do His will, he will know of the teaching, whether it is of God or whether I speak from Myself."* To receive and properly understand the teaching, one must be willing to obey it. And if you receive it in this way, with an open heart, you will know that it came from God; there will be no confusion. The Holy Spirit brings discernment about that which comes from God and what does not. In 1 John 4:1, the Word of God says, *Beloved, do not believe every spirit, but test the spirits to see whether they are from God, because many false prophets have gone out into the world.*

The one who lives by and proclaims the pure teaching of God brings glory to God while the one who alters it for his own interest seeks his own glory. He continues in Verses 22-24 to cite a situation where the Jews have made a lesser law, like circumcision, more important than healing a man completely on the Sabbath. This reference may be related to the man Jesus healed on the Sabbath at the gate of Bethesda in John 5. Motivation from the heart of God will always allow the believer to discern the right response to the circumstances at hand.

OVERCOMING SHORTCOMINGS

If we are to speak as God's representative, God and not man-made precepts must be the teacher. God promises to fill our mouths through His teaching. A fitting example of this is Moses, who was insecure about his ability to speak to Pharaoh as God had commanded. In Exodus 4:10-17, Moses pleads with the Lord not to have to speak since he has never been able to speak eloquently (some scholars suggest he had a speech impediment). The Lord assured him that whatever shortcomings Moses had with his speaking abilities would be no problem to overcome. He promised Moses that *"I, even I, will be with your mouth, and teach you what you are to say."* When Moses' doubts continued, the Lord reminded Moses that his brother, Aaron would be there also, and the Lord would speak through Aaron as well. In Verse 15, *"You are to speak to him and put the words in his mouth; and I, even I, will be with your mouth and his mouth, and I will teach you what you are to do."* God was promising to teach Moses and Moses was to teach Aaron what to say. And to reveal the authority of Moses and Aaron, the Lord would perform three signs or miracles. A similar issue existed with the Apostle Paul, and he wrote about it in his first letter to the Corinthians.

Paul recognized that he had shortcomings related to being able to speak with eloquence, but he did not let that deter him from being God's spokesman to establish the New Testament church in the Gentile world. In fact, he states in 1 Corinthians 2:4-5, that his weakness in this area was to manifest the power of God over the giftedness of man which would point men's faith toward God and away from man. Verse 2 is the key, *For I determined to know nothing among you except Jesus Christ, and Him crucified*. The significant point is that Paul placed importance not on anything he knew, but on the mysteries that God would reveal through him as he focused his attention on Jesus Christ, the person, and Him crucified, the message of the gospel. In this way, Paul was emphasizing that God would give him everything he needed for each situation he faced. God wants to use His people as His mouthpiece, that the work of Christ would continue throughout the New Testament age. God will use anyone who agrees to be taught by God.

Continue in the Teaching

Anyone who goes too far and does not abide in the teaching of Christ, does not have God; the one who abides in the teaching, he has both the Father and the Son. If anyone comes to you and does not bring this teaching, do not receive him into your house, and do not give him a greeting; for the one who gives him a greeting participates in his evil deeds. **2 John 9-11**

The apostle John goes on in his second letter to explain that the teaching of God is not a one-time event, but something that becomes a way of life. He uses the Greek word "*meno*" which is translated abide, remain, or continue in. When the believer allows himself to be taught by God as a lifestyle, he "*has the Father and the Son.*" Anyone who comes to you in the name of the Lord yet is not speaking only from God as if God were his teacher, one should not receive such a one into his house. There were many false teachers in the days when John wrote this letter, and that condition is also prevalent today.

False teaching in the name of the Lord takes on many forms and Paul identifies them as *philosophy and empty deception, according to the tradition of men, according to the elementary principles of the world* in Colossians 2:8. They are intended to take you captive, removing you from the power that God manifests through believers who are personally connected to Christ in mind (teaching) and spirit. When Christ is our all in all, we complete and therefore need nothing else. It reminds us of David's statement in Psalm 23, *The Lord is my shepherd, I shall not want.* When believers are circumcised to Christ, they are fully satisfied.

Chapter 21

THE TEMPLE

The Passover of the Jews was near, and Jesus went up to Jerusalem. And He found in the temple those who were selling oxen and sheep and doves, and the money changers seated at their tables. And He made a scourge of cords, and drove them all out of the temple, with the sheep and the oxen; and He poured out the coins of the money changers and overturned their tables; and to those who were selling the doves He said, "Take these things away; stop making My Father's house a place of business." His disciples remembered that it was written, "ZEAL FOR YOUR HOUSE WILL CONSUME ME." The Jews then said to Him, "What sign do You show us as your authority for doing these things?" Jesus answered them, "Destroy this temple, and in three days I will raise it up." The Jews then said, "It took forty-six years to build this temple, and will You raise it up in three days?" But He was speaking of the temple of His body. So, when He was raised from the dead, His disciples remembered that He said this; and they believed the Scripture and the word which Jesus had spoken. **John 2:13-22**

As Jesus was introducing the new covenant, he was constantly redefining the meaning of words, trying to reveal a new covenant understanding on an Old Testament concept. One of these concepts was the temple. In Old Testament times, the temple was the center of the Jewish spiritual life since the majority of the ceremonies and rites were celebrated in and around the temple itself. To the Old Testament believer, it was a very meaningful place and it molded and shaped the believers' vision of God, Himself.

Cleansing the Temple

I took an Art & Architecture course in college, and we looked extensively at cathedrals and other Christian churches from the Middle Ages and beyond. Since people from the Middle Ages were ignorant of the language of the church (Latin) and did not have any exposure to places other than their own homes and fiefdoms, their only perspective of God came from the church or cathedral. As a result, the churches were so constructed to create an awe-inspiring experience for each church goer as they attended church service or other religious events. The height of the ceilings, windows, and doors, the gold and gold-plated icons and utensils, and the large statues of the various saints of old were an integral part of shaping the mental images of God and His closest friends! The Old Testament temples in their magnificence are a model for the cathedral/church.

In the above passage in John's gospel, Jesus is now redefining the temple and its role in the Christian's life. First, He says it should never be a place of business (Verse 16). We learn from scholars that the money changers were taking tremendous advantage of those from places far away, when required by Jewish law to pay the annual temple tax as well as to purchase any animal sacrifices such as turtle doves brought to the priests in the temple. This unfair treatment of poor outsiders likens itself to the way tax collectors would treat their constituency, charging exorbitant fees that they would keep for themselves. God's house should never profit some at the expense of others' misfortunes or naivete. It is a reminder of the concern Jesus showed to the children (innocent ones) in Matthew 19:14 to not hinder them from coming to God. Evil must be cleansed from the temple!

True Worship

Once the Pharisees challenge Jesus on the authority that He was exercising to make this scene in the temple, Jesus made an extraordinary statement about the destruction of the temple and then rebuilt in three days. Of course, they did not understand what He was talking about, but we now understand from other New Testament Scripture that He was changing the meaning of the temple to the body, first His body, then the believer's body. The temple of the old covenant, a large structure set apart for worship of God, was no longer the temple in the new covenant. According to John 4: 20-24, the place of worship was no longer the principal issue, but the heart behind the worship, within each believer, the new covenant temples. In Verse 21, Jesus made the following statement to the Samaritan woman, *"Woman, believe Me, an hour is coming when neither in this mountain nor in Jerusalem will you worship the Father."* Jesus later emphasizes in Verse 24, *"God is spirit, and those who worship Him must worship in spirit and truth."* Worship is according to *"spirit and truth"* and not ritual.

How much do we emphasize the place of worship over the inner quality of that worship? For many traditional Christians, if the church did not have a steeple with an organ and stained glass, then it was not really a church, and the lack of these physical things would negatively affect their sense of being in God's presence. But Jesus was trying to teach that the physical characteristics of a place of worship or a particular location are not what really matters. The Greek word for worship, *"proskuneo,"* means to blow a kiss to show respect or homage. The basics of worship are not inherent in the physical place, but the hearts of the worshippers. These are the ones the Father is seeking!

The Archbishop of Canterbury in 1941 was William Temple and he made this statement about worship: *"for to worship is to quicken the conscience with the holiness of God, to feed the mind on the truth of God, to purge the imaginations by the beauty of God, to open the heart to the love of God, and to devote the will to the purpose of God."* Many have this idea that worship is the time we sing in church, led by a song leader, and sing familiar Christian hymns and contemporary songs. The biblical premise of worship is that it is so much more than that, encompassing our life beyond the time in church services. It involves the way we live our lives!

BOUGHT WITH A PRICE

All things are lawful for me, but not all things are profitable. All things are lawful for me, but I will not be mastered by anything. Food is for the stomach and the stomach is for food, but God will do away with both of them. Yet the body is not for immorality, but for the Lord, and the Lord is for the body. Now God has not only raised the Lord but will also raise us up through His power. Do you not know that your bodies are members of Christ? Shall I then take away the members of Christ and make them members of a prostitute? May it never be! Or do you not know that the one who joins himself to a prostitute is one body with her? For He says, "THE TWO SHALL BECOME ONE FLESH." But the one who joins himself to the Lord is one spirit with Him. Flee immorality. Every other sin that a man commits is outside the body, but the immoral man sins against his own body. Or do you not know that your body is a temple of the Holy Spirit who is in you, whom you have from God, and that you are not your own? For you have been bought with a price: therefore, glorify God in your body. **1 Corinthians 6:12-20**

Paul is trying to expound upon the revelation of the body being the temple in this passage. In Verses 19-20, he asks if we know that our body is the temple of the Holy Spirit, that we no longer belong to ourselves because Jesus Christ purchased us at Calvary. This is a reality that he wants us to understand and therefore live by glorifying God in our bodies. The new covenant believer recognizes that his spiritual life lives before God in the body, and he is to treat his body as he would any holy place of worship. When Jesus began turning over the tables of the money changers in the temple, he was symbolically speaking to us that we must also turn over the tables of the money changers in our lives and recognize the holiness that God intends for us. And how is this possible?

Paul indicates in Verse 12 that we decide for ourselves what is lawful and what is not lawful for us, the standards we are to live by. Those standards allow us to live lives that are profitable (advantageous, to our benefit) and keeps us from some unseemly behavior mastering the believer. By recognizing the higher standards that God has decreed for all believers, we are joining ourselves to the Lord and become one spirit with Him (Verse 17). The evil of the money changers represents itself by self-centeredness and the standards of God free us from the bondage of all that self-centeredness can produce in our lives.

Rebuilding the Temple

In Ezra 5, the Jews who returned to Jerusalem were desirous to rebuild the temple that Nebuchadnezzar had destroyed seventy years earlier when he took numerous into captivity to Babylon. They had met much opposition and King Artaxerxes of Persia had issued a decree stopping any building of the temple. When Darius became King of Persia, the Jews began rebuilding the temple again and Darius received a letter about the situation from Tattenai, the governor of the province, indicating that a previous king of Persia, King Cyrus had ordered the rebuilding many years earlier. Cyrus had taken the gold and silver utensils taken from the temple by the Babylonians upon their capture of Jerusalem and put them in the hands of the Sheshbazzar, the appointed governor of the province at the time. There was hope that the Jews would be allowed to complete the rebuilding if King Darius would confirm King Cyrus' decree from many years earlier. And in Ezra 6, we find out that Darius did find the decree within the archives and approved the work in Jerusalem.

In Ezra 7, we see Ezra as a man skilled in the law of Moses and given permission by King Artaxerxes to return to Jerusalem with a few followers to reestablish God's work in Judah. The passage tells us that *the hand of the Lord his God was upon him*. Verse 10 also reveals that his heart was set to study and teach the Word of God. Ezra is a type of

Jesus Christ, sent to the Jews to teach the Word of God and to live it! Jesus and His words lead the rebuilding of the temple.

THE DISCIPLINE OF THE LORD

This historical record of the rebuilding of the temple is symbolic of the rebuilding of our temple after we have failed God. God's plan to rebuild our temple is also known as the discipline of the Lord, the Lord's way of reestablishing His supremacy in our lives.

The writer of Hebrews explains the importance of God's discipline in the believer's life in Hebrews 12:5-11. The Greek word translated discipline in this passage is *"paideia"* and it means training and instruction with the intention of raising virtue. In Hebrews 12:10, the discipline of the Lord allows the believer to *share His holiness*. The new covenant brings us into deeper fellowship with Jesus Christ and His discipline is a necessary work of God in our lives to bring about *the peaceful fruit of righteousness*. Without this training, we are only illegitimate children (Hebrews 12:8).

JESUS, OUR PRECIOUS CORNERSTONE

The foundation of the temple, the precious cornerstone is meant to be Jesus Christ, Himself (1 Corinthians 3:11) and this building is a work of God (Psalm 127:1) and supported by other like believers (1 Corinthians 12:27-28), growing together into a holy temple in the Lord. When believers come together in agreement that Jesus is the center of their lives, then their temples become a temple, speaking of the universal church of believers, the body of Christ and Jesus leads His work in the new covenant age through this holy entity.

Chapter 22

FRUITFUL

*"I am the true vine, and My Father is the vinedresser. Every branch in Me that does not **bear fruit**, He takes away; and every branch that bears fruit, He prunes it so **that it may bear more fruit**. You are already clean because of the word which I have spoken to you. Abide in Me, and I in you. As the branch cannot bear fruit of itself unless it abides in the vine, so neither can you unless you abide in Me. I am the vine, you are the branches; he who abides in Me and I in him, **he bears much fruit**, for apart from Me you can do nothing. If anyone does not abide in Me, he is thrown away as a branch and dries up; and they gather them and cast them into the fire and they are burned. If you abide in Me, and My words abide in you, ask whatever you wish, and it will be done for you. My Father is glorified by this, **that you bear much fruit**, and so prove to be My disciples."* **John 15:1-8**

When Jesus says that *"I am the true vine and My Father is the vinedresser,"* He was laying the foundation for the fruitful life. The vinedresser was responsible for the overall care of the vineyard, including the nurturing, trimming, and defending for its ultimate growth in fruitfulness. The vine was the source of nutrition and life to the branches; without that source the branches could not bear fruit (see

Verse 5). The use of the vine metaphor is not uncommon to the Jew; God regularly referred to them as His vineyard.

FRUIT, MORE FRUIT, MUCH FRUIT

One of the most important lessons Jesus taught His disciples during the last week of His life was how to be fruitful. In John 15, the principle at the center of spiritual fruitfulness is the principle of abiding. The Greek word is *meno* and it means *to remain, to continue, to dwell*. Spiros Zodhiates defines it as **to be and remain united with him, one with him in heart, mind, and will**. The idea is that a branch cannot exhibit spiritual life unless there is a continual feeding from the vine. Jesus says He is the true vine, meaning genuine or real, suggesting that there are false vines (foreign vines in Jeremiah 2:21). The more connected a believer is to the true vine, the more production of fruit. When the vinedresser sees there is no fruit, He removes the branch and the one that bears fruit, He prunes it so that it bears more fruit (Verse 2). The vinedresser is not satisfied with just fruit, but he wants more fruit (Verse 2). The true disciple proves it by bearing much fruit (Verse 8).

Verse 7 has the key to discipleship and bearing fruit where Jesus includes the Word of God as part of the equation: *"If you abide in Me, and My words abide in you, ask whatever you wish, and it will be done for you."* In John 8:31-32, *"So Jesus was saying to those Jews who had believed Him, 'If you continue* [meno] *in My word, then you are truly disciples of Mine; and you will know the truth, and the truth will make you free.'"* Jesus says if the believer vitally connects himself to not only the life of Jesus, but also His Word, he can ask of God, and it will happen. This fruitfulness is the proof of discipleship.

A FAITHLESS HEART

Through the prophet Isaiah (5:1-7), God used the vineyard metaphor to illustrate not only the care of the vinedresser (the Father), but also the failure of Israel to produce good grapes. God asks the question, *"What more was there to do for My vineyard that I have not done in it?"*

The conclusion, found in Verse 7 is that the good grapes of justice and righteousness were not present, so God's verdict was that they were *worthless ones.* There is an interesting interplay when you look at the original Hebrew. "Justice" (*mispat*) instead of "bloodshed" (*mispoh*), and "distress" (*tsaaqa*) replaced "righteousness" (*tsedaqa*). So, what happened? God removed His hedge of protection and allowed outside forces to corrupt the heart of the nation and stopped pruning and ceased the clouds from raining. In Isaiah 1:21, *How the faithful city has become a harlot, she who was **full of justice! Righteousness once lodged in her**, but now murderers.* For Israel, the fruit of a healthy relationship with God is justice and righteousness since He is actively caring for it.

Hosea exposes the *heart* of the problem in Hosea 10:2; it was a faithless heart. The Hebrew word translated faithless is *chalaq* and it means divided. When Israel allied itself with unholy nations, their hearts became divided, and they thus became faithless. In James 1:8, Scripture tells us that a double-minded man is unstable in all his ways. When Israel was in bondage to Egypt, the Lord became the object of the people's alliances out of their pressing need for deliverance and God was always aware of their needs, as Psalm 105:24 says, *And He caused His people to be very fruitful and made them stronger than their adversaries.* The fruitful life derives itself from centering each believer on the strength and ability of God, the ultimate producer of spiritual fruit.

The Surviving Remnant

In Isaiah 37, Assyrians led by King Sennacherib surrounded Jerusalem with the intention to get the inhabitants, led by King Hezekiah to surrender. King Hezekiah reached out to the prophet Isaiah for Godly counsel. Although Sennacherib's army greatly outnumbered the Jews, Isaiah told him that God would deliver Israel from the hands of the Assyrians and Hezekiah went to the temple to pray. In Verse 20,

"Now, O Lord our God, deliver us from his hand that all the kingdoms of the earth may know that You alone, Lord, are God." God's response came in Verse 21, when God answered, *"Because you have prayed to Me about Sennacherib, king of Assyria"*, God answered the prayer by promising His care of Jerusalem while her enemy surrounded Jerusalem. In Verse 30 God promises that the inhabitants will have enough food to feed themselves without going outside the city walls to plant and reap in the first and second years. In the third year, they could plant and reap their harvest. The key Verse is 31, which is the fulfillment of God's care, that *the surviving remnant of Judah will again take root downward and bear fruit upward.* By rooting themselves deep into the provisions of God, Jerusalem would bear fruit visible to all.

In Matthew 21:33-45, Jesus spoke a parable to illustrate how the Jewish nation was rejecting their prophets and their Messiah (John 1:11), again using the vineyard as a means to teach the fruitfulness of God's kingdom. It is clear that the reference is to Israel as the vine growers and their progressive rejection of prophets (slaves) and then even the Messiah (landowner's son) in order to *"seize his inheritance"* (Verse 38). Verse 39 says that they threw him out of the vineyard and killed him, a reference to the cross located outside the city of Jerusalem. The verdict against the vine-growers would be *a wretched end*, a reference to the destruction of the Jewish leadership of Jesus's day in 70 AD. Then in Verse 43, the kingdom of God is taken away from this wicked generation and given to a people that will produce the fruit of it which is a reference to the church, made up of both Jews and Gentiles. Fruitfulness is the ultimate measure of success in the kingdom of God.

NO FRUIT, BAD FRUIT

In various Old Testament verses (Jeremiah 8:13, Hosea 9:10, 16), the fig tree is a symbol of Israel. Jesus was illustrating the reality that Israel was alive because it had leaves, but it had no fruit. He was teaching His disciples that Israel's lack of fruit would result in the ultimate destruction of the Jewish leadership and national entity in 70 A.D. when the Romans would destroy the temple in Jerusalem.

Fruitfulness is the by-product of faith and a willingness to trust God for all things.

In the Sermon on the Mount (Matthew 7:17-20), Jesus teaches on the subject of fruitfulness by looking at the tree bearing the fruit and the quality of that fruit. A good tree always bears good fruit while a bad tree always bears only bad fruit. The ultimate verdict for the bad tree is that it must be *"cut down and thrown into the fire,"* speaking about judgment. Most scholars agree this is a reference to the Pharisees, who were not teaching the Law of Moses, but were *"transgressing the commandment of God for the sake of your tradition"* (Matthew 15:3). In Jeremiah 12:10, it says, *Many shepherds have ruined My vineyard, they have trampled down My field; they have made My pleasant field a desolate wilderness.* When Matthew 7:20 says *"you will know them by their fruit,"* He was teaching that fruit is the basis of evaluating a teaching ministry.

Righteousness Yields Fruit

The foundation of abiding in the vine is trust. Mount Zion, another name for Jerusalem, is symbolic of a believer's vertical relationship with God. In Psalm 125, the writer exalts that relationship as eternal (abides forever) and that it is the source of those who are upright in heart. Abiding produces a victorious life because it puts its total trust in God and His ability rather than man's. The believer experiences righteousness as he operates by faith in the gospel, trusting in the Righteous One, Jesus Christ, rather than himself. In Romans 1:17, Paul speaks of the gospel saying, *For in it the righteousness of God is revealed from faith to faith; as it is written, "BUT THE RIGHTEOUS man SHALL LIVE BY FAITH."* The righteous man is a fruitful man as Proverbs 12:12 relates, *The wicked man desires the booty of evil men, but* **the root of the righteous yields fruit**.

Chapter 23

DEVOTION AND PRAYER

Jesus, therefore, six days before the Passover, came to Bethany where Lazarus was, whom Jesus had raised from the dead. So, they made Him a supper there, and Martha was serving; but Lazarus was one of those reclining at the table with Him. Mary then took a pound of **very costly perfume of pure nard** *and anointed the feet of Jesus and wiped His feet with her hair; and the house was filled with the fragrance of the perfume. But Judas Iscariot, one of His disciples, who was intending to betray Him, said, "Why was this perfume not sold for three hundred denarii and given to poor people?" Now he said this, not because he was concerned about the poor, but because he was a thief, and as he had the money box, he used to pilfer what was put into it. Therefore, Jesus said, "Let her alone, so that she may keep it for the day of My burial. "For you always have the poor with you, but you do not always have Me."*
John 12:1-8

As Jesus approaches the final week of his life, He visits again with His close friends, Martha, Mary, and Lazarus in Bethany for a meal. Along with Him are many of His disciples (see Matthew 26:8), including Judas Iscariot, who was soon to betray Him. The highlight of the meal was the costly perfume with which Mary chose to anoint the feet of Jesus, prompting a negative response from Judas Iscariot and some other disciples, according to the account in Matthew's gospel. Jesus's response to the disciples' objections gives us deeper understanding into the importance of this moment with reference to His upcoming death. *"For you always have the poor, but you do not always have Me."* Mary was demonstrating a devotion to Jesus that challenged even His closest disciples.

The pure nard was a fragrant oil prepared from the roots and stems of an aromatic herb from northern India. It was an expensive perfume, imported in sealed alabaster boxes or flasks which were opened only on special occasions. Mary's lavish gift expressed her love and thanks to Jesus for restoring Lazarus to life. The fragrance filled the house. Our willingness to sacrifice our best is a sweet aroma to God! We can glean from the implications of the fragrance by taking a look at the Old Testament and in particular, the tabernacle.

Holy Anointing Oil

In Exodus 30:22-33, God instructed Moses to create the *holy anointing oil to Me (to be used) throughout your generations* (Verse 31). It consisted of four fragrant spices used to dedicate, to consecrate the high priest, Aaron, and his sons to minister as priests as well as to anoint the tent of meeting, the ark of the covenant, and all of the altars, tables, lampstands, and utensils. The sweet aroma of the mixture is representative of the fragrance God smells when a believer lives a life that commands devotion, consecration, holiness, if you will. Our purpose-filled life to honor God's personal investment in each of us in the midst of a corrupt world and a fallen nature produces a sanctified commitment to the Divine Will. The structure of the new covenant provides each believer, through the sacrificial offering of Christ, an ability to operate as forgiven priests of the Most High God.

Not only was the holy anointing oil made to have a fragrant aroma, but God's instructions to create the incense offered on the altar of incense and made like a perfume, *the work of a perfumer* (Exodus 30:34-38). The particular mixture was meant to be only for the Lord, holy, meaning that it was reserved for God. When we set aside something important as unto the Lord, it creates a sweet aroma in God's nostril. In Ephesians 5:1-2, *Therefore be imitators of God, as beloved children; and walk in love, just as Christ also loved you and gave Himself up for us, an offering, and a sacrifice to God as **a fragrant aroma.*** Our commitment to walk in His love represents our willingness to sacrifice ourselves to God's highest priority: loving others.

THE GOOD PART

One definition of devotion is "an earnest attachment to a cause or person." In Luke's gospel, Mary revealed this devotion to Jesus in Luke 10:38-42. Jesus visited this same house of Martha and Mary and found Martha preparing for the meal they were about to partake in, but Mary was *seated at the Lord's feet, listening to His words*. Martha complained that Mary was not helping with the work, but Jesus pointed out Martha's error by saying, *"Martha, Martha, you are worried and bothered about so many things, but only one thing is necessary."* In the midst of many details, Mary had chosen the right priority, *"the good part."* Her devotion was on display for all of us to observe.

> *"Sanctify them in the truth; Your word is truth. As You sent Me into the world, I also have sent them into the world. For their sakes I sanctify Myself, that they themselves also may be sanctified in truth."* **John 17:17-19**

Jesus's prayer to His Father the night before He died in John 17 reveals His heart for His disciples and the need for sanctification (*hagiozoe* – set apart for a sacred purpose), and that the Word of God would accomplish it (Verse 17). Jesus Christ sends each disciple into the world as His representative for a divine purpose through the truth of God's Word to fulfill His will as His witness (Acts 1:8). This consecration accompanies God's ability, His power, His anointing. When the divine covering sends the disciple out, the results will always belong to God and not to him (Ephesians 2:10).

Do not be Entangled

Paul helps us understand an important principle in being set apart for a higher purpose. In 2 Timothy 2:3-7, he uses a soldier and his willingness to give up his freedoms to accomplish his superior's purpose by not allowing entanglement in the affairs of everyday life. It reminds me of the parable of the sower and the seed in Matthew 13 and the seed sown among the thorns that represent *"the worry of the world and the deceitfulness of wealth choke the word."* The second metaphor is as an athlete who commits himself completely to the rules, to the game, to the ultimate goal, not allowing distractions to keep him from God's intentions.

> *Do you not know that when you present yourselves to someone as slaves for obedience, you are slaves of the one whom you obey, either of sin resulting in death, or of obedience resulting in righteousness? But thanks be to God that though you were slaves of sin, you became obedient from the heart to that form of teaching to which you were committed, and having been freed from sin, you became slaves of righteousness.* **Romans 6:16-18**

Paul defines for us the key ingredient in finding devotion to the Divine Will and therefore a real victory over the power of sin in Romans 6 when he says, *you became obedient from the heart to that form of teaching to which you were committed.* It means that a sincere, wholehearted, and honest commitment to the teaching (doctrine) received as truth will result in a victory over sin's corruption and the believer will begin to experience in a practical way the righteousness of God. In Romans 1:17, Paul is referring to the gospel when he says, ***In it** the righteousness of God is revealed from faith to faith, as it is written, 'BUT THE RIGHTEOUS man SHALL LIVE BY FAITH.'* Every moment we live by faith, trusting God, we experience God's righteousness.

Effective Prayer

The effective prayer of a righteous man can accomplish much.
James 5:16

The righteous man has found the devotion that draws him near to His God and it brings him to his knees when he realizes that it is God that accomplishes much as a result of effective prayer. The Greek word for effective is *energeo* and it means *operative, at work*. One major way the new covenant believer realizes the Divine Will is that his devotion produces activity, action, work and one major aspect of this work is prayer. Devotion produces an earnestness as it says in Verse 17 that results in God answering prayers. In 1 John 5:14-15, John declares, *This is the confidence which we have before Him, that, if we ask anything according to His will, He hears us. And if we know that He hears us in whatever we ask, we know that we have the requests which we have asked from Him.* The prayers of the saints are like the burning of incense in the tabernacle as Revelation 5:8 defines, and they produce a wonderful aroma to God.

Jesus taught His disciples about the importance of prayer in Luke 18:1-8 by emphasizing the principle of unceasing prayer. In 1 Thessalonians 5:17, the Scriptures teach us to pray without ceasing. There is no guarantee that God will answer our prayers within a certain timeframe; in fact, He usually wants us to learn how to wait. Our persistence in prayer ties us to the perfect will of God since we have learned how to wait for it by continuing to pray. In Luke 18:8, Jesus wants us to exhibit this kind of faith; this kind of faith is contagious.

Jesus, our Intercessor

We take our example to pray from Jesus Himself, who was continually praying for His Father's will while here as the Son of Man. Now, seated at the right hand of the Father, He is always making intercession for *"those who draw near to God"* (Hebrews 7:25) as part of His Eternal High Priesthood. Our devotion to Him in prayer is possible because of His demonstrated devotion to each believer. In Romans 8:34, Paul says, *who is the one who condemns? Christ Jesus is He who died, yes, rather who was raised, who is at the right hand of God, who also intercedes for us.* It is that kind of support that gives each believer the devotion to stay the course.

> *But thanks be to God, who always leads us in triumph in Christ, and manifests through us the sweet aroma of the knowledge of Him in every place. For* **we are a fragrance of Christ to God** *among those who are being saved and among those who are perishing; to the one an aroma from death to death, to the other an aroma from life to life. And who is adequate for these things?* **2 Corinthians 2:14-16**

Paul tells us that the one who stays the course is being led in triumph in Christ, within the veil of that sacred relationship and produces that fragrance not only to God, but as a ministry to the present world he occupies. His fragrance reflects the sweet aroma that Christ manifests to His Father and this new covenant relationship makes us adequate as His representatives in this present world.

Chapter 24

DISCIPLINE OF THE LORD

"But now I am going to Him who sent Me; and none of you asks Me, 'Where are You going?' But because I have said these things to you, sorrow has filled your heart. But I tell you the truth, it is to your advantage that I go away; for if I do not go away, the Helper will not come to you; but if I go, I will send Him to you. And He, when He comes, **will convict [convince]** *the world concerning* **sin and righteousness and judgment**; *concerning sin, because they do not believe in Me; and concerning righteousness, because I go to the Father and you no longer see Me; and concerning judgment [krisis – determination, distinguish], because the ruler of this world has been judged."* **John 16:5-11**

As Jesus introduces the Holy Spirit to the disciples in John 14-16, He defines for them various roles that the Holy Spirit will play in the life of the new covenant believer. One of the most important is the role of convicting the world. This Greek word for convict is *elegchoe* and it means *to prove or convince one in the wrong and thus to shame him*. Jesus says that He must leave so that the Holy Spirit will come to do this splendid work on behalf of the entire world. This work is necessary so that, just as Jesus came to reveal the light in the midst of darkness, the Holy Spirit would continue to expose darkness through the light of the Gospel. In the passage above, Jesus introduces for us three aspects of the Lord's discipline: convicting the world concerning sin, righteousness, and judgment.

Conviction of Sin

Experiencing God cannot take place without this holy work of God. The conviction of the world concerning sin (*hamartia* – an offense in relation to God with emphasis on guilt) is necessary to bring one to faith. In Romans 4:23b, Paul states, **and whatever is not from faith is sin**. Once a person recognizes his need for a solution to sin and guilt, Christ's work on Calvary becomes evident. It is faith (trust) in the substitutionary work of Jesus that provides the victory over sin and the door to spiritual life.

In his message at Pentecost, Peter said in Acts 2:36, "*Therefore let all the house of Israel know for certain that God has made Him both Lord and Christ—**this Jesus whom you crucified**.*" In response to this conviction, Verse 37 says that the people were *pierced to the heart*, acknowledging their responsibility, and therefore asked Peter what they should do about it. Peter responded, "**Repent** [change the mind, reverse direction], *and each of you be baptized in the name of Jesus Christ for the forgiveness of your sins; and you will receive the gift of the Holy Spirit.*" He was telling them that the Law of Moses was no longer the avenue to God, but faith in Jesus as the Christ, the Messiah.

In Romans 6:8-11,

Now if we have died with Christ, we believe that we shall also live with Him, knowing that Christ, having been raised from the dead, is never to die again; death no longer is master over Him. For the death that He died, He died to sin once for all; but the life that He lives, He lives to God. Even so, consider yourselves to be dead to sin, but alive to God in Christ Jesus.

The believer experiences the victory over sin as he considers himself dead to sin in identification with Jesus's death. The end result is that he shares in the life of Jesus.

Convince of Righteousness

Jesus was tried by both Jews and Romans and found guilty as a criminal, and then sentenced to crucifixion. One of the two thieves crucified with Him recognized that Jesus was not a criminal like he was, saying in Luke 23:41, *"And we indeed are suffering justly, for we are receiving what we deserve for our deeds; but this man has done nothing wrong."* The centurion observing the crucifixion exclaimed *"Truly this was the Son of God!"* The Holy Spirit is the one who convinces men of the righteousness of Christ. The Apostle Paul, who had a similar experience on the Damascus Road in Acts 9, utilized the description "in Christ" or "in Him", more than one hundred times in his letters as defining the relationship of the believer to Christ. In 2 Corinthians 5:21, he states, *He made Him who knew no sin to be sin on our behalf,* ***so that we might become the righteousness of God in Him***. Although Jesus is no longer here, the believer experiences His righteousness within the spiritual connection to Christ.

The Jews had a problem with this since they thought they could derive their own righteousness by keeping the Law. Paul exposes the shortcoming of this thinking in Romans 10:2-4,

> *For I testify about them that they have a zeal for God, but not in accordance with knowledge. For not knowing about God's righteousness and seeking to establish their own, they did not subject themselves to the righteousness of God. For Christ is the end of the law for righteousness to everyone who believes.*

Paul further explains in Romans 4:4-6 that God gives righteousness as a gift and is not earned, a by-product of faith in God. Isaiah spoke of this righteousness in Isaiah 45:24-25, *They will say of Me, "Only in the Lord are righteousness and strength." Men will come to Him, and all who were angry at Him will be put to shame. In the Lord all the offspring of Israel will be justified and will glory.*

Convince of Judgment

The basic meaning of *krisis* is a legal judgment resulting in punishment, In John's Gospel, the meaning and intention of judgment shifts to God's interest in setting things in their proper place. In John 3:17, *"For God did not send the Son into the world to judge the world, but that the world might be saved through Him."* The work of Jesus on the cross was meant to *destroy the works of the devil* (1 John 3:8). For the rest of us, He wishes to put things in their proper order. This responsibility to judge belongs to Jesus alone (James 4:12) and the New Testament warns not to become a judge of others. In Verse 11, *Do not speak against one another, brethren. He who speaks against a brother or judges his brother, speaks against the law, and judges the law; but if you judge the law, you are not a doer of the law but a judge of it.*

1 John 5:19 says, *We know that we are of God, and that the whole world lies in the power of the evil one.* The impact of that power is the continued corruption and disruption of things from their proper place. As a result, the Holy Spirit's work of conviction is an ongoing work, and the Lord wishes to rescue His loved ones from the effects of sin in the world. In John 12:31, *"Now judgment is upon this world;* **now the ruler of this world will be cast out."** Paul tells us that *the flesh sets its desire against the Spirit, and the Spirit against the flesh; for these are in opposition to one another, so that you may not do the things that you please. But if you are led by the Spirit, you are not under the Law* (Galatians 5:17-18). The discipline of the Lord is necessary to reach the believer not following the Holy Spirit.

Training

and you have forgotten the exhortation which is addressed to you as sons, "MY SON, DO NOT REGARD LIGHTLY THE DISCIPLINE OF THE LORD, NOR FAINT WHEN YOU ARE REPROVED BY HIM; FOR THOSE WHOM THE LORD LOVES HE DISCIPLINES, AND HE SCOURGES EVERY SON WHOM HE RECEIVES" [Prov 3:11-12]. *It is*

for discipline that you endure; God deals with you as with sons; ***for what son is there whom his father does not discipline*** *[paideuo* – to train children]*? But if you are without discipline, of which all have become partakers, then you are illegitimate children and not sons. Furthermore, we had earthly fathers to discipline us, and we respected them; shall we not much rather be subject to the Father of spirits, and live? For they disciplined us for a short time as seemed best to them, but He disciplines us* ***for our good, so that we may share His holiness****. All discipline for the moment seems not to be joyful, but sorrowful; yet to those who have been trained by it, afterwards it yields the peaceful fruit of righteousness.*
Hebrews 12:5-11

The writer of Hebrews introduces this principle by quoting Proverbs 3:11-12, indicating that this work addresses *My son* and *those whom the Lord loves*. When the believer understands that the Lord is a hard taskmaster, any conversation about the Lord's discipline produces real fear. In fact, the Lord ties discipline or training to sonship since no discipline suggests illegitimate children. This passage also tells us that a father's discipline produces respect while our heavenly Father's training brings us into life, *zao* which is referencing the benefits of eternal life, kingdom life. One of those benefits is that *we may share in His holiness* and, the *peaceful fruit of righteousness*. It is a partnership with the Lord in the cleansing from all defilement of flesh and spirit, thus perfecting His holiness as believers fear the Lord (2 Corinthians 7:1).

HIGHWAY OF HOLINESS

A highway will be there, a roadway, and it will be called the Highway of Holiness. The unclean will not travel on it, but it will be for him who walks that way, and fools will not wander on it. No lion will be there, nor will any vicious beast go up on it; these will not be found there. But the redeemed will walk there, And the ransomed of the Lord will return and come with joyful shouting to

Zion, with everlasting joy upon their heads. They will find gladness and joy, and sorrow and sighing will flee away. **Isaiah 35:8-10**

The above passage is a prophecy of the coming Kingdom Age, but it also defines for each new covenant believer the value of allowing the Lord to bring him into a depth in the relationship as defined by *the Highway of Holiness*. This believer finds gladness and joy where sorrow and sighing flee away. It happens when he recognizes that the Lord's discipline is *for our good*.

Chapter 25

LIFE IN THE BODY OF CHRIST

The Messiah's time on earth consisted of thirty or so years with the last three representing His public ministry. This meant that within those three years, He would have to identify and train His disciples, demonstrate His messiahship to them not only through teaching, but also through many miracles. He would need to lay a foundation for the entire church age. This foundation would include introducing the supernatural work of the Holy Spirit by the empowering of His followers as well as being the inspiration of New Testament writers. The indwelling Holy Spirit directs the believer to walk in God's will and teaches him the dynamics of a progressive relationship with Jesus Christ and to be His witness. Just as Old Testament leaders were anointed to fulfill their obligations, the new covenant believer requires an anointing, God's ability to complete.

The Apostle Paul uses the terminology "in Christ" or "in Him' nearly one hundred times as a representation of the relationship ordained by the finished work of Christ for each believer. In Colossians 2:10, we are complete *in Him*. Another part of the new covenant believer's spiritual empowerment is found "in the Beloved" (Ephesians 1:6), a reference to the supernatural unity ordained by God for all believers as members of the universal body of Christ. Paul lays out the particular dynamics of this spiritual body in 1 Corinthians 12 and Romans 12. In 1 Corinthians 12:12-14, *For even as **the body is one and yet has many members**, and all the members of the body, though they are many, are one body, so also is Christ. For by one Spirit, we were all baptized into one body, whether Jews or Greeks, whether slaves or free, and we were all made to drink of one Spirit. For the body is not one member, but many.*

One Body

How can a diverse group of people with varying abilities, gifts, cultures, etc. become so united? This passage and others tell us that it is due to a series of ones: one body, one Spirit, one Lord, one faith, one Father, one baptism and one hope (see Ephesians 4:3-6). The unity ordained for members of the body of Christ is produced by one! One body means that no matter which local assembly one attends, he and all true believers are part of one body, with Jesus as its one Lord. One Spirit speaks to the reality that the same Holy Spirit indwells each believer, and it is this Spirit who baptizes the believer into the body of Christ at salvation, sealed for the day of redemption (Ephesians 4:30). One hope promises believers the same future, eternal life, and one faith means that there are certain doctrines or elements of belief, known as cardinal doctrines, that all true believers must accept. Finally, one Father means that all believers are children of the same Father, the God of the Bible.

Prayer for Unity

"I do not ask on behalf of these alone, but for those also who believe in Me through their word; that they may all be one; even as You, Father, are in Me and I in You, that they also may be in Us, so that the world may believe that You sent Me. "The glory which You have given Me I have given to them, that they may be one, just as We are one; I in them and You in Me, that they may be perfected in unity, so that the world may know that You sent Me, and loved them, even as You have loved Me." **John 17:20-23**

During the night before Jesus would be crucified, He prayed to His Father His concerns for the disciples whom He would be leaving behind who would continue the work and establish the church. He was praying to His Father for the same unity that exists between the Father and the Son, *"that they also may be in Us."* The unity between Father and Son produces the oneness of the body of Christ. This unity is as a result of the glory of the Father given to the Son, now given to the disciple. Jamieson, Fausset, and Brown Commentary defines that glory this way:

> *"The glory, then, here meant is all that which Jesus received from the Father as the incarnate Redeemer and Head of His people -the glory of a perfect acceptance as the spotless Lamb-the glory of free access to the Father and the right to be heard always-the glory of the Spirit's indwelling and sanctification-the glory of divine support and victory over sin, death, and hell-the glory of finally inheriting all things."*

A Mystical Body

The body of Christ is an amazing spiritual organism, that one mystical body of which Christ is the sole head, and in the unity of which all saints, whether in heaven, or on earth, or elsewhere, are constituent parts. In 1 Corinthians 5:44, *It is sown a natural body, it is raised a spiritual body. There is a natural body, and there is a spiritual body.* The body of Christ is God's place where the Lord transforms the natural man into a spiritual man. It is the place where each member finds his significance within the eternal work of God. In 1Corthians 12:24-25, *But God has so composed the body, giving more abundant honor to that member which lacked, so that there may be no division in the body, but that the members may have the same care for one another.* The spiritual church provides the environment where the neediest are cared for by other members. It follows the principle that the organism is only as strong as its weakest member, those most in need would receive special attention.

Fellowship

Fellowship demonstrates that life in the body of Christ is spiritual as 1 John 1:7 reveals, *but if we walk in the Light as He Himself is in the Light, we have fellowship with one another, and the blood of Jesus His Son cleanses us from all sin.* To walk in the light of Christ is to walk in the truth of the spiritual relationship with Christ and to recognize our brothers and sisters in Christ as family, as part of each one's spiritual support system in the world. It happens when we know other believers not after the flesh, not after the things that may naturally divide us, but our fellowship is with the life of Christ in each believer (2 Corinthians 5:16). The Greek word translated fellowship is *koinonia* and means that each believer is part of a spiritual community and has a participation in each other's life. God's *agape* (unconditional, self-sacrificing) love motivates life in the body of Christ.

For the believer to find his proper place within the body of Christ is to find fulfillment as a member in particular. In order for the world to understand the gospel, the body of Christ manifests the life of God on earth like nothing else.

Chapter 26

SPIRITUAL WARFARE

*When Jesus had spoken these words, He went forth with His disciples over the ravine of the Kidron, where there was a garden, in which He entered with His disciples. Now **Judas also, who was betraying Him**, knew the place, for Jesus had often met there with His disciples. Judas then, having received the Roman cohort and officers from the chief priests and the Pharisees, came there with lanterns and torches and weapons. So, Jesus, **knowing all the things that were coming upon Him**, went forth and said to them, "Whom do you seek?" They answered Him, "Jesus the Nazarene." He said to them, "I am He." And Judas also, who was betraying Him, was standing with them. So, when He said to them, "I am He," they drew back and fell to the ground. Therefore, He again asked them, "Whom do you seek?" And they said, "Jesus the Nazarene." Jesus answered, "I told you that I am He; so, if you seek Me, let these go their way," to fulfill the word which He spoke, "Of those whom You have given Me I lost not one." Simon Peter then, having a sword, drew it and struck the high priest's slave, and cut off his right ear; and the slave's name was Malchus.* **John 18:1-10**

There are many Christians who are not cognizant of the vital role that the devil and his demons play in undermining one's relationship with God and the purpose of a believer in God's ongoing work in the world. Judas Iscariot is a central figure in the passion of Christ and an illustration of how Satan's opposition to the perfect plan of the redemption of man can infect a man. The story of Jesus's betrayal (*paradidomai* – the delivering of another with evil intent) is the fulfillment of an Old Testament prophecy in Psalm 41:9, *Even my close friend in whom I trusted, who ate my bread, has lifted up his heel against me.* Jesus was prepared for it, but the effect it had on Him was still difficult. Understanding that evil is not only present in the world, but also active, means that the believer needs to learn to recognize spiritual warfare.

Luke 22:3 tells us that Satan, himself entered into Judas, not delegating that responsibility to his demons. Not only is demon possession possible, but also demon obsession, meaning that even a believer's mind can be preoccupied with evil; only non-believers can be demon possessed. It is my conviction that Judas was a thief (John 12:6) and his heart condition among others opened the door for the satanic possession.

Kakos and Poneros

There are 2 Greek words for evil and Vines Dictionary has a good explanation of the two. "*kakos* stands for '*whatever is evil in character, base,*' in distinction (wherever the distinction is observable) from *poneros*, which indicates '*what is evil in influence and effect, malicious, malignant.*' *Kakos* is the wider term and often covers the meaning of *poneros*. *Kakos* is antithetic to *kalos*, '*fair, advisable, good in character,*' and to *agathos*, '*beneficial, useful, good in act;*' hence it denotes what is useless, incapable, bad; *poneros* is essentially antithetic to *chrestos*, '*kind, gracious, serviceable;*' hence it denotes what is destructive, injurious, evil."

In Romans 7:21, *kakos* is the original Greek: *I find then the principle* [law] *that evil* [kakos] *is present in me, the one who wants to do good.* John 7:7 explains, "*The world cannot hate you, but it hates Me because I testify of it, that its deeds are evil* [poneros]." *Kakos* is the general term that represents evil compared to good while *poneros* is that evil which corrupts and is the source of conspiracies. Both are representative of the methods used by the devil and his kingdom.

> *the one who **practices sin is of the devil**; for the devil has sinned from the beginning. The Son of God appeared for this purpose, **to destroy the works of the devil**. No one who is born of God practices sin because His seed abides in him; and he cannot sin, because he is born of God. By this the children of God and the children of the devil are obvious: **anyone who does not practice righteousness is not of God**, nor the one who does not love his brother.* **1 John 3:8-10**

The emphasis of John's teaching is the word *practice* [present active participle of *poieo*, to make or to do]. It speaks of continuous action. The devil wishes to keep believers preoccupied with sin without experiencing victory. It is God's plan that believers live continuously in doing righteousness, doing what is right. This controversial passage is not teaching sinless perfection, but that when the believer is operating in his old self (see Ephesians 4:22-24), he is influenced to sin. On the other hand, the new self, the new man cannot sin since he is under the influence of the Holy Spirit. The believer chooses the life in which he functions day by day. Paul testifies in 1 Corinthians 15:31, *I die daily.*

THE DEVIL IS A LIAR

Jesus deals with the Pharisees regarding this matter in John 8 when He challenges their ability to understand [literally *hear*] His word (Verse 43). He tells them that they are of their father, the devil and as a result, they are preoccupied with doing his desires. In Verse 44, "*He was a murderer from the beginning and **does not stand in the truth because there is no truth in him**. Whenever he speaks a lie, he speaks from his own nature, for he is a liar and the father of lies.*" Jesus places the whole matter on the altar of the **truth** verses a **lie**. The true believer, operating under the power of the Holy Spirit is only interested in the truth. The new covenant believer is all about truth and the Holy Spirit, the Spirit of Truth, is always communicating that which is true. The Greek word for truth is *aletheia* and also means "reality," so the things that the believer hears is reality from God's perspective.

> ***Truthful lips will be established forever***, *but a lying tongue is only for a moment. Deceit is in the heart of those who devise evil, but counselors of peace have joy.* **Proverbs 12:19-20**

The Apostle Paul helps us understand the nature of that warfare in 2 Corinthians 10:3-5,

> *For though we walk in the flesh,* ***we do not war according to the flesh****, for the weapons of our* ***warfare*** *are not of the flesh, but divinely powerful for the destruction of fortresses. We are destroying speculations and* ***every lofty thing raised up against the knowledge of God****, and we are taking every thought captive to the obedience of Christ.*

So much of this warfare surrounds one's thought life and that battle takes place around thoughts, speculations [*logismos* – considerations, reflections] that devalue the things of God, the knowledge of God, placing something or someone else in His place. This battle is fought in the spiritual realm, empowered by the Holy Spirit, and intends to destroy fortifications or strongholds that have successfully invaded the believer's mind.

> *Finally, be strong in the Lord and in the strength of His might. Put on the full armor of God, so that you will be able to* ***stand firm*** *against the schemes of the devil. For our struggle is not against flesh and blood, but against the rulers, against the powers, against the world forces of this darkness, against the spiritual forces of wickedness in the heavenly places. Therefore, take up the full armor of God, so that you will be able to resist in the evil day, and having done everything, to* ***stand firm****. Stand firm therefore, HAVING GIRDED YOUR LOINS WITH TRUTH, and HAVING PUT ON THE BREASTPLATE OF RIGHTEOUSNESS, and*

having shod YOUR FEET WITH THE PREPARATION OF THE GOSPEL OF PEACE; in addition to all, taking up the shield of faith with which you will be able to extinguish all the flaming arrows of the evil one. And take THE HELMET OF SALVATION, and the sword of the Spirit, which is the word of God. With all prayer and petition pray at all times in the Spirit, and with this in view, be on the alert with all perseverance and petition for all the saints. **Ephesians 6:10-18**

Stand Firm

In Ephesians 6, Paul defines for us the weapons of the battle as armor. He begins by reminding the believer that the ability to overcome evil is not inherent in man, but it comes from God; **the battle is the Lord's**. In putting on the full armor of God, we put on His strength. The believer's role is to stand firm [*hestemi* – stand fast], having adorned the spiritual armor, including the loins girded with truth. It means that the truth [reality] of God and His Word is the core (loins) of a believer's life so he operates with integrity. He also puts on the breastplate of righteousness, armor that covers the body from the neck to the waist and speaks to the believer who chooses to live his life according to God's righteousness, that which is right. Feet (with the preparation of the gospel of peace) speaks not only of one's walk with God as one of peace (Romans 5:1), but also one's willingness to share it with others.

There is also the shield of faith and the helmet of salvation. One's individual faith in the promises of God protects him from the flaming arrows of the devil; his assurance of his salvation protects his mind from evil thoughts. The sword of the Spirit, a reference to the Word of God gives us both an offensive and defensive weapon against that which is not true. When Hebrews 4:12 speaks of the Word of God as living and powerful and sharper than any two-edged sword, it does its work in the heart and the mind to separate the soulish thoughts from the spiritual ones, allowing the believer discernment in warfare. Over and over again, Jesus utilized the truth of the Word of God when confronted by His enemies (and even the devil in Matthew 4:1-11) with the statement, *it is written*. He recognized the authority that it conveyed in challenging those who would question God's dominion over all things.

Finally, the emphasis in *all prayer and petition pray at all times in the Spirit* calls on the spiritual power of God to respond to every attack meant to dethrone God in the believer's heart and His rightful place. It is prayer that provides the energy to *stand firm against the schemes of the devil*. It is the power of the Holy Spirit that,

> *also helps our weakness; for we do not know how to pray as we should, but the Spirit Himself intercedes for us with groanings too deep for words; and He who searches the hearts knows what the mind of the Spirit is, because He intercedes for the saints according to the will of God.* **Romans 8:26-27**

Resistance

Submit [to be placed in subjection under] *therefore to God. Resist* [to stand against] *the devil and he will flee from you* (James 4:7). This encouragement to resist contrasts with Verse 6, where God is doing the resisting of the proud, while giving grace to the humble. This resistance comes from a firmness in the faith (1 Peter 5:9), and a full reliance on the power of God.

Chapter 27

THE KINGDOM OF HEAVEN

As Scripture testifies in Matthew 2:2, the magi came from the east looking for the Messiah by saying, *"Where is He who has been born King of the Jews? For we saw His star in the east and have come to worship Him."* Although there is no consensus on who the magi were or where they came from, it is more likely they were Gentiles of prominent position from a country, perhaps Parthia, northeast of Babylon, and given a special revelation by God of the birth of the King of the Jews. This occurred at a time when the prophecy of Daniel 9:25-27 was creating an expectation of the Messiah's imminent coming within Judaism and beyond (i.e., Herod). The idea that Messiah was to be a king and take charge of the existing government on behalf of the Jewish nation was a collective understanding among the Jewish masses and this paradigm became a theme of his entire public ministry.

Before Jesus's baptism, John the Baptist was preaching, *"Repent, for the kingdom of heaven is at hand"* (Matthew 3:2). Jesus assumed this same mantle in Matthew 4:17 as he began speaking to the masses and then extended it to His disciples' charge in Matthew 10:7, *"And as you go, preach, saying, 'The kingdom of heaven is at hand.'"* But what did this all mean? Was Messiah ready to demonstrate his physical authority or was there another, more profound meaning of the kingdom of heaven? To answer this question, we need to look at His entire public ministry, particularly his response to the Jewish accusations against Him when brought to Pilate.

KING OF THE JEWS

When confronted with the accusation that He was the *"King of the Jews"* in John 18:33, Jesus first inquired of Pilate by questioning his own personal belief in the charges, that somehow Jesus was a threat to the Roman authority of the Jewish nation. Jesus's reply to Pilate was, *"My kingdom is not of this world"* (Verse 36), thus redefining the kingdom as not a physical reality, but a spiritual one. Jesus reiterates to Pilate that He is a king, but that the defining element of His kingdom is *"the truth"* and that those who are of the truth hear the voice of their king (Verse 37). Pilate understood that this was not Rome's problem (*"I find no guilt in Him,"* Verse 38) and intended to turn Jesus loose, but the Jewish leaders had something else in mind. This King needed to die!

The interaction of the two thieves on the cross next to Jesus (see Luke 23:39-43) illustrates this principle of the kingdom. One of the thieves was only looking for a solution to his present situation, while the other comprehended the gravity of the moment. He understood that legitimate condemnation had come to both for things they did while Jesus was innocent of His charges. This thief asked Jesus to remember him *"when you come in Your kingdom."* Jesus's response was to acknowledge that this thief would soon be in Paradise. The crux of the matter was that this thief recognized Jesus as a king since He was about to come to His kingdom. He was confirming that the truth of his statement, *"this man has done nothing wrong"* allowed him to recognize the king and a kingdom. This criminal became a believer!

IN YOUR MIDST

The Pharisees ask Jesus about the kingdom of God in Luke 17:20-21 and His response is enlightening. He tells them that the kingdom is not recognizable by physical signs that are observable, but that the kingdom is *"in your midst."* The Greek word, *entos* means *inside* and that the kingdom of God is a reality that exists inside each one who recognizes the king and is therefore of the truth. The Pharisees were never able to grasp this principle.

> *And the disciples came and said to Him, "Why do You speak to them in parables?" Jesus answered them, "To you it has been granted* **to know the mysteries of the kingdom of heaven**, *but to them it has not been granted. "For whoever has, to him more shall be given, and he will have an abundance; but whoever does not have, even what he has shall be taken away from him. "Therefore, I speak to them in parables; because while seeing they do not see, and while hearing they do not hear, nor do they understand."*
> **Matthew 13:10-13**

Once the Jewish leadership had accused Jesus of being demon possessed in Matthew 12:24, Jesus began teaching in parables. The disciples were confused that Jesus would begin speaking in parables instead of the normal teaching methods; Jesus explained that the mysteries (secrets) of the kingdom are understood only in the light of the Truth (see John 14:6). The Jewish leadership had rejected the Truth. By accusing Jesus as being of Beelzebul, Jewish leaders were saying that He could not be Messiah even though He had performed a series of miracles that only the Messiah could perform, including casting out the demon in the blind and mute man in Matthew 12:22-23. In Verse 23, the people responded to this miracle by saying, *"This man cannot be the Son of Man, can He?"* [The Son of Man is a term used to reference Messiah].

HUMILITY AND MERCY

In Matthew 18:1-4, Jesus helps us to understand that success in the kingdom depends on **humility** and He uses a child to illustrate the point. When asked about *"Who then is greatest in the kingdom,"*

He explained that becoming like children represents innocence and a lack of pride and haughtiness. Jesus was answering the question by concluding that selflessness which produces humility is the key. It defines greatness.

Jesus also addressed greatness in the kingdom in the Sermon on the Mount. In Matthew 5:19,

"Whoever then annuls one of the least of these commandments, and teaches others to do the same, shall be called least in the kingdom of heaven; but whoever keeps and teaches them, he shall be called great in the kingdom of heaven."

Since these commandments represent the very mind of God, to disregard them would be detrimental while to honor and teach them would result in kingdom greatness.

In Paul's first letter to Timothy, Paul was applying the principle of Hebrews 2:9 in his encouragement to Timothy by acknowledging the King eternal (1 Timothy 1:17), crowning Him with glory and honor. Recognizing that Paul's giftedness and natural abilities did not get him anywhere in the Kingdom, it was acknowledging that **mercy** opened the door for him to see the King and be a giant in the Kingdom! This instruction was consistent with what Jesus taught in Matthew 5:20 when He said, *"For I say to you that unless your righteousness surpasses that of the scribes and Pharisees, you will not enter the kingdom of heaven."* Jesus was teaching that human effort to meet the religious demands of a Holy God does not work. It requires God's perfect righteousness.

THE WORD OF THE KINGDOM

In Jesus's day, the Pharisees were dividing the Law of Moses into a hierarchy, with some being greater than others. Yet Jesus had quoted a Scripture from the Law of Moses (Deuteronomy 8:3) in Matthew 4:4 when He stated, *"It is written, 'MAN SHALL NOT LIVE ON BREAD ALONE, BUT ON EVERY WORD THAT PROCEEDS OUT OF*

THE MOUTH OF GOD.'" Jesus was teaching the importance of every Word, that all Scripture is necessary food.

In His public ministry, Jesus taught many parables that address the kingdom of heaven or the kingdom of God. In fact, eight of them appear in Matthew 13. He was teaching the dynamics of this kingdom in which all of His disciples and followers need to understand. These principles allow us not only to grasp the conditions of entry, but also how to function and thrive within the kingdom.

> *"Hear then the parable of the sower. When anyone hears **the word of the kingdom** and **does not understand it**, the evil one comes and snatches away what has been sown in his heart. This is the one on whom seed was sown beside the road. The one on whom seed was sown on the rocky places, this is the man who hears the word and immediately receives it with joy; **yet he has no firm root in himself, but is only temporary**, and when affliction or persecution arises because of the word, immediately he falls away. And the one on whom seed was sown among the thorns, this is the man who hears the word, and **the worry of the world and the deceitfulness of wealth choke the word**, and it becomes unfruitful. And the one on whom seed was sown on the good soil, this is the man who hears the word and **understands it, who indeed bears fruit** and brings forth, some a hundredfold, some sixty, and some thirty."* **Matthew 13:18-23**

Receiving the Word

The first of the eight parables from Matthew 13 are a direct reference to the Word of God, *the Word of the kingdom*. The King's primary method of communication in the kingdom is the Word. Hearing the Word and understanding it produces success in the kingdom. The parable defines that the condition of the heart is the primary criterion that determines success. The seed sown beside the road has no room to establish its roots and therefore is easy pickings for the devil. This condition of the heart is determined by how one receives the Word.

In 1 Thessalonians 2:13, Paul says, *For this reason we also constantly thank God that when you received the word of God which you heard from us,* **you accepted it not as the word of men**, *but for what it really is, the word of God, which also performs its work in you who believe.* The Word has an intended work (see Isaiah 55:11), but it must be received from God (the King) with the authority that should accompany it. According to Hebrews 4:2, the Word accomplishes what God intends when united by faith.

The rocky places speak of the one whose heart has not fully accepted the Word as truth and therefore trials of life cause him to fall away. The thorns represent the cares of life that can interfere with the Word and the Word therefore is unfruitful. The good soil is the environment where the Word when understood produces great fruit. The critical point made through this parable is that the environment of the heart when receiving the Word determines the quality and volume of the fruit it will produce.

Serving Others

From the Mount of Olives (Matthew 25:31-36), Jesus taught the disciples about the coming judgment of all nations, promising that the blessed ones would inherit the kingdom. This kingdom was *"prepared for you from the foundation of the world"* and offered to those who have a ministry to the King through their relationship to those in need and their willingness to give of themselves to meet those needs. It was the plan of God from the very beginning that men would inherit the kingdom as a result of their willingness to serve the needs of others on behalf of the King.

In conclusion, the promise of Hebrews 12:28 is that each believer receives *a kingdom which cannot be shaken*. When he recognizes the kingdom by crowning the King (Jesus) with glory and honor (Hebrews 2:9) in his heart, he experiences kingdom life. As such, he should hold fast to the grace of God, the environment in which we have received that permanent kingdom by showing gratitude to God in reverence and awe. Remember, Jesus died with a crown (of thorns) on His head.

Chapter 28

THE WORK IS FINISHED

The night before His crucifixion, Jesus prayed to His Father, *"I glorified You on the earth, having accomplished the work which You have given Me to do"* (John 17:4). Throughout His public ministry, Jesus was preoccupied with this work as He said that His food was to do the will of His Father and *"to accomplish His work"* (John 4:34). This divine work, planned before the foundation of the world by *the predetermined plan and foreknowledge of God* (Acts 2:23), is the central part of God's plan of redemption for all mankind. It requires a victorious Messiah to be the Paschal Lamb (1 Corinthians 5:7). When Jesus said on the cross, *"It is finished!"* in John 19:30, He was speaking about more than His work on earth.

THE PASSOVER FULFILLED

So much of Jesus's last week of human life was the fulfilling of many Scriptures. The Last Supper was a Passover Seder and at the center of the service was an unblemished lamb slain to shed blood. When Paul identified Christ as our Passover, he was linking the events of that last week to the requirements of the first Passover from Exodus 12. Jay Mack's "Life of Christ Commentary" below captures the fulfillment of the Passover lamb:

At the feast of the Passover, the man of the house was commanded to examine a lamb for the Passover meal (Exodus 12:3-6). For five days, from the tenth of Nissan to the fourteenth he was to examine the lamb to make sure it was without defect or blemish and worthy to be the Pesach sacrifice. Jesus entered Jerusalem on Sunday, the tenth of Nissan and was examined by the Jews for five days. As far as the Jewish religious leaders were concerned, they had two goals. They would question Yeshua in front of the multitude to turn the people against Him, and they looked for a specific way to charge Him with a crime so they could put Him to death by Roman law. But it was not successful. After those five days of examination by the Pharisees, by the Sadducees, by the Torah-teachers and by the Herodians, Jesus answered all their objections and questions; therefore, He was found to be without defect or blemish. Christ ate the Seder meal on the night of the Passover, the same night that all the Jewish people ate it. But because the Son of God qualified as the Pesach Lamb, He was slaughtered on the day of the Passover, the fifteenth of Nissan.

When John the Baptist saw Jesus approaching him for the baptism in John 1:29, he said, *"Behold the Lamb of God who takes away the sins of the world."* Long before Jesus fulfilled the promise of being the Passover lamb, John the Baptist already recognized Jesus that way. But what is the significance of being the Lamb of God? The importance of the lamb was defined for us by Isaiah in 53:7 when referring to the coming Messiah he said, *"Like a lamb that is led to slaughter, and like a sheep that is silent before its shearers, so He did not open His mouth."* The significance of a lamb is that it must be slaughtered.

Ransom

The concept of redemption in Greek is *exagorazo* and means *to release on receipt of a ransom*. Jesus acknowledged to His disciples that He came *"not to be served, but to serve and give His life a ransom for many"* (Mark 10:45). Jesus was the ransom that releases the believer from the curse of sin as Paul defines it in Galatians 3:13-14. The result of that redemption is to open up the blessings of Abraham to all believers, Jews, and Gentiles, who put their trust in the completed work of Christ and may now receive the Holy Spirit by faith. It also means that believers have been *bought at a price* (1 Corinthians 6:20) so that they may recognize that they no longer belong to themselves, but to the Redeemer.

A remarkable passage in the Talmud says:

"It was a famous and old opinion among the ancient Jews that the day of the new year which was the beginning of the Israelites' deliverance out of Egypt should in future time be the beginning of the redemption by the Messiah."

The foundation of the new covenant is that redemption of men requires nothing more and therefore, *"FOR I WILL BE MERCIFUL TO THEIR INIQUITIES, AND I WILL REMEMBER THEIR SINS NO MORE"* (Hebrews 8:12). Forgiveness of sins for all new covenant believers is dependent on the completion of the work of redemption.

WORTHY IS THE LAMB

From the time of calvary forth, Jesus was recognized as the slain Lamb in honor of His fulfilled sacrifice, the innocence of the lamb speaking to the fact that He remained silent in spite of the false accusations. In Revelation 5:5-12, taking place in heaven during the Tribulation period, the elders with the four living creatures recognize Messiah first as the Lion of Judah (Verse 5), representing His second coming and then as the Lamb slain, representing His first coming. It is important to note that the book in Verse 7 is a symbol of the future and could only be opened by the Lamb. In Verse 9, they sang a new song: *Worthy is the Lamb!* Why? Because the slain Lamb had *"purchased for God with Your blood from every tribe and tongue and people and nation."* And in Verse 10, the Lamb has *"made them to be a kingdom and priests to our God"*. This is a powerful passage illustrating the completed work of the Paschal Lamb resulting in worship, not just from men, but from angels as well. When Jesus said, *"It is finished,"* He was opening the door for all men, Jews, and Gentiles, to be able to *reign in life through the One, Jesus Christ* (Romans 5:17) as referenced in Verse 10 above.

> *And behold, the veil of the temple was torn in two from top to bottom; and the earth shook, and the rocks were split. The tombs were opened, and many bodies of the saints who had fallen asleep were raised; and coming out of the tombs after His resurrection they entered the holy city and appeared to many. Now the centurion, and those who were with him keeping guard over Jesus, when they saw the earthquake and the things that were happening, became very frightened and said, "Truly this was the Son of God!"* **Matthew 27:51-54**

The moment of Jesus's death on the cross caused a series of profound things to take place, as the Matthew account above reveals. In Verse 51, *the veil of the temple was torn in two from top to bottom*. This is a profound statement since that veil was the curtain that separated the Holy of Holies from the Holy Place in the temple. It also was torn from the top, not the bottom signifying that it was God's work and not men. The Holy of Holies was the place restricted to God, Himself and only available to the High Priest one day of each year, the Day of Atonement (Yom Kippur). The moment of Jesus's death opened the Holy of Holies, the presence of God to all believers. Hebrews 10:20 further illuminates this principle when the writer tells us that the veil is symbolic of Jesus's flesh, providing *a new and living way*! It is the completed work of Christ at calvary through the sacrifice of His flesh that immediately gave each believer full access to God (Ephesians 2:18).

More Evidence

At the same time, some type of earthquake occurred, resulting in rocks being split. Jesus's sacrificial death resulted in a statement to all living beings, not just the religious crowd. The Matthew account is the only one that includes the raising of many bodies of dead believers to enter Jerusalem after His resurrection, *"appearing to many."* The earthquake caused the graves to be opened and they were resurrected from their graves after the resurrection of Christ. Since they were recognizable to many, these saints are the demonstration of the victory that Jesus won over death. All of these events caused those Roman soldiers (probably pagans) who were keeping guard to testify, *"Truly this was the Son of God."* The power of this event was on display for all interested to observe!

> *And his father Zacharias was filled with the Holy Spirit, and prophesied, saying: "Blessed be the Lord God of Israel, for He has visited us and* **accomplished redemption for His people***, and has raised up a horn of salvation for us in the house of David His servant..."* **Luke 1:67-69**

The prophecy of Zacharias was that the Redeemer was to visit, and He would *"accomplish redemption for His people."* Although His own would reject Him (John 1:11), He still came for His people which defines the greatest work of redemption! The accomplished work of the Redeemer at Calvary leaves no one behind, not even those who have completely rejected Him. The believer can have full assurance that there is nothing required by God on his/her behalf to complete redemption. By faith in His work, *"It is finished."*

Chapter 29

RECOGNIZING THE RISEN LORD

There are a series of accounts of disciples encountering the risen Lord that, like Mary Magdalene in the John 20 account, did not recognize Jesus right away. In fact, in each of the accounts, it was a different stimulus that caused the disciple to finally know it was Him. In Mary's case, it was when Jesus said her name, *"Mary"* in Verse 16. She had originally thought Him to be the gardener even after he asked her why she was weeping. It is clear from this and other accounts of Mary that the relationship was a close and meaningful one to her. Jesus's use of her name, not just the name, but the unique way he spoke it was so familiar to her and caused a light to go off in her mind: this is not the gardener. It is Rabboni, my teacher.

Once she recognized Him, there was His command, *"stop clinging to Me."* Scholars do not agree on the reason for this command. One thing is clear, Jesus had not yet ascended to His Father. We also notice that Jesus tells Mary to go to *"My brethren,"* not friends or other intimate terms. This signifies that the relationship with the risen Jesus was to be different than before, thus *brethren*. The nature of an intimate relationship with the risen Lord was to be much different than before, no longer physical, and His disciples needed to learn that. It would take the experiences of watching Jesus ascend to heaven from

Mount Olivet (Acts 1:9), meeting in the upper room in anticipation of Pentecost (Verses 13-14), and the moving of the Holy Spirit on that special day (Acts 2) to initiate that change.

My Lord and My God

In the same chapter there was Thomas, doubting Thomas. Jesus had visited with most of His disciples on a day when Thomas was not present. As his friends told Thomas about the risen Lord with excitement, he admitted to them that this was just too difficult to believe. He would have to have the physical evidence, or he could not accept it. When finally confronted directly with the risen Lord, Jesus told him to get the proof he needed by putting his finger and hand in the wounds and this would be enough for Thomas to answer, *"My Lord and my God!"* Thomas could now acknowledge Jesus as Lord and God, a statement that he had never made before. Then Jesus addresses us, future believers who have never had this opportunity to see yet could believe Jesus as Lord and God. Like the disciples, we must believe that Jesus is risen in order to recognize Him as Lord!

Burning Hearts

And then there were the two disciples traveling on the road to Emmaus who had an experience with the Risen Lord in Luke 24. As Jesus begins walking with them, the account from Luke tells us in Verse 16 that *their eyes were prevented from recognizing him* without any explanation as to why. The same event (we believe) covered by Mark in 16:12 says that he appeared *in a different form,* so He looked differently than they were used to. But according to Luke's account, He was just a normal guy walking on the same road, and they started this conversation about the events that had just taken place in Jerusalem. The disciples admitted that they had been hoping that Jesus was to be the one who *was going to redeem Israel* (Verse 21). It was clear from their testimony that they did not yet believe that Jesus was the One who would redeem Israel. Since they had not yet fully grasped the events and that this was Jesus, He began to explain to them *the things concerning Himself in all the Scriptures* (Verse 27).

And their response to His commentary was, *"were not our hearts burning within us while He was speaking to us on the road"* (Verse 32). It was not until they broke bread with Jesus that they finally recognized Him (Verse 31). If we are to see Jesus as the Risen Lord, we must understand that Jesus Christ is the fulfillment of the Old Testament Scriptures. As Jeremiah specifies in Jeremiah 15:16, *Your words were found and I ate them, and Your words became for me a joy and the delight of my heart; for I have been called by Your name, O Lord God of hosts.* The Word of God, if understood accurately, becomes food for the believer. Jesus's words in Matthew 4:4, *"MAN SHALL NOT LIVE ON BREAD ALONE, BUT ON EVERY WORD THAT PROCEEDS OUT OF THE MOUTH OF GOD"* are applicable. The Word of God is our spiritual food!

Recognizing the Miraculous

Finally, we have the disciples fishing in the Sea of Galilee in John 21, something they had done many times before and Jesus appears on the beach. Knowing that they had not yet caught any fish, Jesus encouraged them to put their nets in a different place and *"you will find a catch."* I am sure this event was reminiscent of an earlier time found in Luke 5:4-7 where Jesus had instructed Peter to put down his nets in deep water for a great catch and it happened just as Jesus said. In John 14:11, *"Believe Me that I am in the Father and the Father is in Me; otherwise believe because of the works themselves."* Our ability to fully understand that Jesus is the Risen Lord depends on our experiences as Jesus has made Himself real in our lives through miraculous conclusions. He is the God of the impossible (Matthew 19:26) and He wants us to recognize Him this way.

Living for the Risen Lord

2 Corinthians 5:14-17 addresses how one recognizes the Risen Lord, that we recognize no one according to the flesh, not even Jesus. The apostle Paul wrote these words from personal experience, that he, as Saul of Tarsus and a contemporary of Jesus's public ministry, did not recognize Jesus as Messiah until he had a personal experience with the Risen Lord in Acts 9:3-6. It took Saul of Tarsus' confrontation with Jesus of Nazareth for him to finally recognize the Risen Lord and become almost immediately commissioned as the apostle Paul. In the same way, Paul encourages believers to *know Him in this way no longer*. Verse 15 gives us the key, *that they who live might no longer live for themselves, but for Him who died and rose again on their behalf,* the Risen Lord. In Verse 17, *new things have come.*

Jesus's personal love for the believer, as demonstrated by His death on our behalf (Romans 5:8), is the foundation of this relationship. This type of love is self-sacrificing yet a motivating love (2 Corinthians 5:14) and it takes a real faith in this personal love of Jesus to bring one to this dynamic relationship where His priorities become the believer's priorities. Any dramatic change in the depth of a relationship with Jesus can only happen in the light of a newfound appreciation of His personal love. In Romans 14:7-9, *For not one of us lives for himself, and not one dies for himself; for if we live, we live for the Lord, or if we die, we die for the Lord; therefore, whether we live or die, we are the Lord's. For to this end Christ died and lived again,* **that He might be Lord both of the dead and of the living.**

Set Your Mind on God's Interests

Peter's amazing response to Jesus when asked, "*and who do you say that I am?*" is noteworthy when Peter said, "*you are the Christ, the Son of the living God*" and Jesus acknowledged that flesh and blood did not reveal it to Peter, but the Father. Yet within a brief period of time, Peter rebukes Jesus when He told the disciples He would need to suffer and die at the hands of the scribes and Pharisees yet raised on the third day (Matthew 16:21). In Verse 23, we get the real reason behind Peter's rebuke when Jesus points out to him that, *"you are not setting your mind on God's interest, but man's."* The Greek word is *phroneo* and it has the meaning of **being mindful of or devoted to** according to Spiros Zodhiates. This passage demonstrates that man decides what concern upon which he is setting his mind. In one moment, Peter speaks the testimony of the Father and then the next, his own self-interest that Jesus could not leave the disciples behind. These are decisions of the will, the affections, and the conscience.

The Apostle Paul sums it up for us in Romans 8:5-6 (same Greek word) by comparing and contrasting two mindsets, the one on fleshly, earthly, and natural things versus the mind set on spiritual things. The natural, fleshly, earthy mindset results in death while the spiritual mindset produces life and peace. In Philippians 3:18-20, Paul says,

> *For many walk, of whom I often told you, and now tell you even weeping, that they are enemies of the cross of Christ, whose end is destruction, whose god is their appetite, and whose glory is in their shame, who set their minds on earthly things. For our citizenship is in heaven, from which also we eagerly wait for a Savior, the Lord Jesus Christ.*

This fleshly mindset is an enemy of the cross since it never recognizes the greatest work of God on our behalf, Christ's death and resurrection which is the evidence of our heavenly citizenship. This new citizenship produces a new mindset with the believer living in great expectation, eagerly awaiting the Savior.

UPWARD CALL

Paul acknowledges in his pastoral epistles that the work of the Lord has purchased for us a new position, seated above, in heavenly places (Ephesians 2:6) and that this position raises us up by faith in God's work: In Colossians 2:12, *having been buried with Him in baptism, in which you were also raised up with Him through faith in the working of God, who raised Him from the dead.* This position is an ascending position and brings with it an ascending experience in God. Paul says in Philippians 3:14, *I press on toward the goal for the prize of the **upward call** of God in Christ Jesus.* This new mindset keeps the believer pressing on to the upward call of God which is the ultimate prize this life has to offer.

The risen Lord ordains a path for each of us to follow which Paul defines as "in Him,' or "in Christ," etc. This path is a place to walk, and it establishes us in the faith and produces gratitude. Paul warns us of the war that is constantly trying to arrest our minds from the life and peace of the spiritual mindset. In Colossians 2:8-10, the god of this world uses philosophies and empty deceptions according to the traditions of men to keep men attached to worldly interests so that they never come to know the fullness of God found in a spiritual relationship with the Lord Jesus Christ.

Fellowship in Suffering

I believe Philippians 3:10 to be Paul's signature statement about his relationship with God, that it was about knowing Him. This Greek word, *ginosko* has the sense of coming to know as a process, through experience. Paul was saying that this coming to know Jesus is the process of experiencing the power of His resurrection and the fellowship of His suffering. Both experiences are essential for the believer to truly know God in all of His fullness. Before Easter Sunday, there was Good Friday; before the resurrection, there was His suffering. To experience the risen Lord, we must identify with the One who suffered and the conforming process to His death. Suffering then becomes an integral part of a spirit-filled believer's life.

> *But if anyone suffers as a Christian, he is not to be ashamed, but is to **glorify God in this name**. For it is time for judgment to begin with the household of God; and if it begins with us first, what will be the outcome for those who do not obey the gospel of God? AND IF IT IS WITH DIFFICULTY THAT THE RIGHTEOUS IS*

SAVED, WHAT WILL BECOME OF THE GODLESS MAN AND THE SINNER? Therefore, those also who suffer according to the will of God shall **entrust their souls to a faithful Creator in doing what is right**. *1 Peter 4:16-19*

The Greatest Evidence

The greatest evidence that a disciple has experienced the risen Lord is his willingness to suffer. When we look at the first century disciples after Pentecost, we see men who were willing to suffer for their faith. Foxe's Book of Martyrs is a sobering picture of what happened to men and women of faith who were willing to obey to the point of death. Below are various excerpts from the first chapter of this great chronicle:

Stephen - Acts 7 gives us a description of Stephen's execution by stoning and it began a period when about two thousand Christians, with Nicanor, one of the seven deacons, suffered martyrdom during the "persecution that arose about Stephen."

James the Great - one of the Sons of Zebedee and the elder brother of the Apostle John. The account given us by an eminent primitive writer, Clemens Alexandrinus, ought not to be overlooked; that, as James was led to the place of martyrdom, his accuser was brought to repent of his conduct by the apostle's extraordinary courage and undauntedness, and fell down at his feet to request his pardon, professing himself a Christian

Philip - was born at Bethsaida, in Galilee and was first called by the name of "disciple." He labored diligently in Upper Asia, and suffered martyrdom at Heliopolis, in Phrygia. He was scourged, thrown into prison, and afterwards crucified, A.D. 54.

Matthew - whose occupation was that of a toll-gatherer, was born at Nazareth. He wrote his gospel in Hebrew, which was afterwards translated into Greek by James the Less. The scene of his labors was Parthia, and Ethiopia, in which latter country he suffered martyrdom, being slain with a halberd in the city of Nadabah, A.D. 60.

James the Less - the half-brother of Jesus. He was elected to the oversight of the churches of Jerusalem; and was the author of the Epistle ascribed to James in the sacred canon. At the age of ninety-four he was beaten and stoned by the Jews; and finally had his brains dashed out with a fuller's club.

Matthias - Of whom less is known than of most of the other disciples, was elected to fill the vacant place of Judas. He was stoned at Jerusalem and then beheaded.

Andrew - Was the brother of Peter. He preached the gospel to many Asiatic nations; but on his arrival at Edessa, he was taken and crucified on a cross, the two ends of which were fixed transversely in the ground. Hence the derivation of the term, St. Andrew's Cross.

St. Mark - was born of Jewish parents of the tribe of Levi. He is supposed to have been converted to Christianity by Peter, whom he served as an amanuensis [like a scribe], and under whose inspection he wrote his Gospel in the Greek language. Mark was dragged to pieces by the people of Alexandria, at the great solemnity of Serapis their idol, ending his life under their merciless hands.

Peter - among many other saints, the blessed apostle Peter was condemned to death, and crucified, as some do write, at Rome. Jerome saith that he was crucified, his head being down and his feet upward, himself so requiring, because he was (he said) unworthy to be crucified after the same form and manner as the Lord was.

Paul - the apostle, who before was called Saul, after his great travail and unspeakable labors in promoting the Gospel of Christ, suffered also in this first persecution under Nero. Abdias, declareth that under his execution Nero sent two of his esquires, Ferega and Parthemius, to bring him word of his death. They, coming to Paul instructing the people, desired him to pray for them, that they might believe, who told them that shortly after they should believe and be baptized at His sepulcher. This done, the soldiers came and led him out of the city to the place of execution, where he, after his prayers made, gave his neck to the sword.

Jude - the brother of James, was commonly called Thaddeus. He was crucified at Edessa, A.D. 72.

Bartholomew - preached in several countries and having translated the Gospel of Matthew into the language of India, he propagated it in that country. He was at length cruelly beaten and then crucified by the impatient idolaters.

Thomas - called Didymus, preached the Gospel in Parthia and India, where, exciting the rage of the pagan priests, he was martyred by being thrust through with a spear.

Luke - the evangelist, was the author of the Gospel which goes under his name. He traveled with Paul through various countries and is supposed to have been hanged on an olive tree, by the idolatrous priests of Greece.

John - the "beloved disciple," was brother to James the Great. The churches of Smyrna, Pergamos, Sardis, Philadelphia, Laodicea, and Thyatira, were founded by him. From Ephesus he was ordered to be sent to Rome, where it is affirmed, he was cast into a cauldron of boiling oil. He escaped by miracle, without injury. Domitian afterwards banished him to the Isle of Patmos, where he recorded the Book of Revelation. Nerva, the successor of Domitian, recalled him. **He was the only apostle who escaped a violent death.**

Fixing our Eyes on Him

fixing our eyes on Jesus, the author and perfecter of faith, who for the joy set before Him endured the cross, despising the shame, and has sat down at the right hand of the throne of God. For consider Him who has endured such hostility by sinners against Himself, so that you will not grow weary and lose heart. **Hebrews 12:2-3**

Chapter 30

LOVING THE RISEN LORD

So, when they had finished breakfast, Jesus said to Simon Peter, "Simon, son of John, do you love [agapao] *Me more than these?" He said to Him, "Yes, Lord; You know* [oida –intuitive] *that I love* [phileo] *You." He said to him, "Tend My lambs." He said to him again a second time, "Simon, son of John, do you love* [agapao] *Me?" He said to Him, "Yes, Lord; You know that I love* [phileo] *You." He said to him, "Shepherd My sheep." He said to him the third time, "Simon, son of John, do you love* [phileo] *Me?" Peter was grieved because He said to him the third time, "Do you love Me?" And he said to Him, "Lord, You know all things; You know* [ginosko – experiential] *that I love* [phileo] *You." Jesus said to him, "Tend My sheep."* **John 21:15-17**

So much of Jesus's efforts during the last days and weeks of His life on earth were trying to prepare the disciples for life without Him in a physical sense. In this exchange with Peter in Verses 15-17, Jesus is teaching Peter how he and the disciples will be able to express their love to Jesus after He has ascended by asking questions and giving them the answers.

As the disciples finally recognize, *"It is the Lord"* (Verse 7) on the beach, they respond with affection that has been accumulating toward Jesus over the three-year period they were with Him. They eat breakfast together and now Jesus confronts Peter with three similar, but quite different questions that put him on the defensive. To fully understand the passage, we must appreciate that there are four different Greek words that are translated "love" in English. These are: 1. *storge* represents love within the family between siblings, between parents and children, etc., 2. *eros* speaks of love between a man and woman in an intimate relationship, 3. *phileo* is usually related to love between friends, and 4. *agapao* is love between God and man and has an unconditional characteristic. In this exchange, Jesus and Peter use *phileo* and *agapao* which obviously can change the meaning.

HE WHO HAS FOUND HIS LIFE WILL LOSE IT

Jesus's first question to Peter is: Do you love me with God's love more than the physical things in life that you have attached yourself to, including friends, family, money, position, etc.? God is a jealous God (Exodus 34:14) and He desires our primary devotion. In Matthew 10:37-39, Jesus taught this principle when He said,

> *"He who loves father or mother more than Me is not worthy of Me; and he who loves son or daughter more than Me is not worthy of Me. "And he who does not take his cross and follow after Me is not worthy of Me. "He who has found his life will lose it, and he who has lost his life for My sake will find it."*

Notice that Jesus asks about loving with God's love, while Peter answers with *phileo*, speaking of the love he had for Jesus as a friend. Jesus is trying to tell Peter that his friendship love is not going to be enough. In either case, Jesus's answer is, *"Tend my lambs"* meaning the way you take care of the sheep (believers) of God defines the way to express your love for me.

The second question focuses itself completely on the quality of Peter's love for Jesus and is not a comparative. Instead, He asks Peter for the kind of love that is different than Peter had ever experienced before, speaking of total devotion to Jesus. Of course, it needed to be more than friendship. I am sure Peter remembered what happened when they took Jesus away for trial and Peter denied knowing Him three times (Luke 22). The fact is that this kind of love does not reside with man but is only possible when we consider the quality of God's love for us (1 John 4:19). A successful believer is one who learns to live the supernatural life that begins with God's love! Jesus's response was the same as the first: *"Shepherd My sheep."*

TEND MY SHEEP

In the third question, Jesus uses the Greek word *phileo* instead of *agapao*. He is asking Peter if the relationship Peter has with Him has changed since His resurrection. Peter is now grieving at the question because he thinks that Jesus should know (Greek word *ginosko*, meaning knowledge by experience) that Peter is a devoted friend. Again, the answer Jesus gives is *"Tend My sheep."* Whatever type of love we have for Jesus, the answer is always the same, take care of the sheep. This reminds us of Jesus's teaching in Matthew 25:34-40 which concludes with the statement, *"Truly I say to you, to the extent that you did it to one of these brothers of Mine, even the least of them,* **you did it to Me.***"* In the passage, Jesus speaks of feeding the hungry and thirsty, visiting the stranger, clothing the naked, and visiting the sick and imprisoned as some ways we show our personal love of Jesus. In Galatians 5:6, faith works by *agapao* love.

NO LONGER LIVING FOR ME

*For the **love [agapao]** of Christ controls us, having concluded this, that one died for all, therefore all died; and He died for all, so that they who live might no longer live for themselves, but for Him who died and rose again on their behalf. Therefore, from now on we recognize no one according to the flesh; even though we have known Christ according to the flesh, yet now we know Him in this way no longer.* **2 Corinthians 5:14-16**

The apostle Paul teaches this principle of *agapao* love in 2 Corinthians 5:14. This love is meant to "control" us, that love holds us closely. The basis of this happening in a believer's personal life is that he finally concludes that Jesus's death means that he died too. It means that because Jesus was willing to die for each believer personally and therefore a sufficient reality, it means each believer need no longer live for personal interest but *agapao* love controls him. In 1 Corinthians 6:19-20, *...and that you are not your own? For you have been bought with a price.*

Then in Verse 16, he speaks of recognizing or knowing no one according to the flesh, not even Jesus. Our relationship with others, spiritually speaking, should no longer be according to any type of love that is natural, of the flesh, because that kind of love is still conditional. Only God's love is unconditional and therefore the Christian requires this kind of love. This means there needs to be a decision to die to one's own personal interests and only then can he find *agapao* love. This is the very same message Jesus was trying to teach Peter and the disciples on the beach. This *agapao* love is also the basis of the relationship between believers within the body of Christ.

FORGIVENESS

The most obvious evidence a believer has of God's love is knowing God's forgiveness without doing anything other than believe (Romans 5:8). In Luke 7:40-50, the woman who was of questionable character (a sinner in Verse 37) is moved to tears as she wipes her tears and very expensive perfume on Jesus's feet. She is demonstrating love toward Jesus because she believes in who Jesus is and that she has received forgiveness. And the expression of that forgiven condition is loving much. Jesus commends her as an example of one who recognizes the degree of forgiveness and is now divinely enabled to love Jesus with *agapao* love. The opposite condition is also true, as Jesus says, "*but he who is forgiven little, loves little*" (Verse 47). The love cycle begins with God's love toward us ("*We* [agapao] *love because He first* [agapao] *loved us*" – 1 John 4:19).

When we talk about forgiveness, we must also talk about the debt forgiven. Paul says that the only debt we should have in Romans 13:8 is to owe *agapao* love to others. Once we come to grips with the fact that we have no debts because of Jesus, we are ready to take on His debt, which is the *agapao* love of others. In fact, he says that this *agapao* love of others fulfills the law and relates this love to the fulfillment of various of the Ten Commandments. When a scribe asked Jesus *"which is the great commandment in the law?"* His response in Matthew 22:35-40 was that you shall love God and love your neighbor. In Verse 40, *"On these two commandments depend the whole Law and the Prophets."* The essence of our faith in Jesus is the expression of *agapao* love in loving God and loving others.

SECURITY IN GOD'S LOVE

> *I am my beloved's, and his desire is for me. Come, my beloved, let us go out into the country, let us spend the night in the villages. Let us rise early and go to the vineyards; let us see whether the vine has budded, and its blossoms have opened, and whether the pomegranates have bloomed. There I will give you my love. The mandrakes have given forth fragrance; and over our doors are all choice fruits, both new and old, which I have saved up for you, my beloved.* **Song 7:10-13**

Falling in love with God is not something that takes place immediately, but like any relationship it is a process. The Song of Solomon, written by Solomon, is the account of a romance between King Solomon and a Shulammite woman. It is also a picture of the love relationship between the bride (the church) and the bridegroom (Jesus Christ). In looking at this process of love between the two, we can glean from three particular verses what this process looks like from the bride's (Christian's) perspective. In the first (Song 2:16), the bride says, *"My beloved is mine, and I am his."* The expressed idea is that He belongs to me first, then I belong to Him. In Song 6:3, *"I am my beloved's, and my beloved is mine."* Notice that she now recognizes that she belongs to Him first, then He belongs to her. We go through the same process in the growth of our relationship with Jesus, becoming increasingly confident in His love. In the context of Song of Solomon, Song 2:16 takes place before the wedding and Song 6:3 afterwards.

The third verse above completes the process, *"I am my beloved's, and his desire is for me."* The woman is so convinced about the bridegroom's love for her that she does not need to express it. This is the fulfillment of God's love for us and how we become more secure in that love. Our passage above in Song 7 continues with the bride and bridegroom going out into the country, in the villages, going to the vineyards, and looking at the fruit of the vine, the pomegranate, and the mandrake. When the believer is fully convinced of Jesus's personal love for him, he is excited to participate in the work of God in the world to love others, thus producing fruit of all kinds. In Verse 12, *"there I will give you my love."* Loving others becomes an integral part of our relationship to Jesus.

A Way of Life

We see the ultimate picture of *agapao* love in Romans 12:9-13 with the principles of being diligent, devoted to one another, preferring others in honor, devoted to prayer, contributing to the needs of others, and practicing hospitality. This type of love produces a way of life within the believer and is the fulfillment of God's *agapao* love in us (1 John 4:12). The transforming life of the Holy Spirit produces an amazing change in the believer's heart to live the supernatural life of *agapao* love!

Chapter 31

WHY THE LAW OF MOSES?

From the time Abraham received promises from God in response to his faith in Genesis 12:1-3 (approximately 1900 BC) until God gave Moses the entire Law on Mount Sinai in Exodus 20 (approximately 1477 BC), the Hebrew nation functioned spiritually under this covenant God gave to Abraham that He would bless those who bless Abraham. For 430 of those years, pharaohs held the Hebrews in bondage in Egypt until Moses led the nation across the Red Sea into the wilderness. The question arises as to why God would introduce the Law of Moses to His people when it was to be a temporary covenant, until such a time as the Messiah would introduce the new covenant nearly 1,500 years later? What purpose did this old covenant serve?

In Galatians 3:19, Paul asks and then answers the question, *Why the Law then?* Paul concludes that, in the context of the covenant made with Abraham, the inheritance from the promise of God is not based on law but through faith in the promise made to Abraham, the father of our faith (Romans 4:16). The Law, then, is *"added because of transgressions,"* meaning that leading us to Christ was its mission, *so that we may be justified by faith* (Galatians 3:24). In Verse 23, Paul explains that those who put their faith in the Law of Moses are being *"kept in custody"* under (the power of) the Law until Messiah would come. Faith in God's promises and not in the celebration of religious rituals and legal obedience produces great spiritual benefits.

A Different Gospel

The churches of Galatia were struggling with the influence of those who were teaching that Christians need to keep the Law of Moses in order to find justification and the Christian faith. There had been a Council led by James (Jesus's half-brother) held in Jerusalem dealing with this matter and described by Luke in Acts 15. Verses 19-20 report the results of that council,

"Therefore, it is my judgment that we do not trouble those who are turning to God from among the Gentiles, but that we write to them that they abstain from things contaminated by idols and from fornication and from what is strangled and from blood."

Christians do not need to keep the Law of Moses. This conclusion did not end the controversy and there remained those, known as Judaizers, who would continue to require it. Attempts like these continue to this day as men try to complicate the new covenant with old covenant and other man-made requirements.

In Galatians 1:6-7 Paul says, *I am amazed that you are so quickly deserting Him who called you by the grace of Christ, for a different gospel; which is really not another; only there are some who are disturbing you and want to distort the gospel of Christ.* When Jesus said He came to fulfill the Law of Moses (Matthew 5:17), He meant that there was to be a newly defined relationship with God, known as the new covenant (promised to Israel in Jeremiah 31) and enacted on better promises (Hebrews 8:6), therefore making the old covenant obsolete (Hebrews 8:13). The old covenant represents God's perfect justice, but without the spiritual ability to fulfill it. It had to be kept perfectly or the follower would be classified as a transgressor (James 2:10).

Righteousness of the Law

In Romans 7:7-12, Paul further explains that *the Law is holy and righteous and good* (Verse 12), but its intended purpose is to help followers of the Law to understand that righteousness is not derived from the Law, but that the Law makes sin come alive and exposes the sin that is *taking opportunity through the commandment* (Verse 11) and deceives me resulting in separation from God (spiritual death). In 1 Timothy 1:8-10:

> *But we know that the Law is good, if one uses it lawfully, realizing the fact that* **law is not made for a righteous person**, *but for those who are lawless and rebellious, for the ungodly and sinners, for the unholy and profane, for those who kill their fathers or mothers, for murderers and immoral men and homosexuals and kidnappers and liars and perjurers, and whatever else is contrary to sound teaching.*

In Romans 10, Paul addresses the Jewish nation of his day, clearly defining how the Law cannot lead to righteousness because Jews do not *subject themselves to the righteousness of God* (Romans 10:3), but their own ability to keep the law, otherwise known as "righteousness based on the law," and that attempt produces a self-righteousness. No one can earn God's righteousness (see Romans 4:4-5) but receives it by faith in the One who is righteous! Romans 10:4 summarizes the argument when it concludes *For Christ is the end of the law for righteousness to everyone who believes.* For the New Testament Christian, faith in Jesus as the Christ is the only avenue to God's righteousness (see John 14:6).

Righteousness by Faith

According to Galatians 3:12-14, trying to be a Christian and yet attempting to live under the Law of Moses is a curse and the Messiah had become a curse for us so that Jews and Gentiles *would receive the promise of the Spirit by faith.* This promise is only received through a real faith in Jesus as Messiah, having trusted in His sacrificial death and resurrection and not in one's own efforts to be or become righteous. In Verse 11, Paul quotes the Old Testament passage found in Habakkuk 2:4 as his evidence and confidence: *"THE RIGHTEOUS MAN SHALL LIVE BY FAITH."*

Under the old covenant, salvation came from God and realized when one became a part of God's people. Rahab, a Gentile is a good example of this principle, as Joshua 6:25 says, *However, Rahab the harlot and her father's household and all she had, Joshua spared; and she has lived in the midst of Israel to this day, for she hid the messengers whom Joshua sent to spy out Jericho.* She became a Jew by believing in the God of Israel and acting on that faith. According to the Apostle Paul in Romans 9:8, *That is, it is not the children of the flesh who are children of God, but the children of the promise are regarded as descendants.* Faith in the God of Abraham, Isaac & Jacob has always been the avenue of salvation.

Uniting the Jew and Gentile

The new covenant encourages believers to assemble together often and all the more as the time of Jesus's second coming draws near (Hebrews 10:25). This covenant does not define the locations of the gatherings nor the particular means of worship, etc., unlike the old covenant. Yet the new covenant has ordained that both Jew and Gentile will come together since the dividing wall between the two is removed in Christ (Ephesians 2:14) and all are members of God's household. This is only possible because the *Law of commandments contained in ordinances* is no longer a requirement and therefore the two groups experience peace. In Romans 5:1, *Having been justified by faith, we have peace with God through our Lord Jesus Christ.* Faith in Jesus as Christ resolves all divisions.

In Ephesians 2:20, Paul connects the foundation of the apostles [new covenant] and prophets [old covenant] as one foundation, meaning both groups now have the same foundation, and it is not the Law of Moses. In Romans 3:21, Paul states, *But now apart from the Law the righteousness of God has been manifested, being witnessed by the Law and the Prophets*, meaning that the Old Testament Scriptures predicted that it would take a "prophet" (Messiah) Who will speak with God's words as was given to Israel in Deuteronomy 18:15, *The Lord your God will raise up for you a prophet like me from among you, from your countrymen, you shall listen to him.*

Jesus Christ, Our Point of Reference

The fact is that Messiah's arrival did not create a large fanfare among the Jews (John 1:11) and the Jewish leadership fought constantly against His acceptance as the Promised One since it meant the threat to their positions of leadership. Isaiah (53:1) warned of this rejection and Paul quotes it in Romans 10:16-17, *However, they did not all heed the good news; for Isaiah says, "LORD, WHO HAS BELIEVED OUR REPORT?" So, faith comes from hearing, and hearing by the word of Christ.* As Galatians 3:24 states, the Law is meant to lead us to the Messiah. The point of reference is not the Law of Moses, but the person of Jesus Christ.

The Law of Moses included not only the moral law, but also the ceremonial law (Jewish festivals) as well as the worship requirements associated with the tabernacle and later the temple. In Hebrews 9, the writer begins the conversation of the *regulations of divine worship* associated with the tabernacle, including a description of the various elements within the tabernacle that became the center of worship for the nation while in the wilderness. The priestly activities associated with each of these elements points to the Messiah as High Priest, who would be the fulfillment of eternal redemption. As an example, the lampstand represents Jesus as the light of the world (John 8:12) and the table of the sacred bread is a picture of Jesus as the bread of life (John 6:35). The daily priestly activities were always pointing to the coming Messiah! In Psalm 27:5, David says, *For in the day of trouble He will conceal me in His tabernacle; in the secret place of His tent, He will hide me; He will lift me up on a rock* (a reference to Christ in 1 Corinthians 10:4).

Christ is the Fulfillment

The Jewish festivals also have their fulfillment in the first coming and second coming of Christ. For example, the Last Supper fulfilled Passover (Leviticus 23:4-5), Unleavened Bread (Leviticus 23:6-8) at Calvary, First Fruits (Leviticus 23:9-14) on Easter and Feast of Weeks

(Leviticus 23:15-22) at Pentecost in Acts 2 and the coming of the Holy Spirit. These Festivals are all celebrated in the spring. The final three festivals are references to the second coming of Messiah, Trumpets (Leviticus 23:23-25) to be fulfilled at the Rapture (1 Thessalonians 4:16-18), Day of Atonement (Leviticus 23:26-32) speaks of the Tribulation, and Tabernacles (Leviticus 23:33-43) refers to the 1,000-year reign of Messiah (the Millennium). These last three festivals happen in the fall.

The 1,500 years of life under the old covenant was meant to reveal the person of Jesus as Messiah for those who were fully engaged with their hearts. The symbols and types associated with the old covenant worship are a direct link to Jesus Christ as Messiah and Jesus would become recognizable to many because of the connections to the various aspects of regular worship. The new covenant is the only covenant referred to in Scripture as eternal (Hebrews 13:20), meaning it has always existed as the fulfillment of the fullness of God in man.

Chapter 32

FROM LAW TO GRACE

For the Law was given through Moses; grace and truth were realized [came into being] *through Jesus Christ.* **John 1:17**

The conversion from the old covenant to the new covenant is an interesting case study in the progressive revelation of God and His relationship to man. Scripture gives a prophetic picture of the introduction of this better covenant (grace) with the transition of leadership from Moses to Joshua. In his closing commentary to the people in Deuteronomy 31-34, Moses told them that he would not be leading them into their promised land.

> *So, Moses went and spoke these words to all Israel. And he said to them, "I am a hundred and twenty years old today; I am no longer able to come and go, and the Lord has said to me, 'You shall not cross this, Jordan.' "It is the Lord your God who will cross ahead of you; He will destroy these nations before you, and you shall dispossess them. Joshua [Jehoshua – Jehovah saves] is the one who will cross ahead of you, just as the Lord has spoken."*
> **Deuteronomy 31:1-3**

God had already told Moses that he would not enter the promised land and he would die in the wilderness. This is a picture of the old covenant needing to remain in the wilderness and not have any role to play in the new covenant relationship with God. In Hebrews 8:13, *When He said, "A new covenant," He has made the first obsolete. But whatever is becoming obsolete and growing old is ready to disappear.* Instead of Moses, another, Joshua would lead the nation. The Hebrew name of Jesus is Joshua, so the reality is that it took a Joshua to lead the new covenant believer into their promised land. There is no need for the old relationship to promote the new.

INHERITANCE

In Deuteronomy 31:7-8, *Then Moses called to Joshua and said to him in the sight of all Israel, "Be strong and courageous, for you shall go with this people into the land which the Lord has sworn to their fathers to give them, and* **you shall give it to them as an inheritance**. *"The Lord is the one who goes ahead of you; He will be with you. He will not fail you or forsake you."* The inheritance promised to the Jewish nation through Abraham and Moses was a portion of the promised land, but the new covenant promises another inheritance, fulfilled in the relationship with its mediator and confirmed by the pledge of the Holy Spirit (Ephesians 1:10-14). God has reserved a faith-rest as part of our inheritance as Hebrews 4:9 says, *So there remains a Sabbath rest for the people of God.*

The central focus of the old covenant is the law of Moses (Torah) while the new covenant centers on the person of Jesus. When Joshua was readying the people to cross the Jordan River in Joshua 3, the Lord said to Joshua, *This day I will begin to exalt you in the sight of all Israel, that they may know that just as I have been with Moses, I will be with you.* (Verse 7). In the same way, the Father was exalting (lifting up) the Son so that all men would be drawn to Him (John 12:32). Then the priests would enter the river and stand still to allow the people to pass on dry land. In the new covenant, the priest or preacher is vital in communicating the Word of God and the gospel to the people (Romans 10:14). God then commands Joshua to choose twelve men, one from each tribe to lead the nation. This is a picture of the twelve apostles who would lead the new Christians and create the New Testament Scripture once Jesus ascended.

THE FAITHFUL SON

> *Therefore, holy brethren, partakers of a heavenly calling, consider Jesus, the Apostle and High Priest of our confession; He was faithful to Him who appointed Him, as Moses also was in all His house. For He has been counted worthy of more glory than Moses, by just so much as the builder of the house has more honor than the house. For every house is built by someone, but the builder of all things is God. Now Moses was faithful* **in all His house** *as a servant, for a testimony of those things which were to be spoken later; but Christ was faithful as a Son* **over His house**—*whose house we are, if we hold fast our confidence and the boast of our hope firm until the end.* **Hebrews 3:1-6**

In this passage from Hebrews 3, God is revealing that Moses was faithful as a servant (*therapon* – attendant, minister) in all God's house, but Christ (Messiah) was faithful as a Son over His house. So, what is the significance? In Verse 3, Jesus is worthy of more glory than Moses in the same way that the builder of the house (God) deserves more honor than the house. The writer of Hebrews reveals that the Messiah, God incarnate, is not just a member of or servant to God's house (His people) but is its builder and maintains its existence by holding things together (Colossians 1:17) until the end. This becomes the basis of our confidence since our hope is in Jesus as Messiah and the head of the church (Colossians 1:18). On the other hand, Moses served the people of God's house as its leader and a testimony of what man could not accomplish through the law of Moses, but what was to come.

The new covenant has greater strength than the old because it is based on the strength the believer finds in Christ, as 2 Timothy 2:1 says, *You therefore, my son, be strong in the grace that is in Christ Jesus.* Grace depends only on God so that the believer will become the partaker of a heavenly call.

Chapter 33

FROM PENTECOST TO PENTECOST

In Genesis 46:3-4, God told Jacob that the Lord would make him a great nation, promising that He would go with Jacob and his family to Egypt and *"I will surely bring you up again"*. God would birth the nation of Israel beginning with the seventy of Jacob's family as well as Joseph and his family already there and then deliver them. In Exodus 1, Scripture says that the sons of Israel would be fruitful and increase greatly, multiply and become exceedingly mighty for a season. But once the Pharaoh who favored Joseph was gone, a new leader would place them in hard labor for hundreds of years. In fact, Exodus 12:41 tells us that this Hebrew nation remained in Egypt for exactly 430 years. Since Egypt is a symbol of the world, the nation of Israel would be birthed out of the injustices of the world.

When God chose Moses to lead the nation out of bondage and into the wilderness, scholars believe that there were between two million and three million crossing the Red Sea, which is a picture of salvation. They arrived at Mt. Sinai where the Lord gave the Law to Moses on the mountain. The Jewish Festivals within the Law included Passover, in celebration of God's deliverance from Egypt and Pentecost (Greek word meaning fiftieth) signifying that God would deliver the Law of Moses fifty days after their deliverance. The Law of Moses would be the Lord's intended means of His people finding a quality relationship with Him through His perfect justice. They were to put their trust in God's justice over man's injustices.

SHORTCOMINGS OF THE LAW

The Law of Moses may most clearly be represented by Deuteronomy 10:12-13, *Now, Israel, what does the Lord your God require from you, but to fear the Lord your God, to walk in all His ways and love Him, and to serve the Lord your God with all your heart and with all your soul, 13 and to keep the Lord's commandments and His statutes which I am commanding you today for your good?* Of course, this was a tall order, and it turns out that they could not measure up. Living under the standards and regulations of the Law of Moses would not provide the necessary ability to keep the Lord's commandments. As Jeremiah testified in Jeremiah 7:23-24,

> *But this is what I commanded them, saying, "Obey My voice, and I will be your God, and you will be My people; and you will walk in all the way which I command you, that it may be well with you." Yet they did not obey or incline their ear but walked in their own counsels and in the stubbornness of their evil heart and went backward and not forward.*

This failure of the old covenant to bring the old covenant Hebrew into a truly spiritual relationship with God was always God's plan (see Hebrews 7:18). No matter how good man's attempts are in his own efforts, he cannot find righteousness before God. Paul explains in Galatians 3:23-25,

> *But before faith came, we were kept in custody under the law, being shut up to the faith which was later to be revealed. Therefore, the Law has become our tutor **to lead us to Christ**, so that we may be justified by faith. But now that faith has come, we are no longer under a tutor.*

According to Romans 8:3, *For what the Law could not do,* **weak as it was through the flesh***, God did: sending His own Son in the likeness of sinful flesh and as an offering for sin*. The conclusion of the Law of Moses was always to be a living faith in the Messiah, Jesus Christ. If that is so, then what does this transition look like? The answer is a new covenant.

THE MISHNAH

When returning from captivity in Babylon and Persia, the Rabbis assembled to discuss what to do so that this captivity would never occur again. The strategy they came up with was to establish a "fence" around the 613 laws of Moses. By creating laws that would surround the Mosaic laws (more stringent) and enforce them as they would the original 613, Jews would experience punishment for those man-made laws without breaking God's laws. They decided that the oral law, the administrative methods used throughout the old covenant period to implement the Mosaic laws, would serve as the basis for these man-made rules and regulations. Many years later, these laws would be codified as the Mishnah and included in the Talmud. Yet there are Scripture verses that prohibit the addition or subtraction to the Lord's commandments (see Deuteronomy 4:2 and 12:32), but these prohibitions did not stop them from adding to the Law of Moses.

Jesus dealt with this matter in Matthew 15:1-14 when He addressed the "tradition of the elders", a reference to the oral law. In Verse 3, He asks the Pharisees, *"Why do you yourselves transgress the commandment of God for the sake of your tradition?"* The Pharisees and scribes were elevating oral tradition above the Law of Moses. He then quotes Isaiah 29:13, *"This people honors Me with their lips, but their heart is far away from Me. But in vain do they worship Me, teaching as doctrines the precepts of men."* Man's tendency is to want to create rules and regulations to legislate morality, but it never really works. When the religious man attempts this, he undermines the work of the Holy Spirit in bringing the believer into a true spiritual relationship with God in the new covenant age.

Birthing the Church

Luke 10:1-2 tells us that Jesus **appointed seventy others** *and sent them in pairs ahead of Him to every city and place He Himself was going to be laborers in the harvest.* Just as the Hebrew nation began with seventy of Jacob's family (plus Joseph's family already in Egypt), the church began with seventy laborers (in addition to the twelve). This passage tells us that, **seventy returned with joy,** *saying, "Lord, even the demons are subject to us in Your name." And He said to them, "I was watching Satan fall from heaven like lightning. Behold, I have given you authority to tread on serpents and scorpions, and over all the power of the enemy, and nothing will injure you."* **Luke 10:17-19**

The supernatural power of the Holy Spirit accomplishes the work of the new covenant and not by man's obedience alone.

Legalism that had gripped the Jewish leadership, particularly the Pharisees and scribes since the return from Babylonian captivity, was the environment in which the church would come to life. Jesus confronted the Pharisees in Matthew 23:4 when He said, *"They tie up heavy burdens and lay them on men's shoulders, but they themselves are unwilling to move them with so much as a finger."* The times were ripe for a new relationship with God, based upon His grace and the power of the Holy Spirit. The new covenant resolves all the shortcomings of the old covenant since it relies on the work and power of God. This covenant is a covenant of grace and not according to works.

From the Cross to Pentecost

Calvary fulfills the completed work of redemption with Jesus's sacrificial offering of Himself when He said, *"It is finished."* The fiftieth day after His resurrection, the Jewish festival of Pentecost became the day the Holy Spirit was bestowed on all who would believe in Jesus as Messiah, as promised by Jesus as well as other Old Testament prophecies, including Joel 2:28-29. In John 14:26, Jesus said, *"But the Helper, the Holy Spirit, whom the Father will send in My name, He will teach you all things, and bring to your remembrance all that I said to you."*

In Acts 2, the Holy Spirit is given as a gift when three thousand would exercise their faith in Jesus as the Christ, the One who forgives sin as opposed to the sacrificial system of the Law of Moses (Acts 2:38).

Man is not capable of being spiritual apart from the Holy Spirit. In John 3:6, *"That which is born of the flesh is flesh, and that which is born of the Spirit is spirit."* According to Paul in Romans 2:28-29, the spiritual man, the true Jew is the one who has a circumcised heart, *by the Spirit and not by the letter, and his praise is not from men, but from God.* Following the letter of the law can never bring anyone into a spiritual relationship with God, but instead only a religious one. The spiritual man learns the leading of the Spirit of God, becoming His son, His mature one (Romans 8:14). As Jesus taught in John 3:8, *"The wind blows where it wishes and you hear the sound of it, but do not know where it comes from and where it is going; so is everyone who is born of the Spirit."* The spiritual man allows the Holy Spirit to take him where He wishes.

Conclusion

It was no accident that the Jews could not find their spiritual maturity through the Law of Moses since it could not justify anyone, it would only bring one to a knowledge of his sin (Romans 3:20). From the first Pentecost when God delivered the Law of Moses to the people at Mount Sinai, the Hebrew nation struggled in their relationship with God since they could not fully trust Him to be all that they needed Him to be. Human effort is not the secret to a living faith in God, but seeking Him brings one to a place where God is everything he needs to find rest. An intimate relationship with Him brings the believer to rest. In Matthew 11:28-30, Jesus taught,

> *"Come to Me, all who are weary and heavy-laden, and I will give you rest. Take My yoke upon you and learn from Me, for I am gentle and humble in heart, and YOU WILL FIND REST FOR YOUR SOULS. For My yoke is easy and My burden is light."*

Chapter 34

BLESSINGS OF THE NEW COVENANT

There are many blessings of God filling the Old Testament for His people. One of the most important of these resides in Genesis 12:1-3 where God blesses Abraham if he leaves his country of origin for an unknown land. It is there that God would make him a great nation, bless him, make his name great so that Abraham would be a blessing. Through Abraham's willingness to leave his home for one not known to him, God would bless the nations, a new concept since God had just scattered the people from Babel in Genesis 11. The avenue to God's blessing follows this same pathway for all who choose to believe God's promises.

Paul teaches us in Ephesians 1:3, that the Father *has blessed us with every spiritual blessing in the heavenly places in Christ* (the new covenant). The Greek word for blessing is *eulogia* and it means a benefit bestowed on another. God has bestowed (aorist tense meaning something completed in the past) divine benefits on believers who are willing to leave their home as defined by the material world and perceived by the five senses and allow the Holy Spirit to lead them to a spiritual place Paul refers to as "*in Christ*." To know that this promise is real is to look at Abraham. In Genesis 24:1, Scripture says, *Now Abraham was old, advanced in age; and the Lord had blessed Abraham in every way.* As the father of our faith (Romans 4:16), he has paved the way for those who are of the faith of Abraham to also find all the blessings God has intended (see Galatians 3:9).

The Righteous Life

"Blessed are the poor in spirit, for theirs is the kingdom of heaven." "Blessed are those who mourn, for they shall be comforted." "Blessed are the gentle [meek], for they shall inherit the earth." "Blessed are those who hunger and thirst for righteousness, for they shall be satisfied." "Blessed are the merciful, for they shall receive mercy." 'Blessed are the pure in heart, for they shall see God." "Blessed are the peacemakers, for they shall be called sons of God." "Blessed are those who have been persecuted for the sake of righteousness, for theirs is the kingdom of heaven." "Blessed are you when people insult you and persecute you, and falsely say all kinds of evil against you because of Me." **Matthew 5:3-11**

In the Sermon on the Mount, Jesus laid out for the disciples the many blessings associated with the new covenant; there are conditions associated with each. The poor in spirit are those who recognize their spiritual helplessness. In Verse 4, mourners are those who are especially aware of their own sinfulness and the new covenant promises comfort. The gentle or meek have an inwrought grace of the soul, particularly toward God; it is the acceptance of God's unique plan toward the believer. In Verse 6, righteousness is not something that happens, but something that must be pursued. The righteous life is the blessed life.

The Value of Perseverance

The merciful are those who give mercy to those who are suffering; this characteristic is evidence of piety and devotion to God. In Proverbs 11:17, *The merciful man does himself good, but the cruel man does himself harm.* The pure of heart in Verse 8 are those who are completely transparent before God, honest, holding nothing back. And then there are the peacemakers, who, having received peace (Romans 5:1), they bring peace to others. Verses 10 and 11 address the persecuted, who willingly accept mistreatment for the sake of the gospel and their dedicated relationship to God through Christ. In James 1:12, *Blessed is a man who perseveres under trial; for once he has been approved, he will receive the crown of life which the Lord has promised to those who love Him.*

These blessings of God that Jesus spoke about include receiving the kingdom, inheriting the earth, being satisfied, receiving mercy, the ability to see God, and called sons of God. They all speak of a heightened relationship with God and come to the one who acknowledges his own poverty to be able to recognize the riches of God and His kingdom. In James 2:5, Scripture says, *Listen, my beloved brethren: did not God choose the poor of this world to be rich in faith and heirs of the kingdom which He promised to those who love Him?* James' reference to the poor of this world was not speaking of a lack of material things, but more importantly a Biblical evaluation that the value of the Kingdom far exceeds those of worldly things.

Worthy is the Lamb

Jesus had a powerful exchange with Thomas in John 20:28-29, when Thomas finally acknowledged Jesus as His Lord. Jesus made the following statement to him in Verse 29, *"Because you have seen Me, have you believed? Blessed are they who did not see, and yet believed."* Real faith, believing when there is no evidence, is always the primary roadway into the riches of the Kingdom. The object of that faith is in Jesus, the Christ, His identity, His character, and His nature. In Revelation 5:11-13, around the throne, John sees angels as well as the living creatures and elders with multitudes more all saying with their voices, *"Worthy is the Lamb that was slain to receive power and riches and wisdom and might and honor and glory and blessing."* In response, every creature in every place responds with, *"To Him who sits on the throne, and to the Lamb, be blessing and honor and glory and dominion forever and ever."* Jesus has earned the right to receive every blessing! Every blessing God has prepared for the church age is wrapped up in who Jesus is and what He accomplished.

Jesus says, *"blessed are those who hear the word of God and **observe it**"* (Luke 11:28). The Greek word used here is *phulasso* and it means to keep watch. Figuratively, it means to not violate the Word of God. That can only happen when we esteem and treasure the Word more than our necessary food (Job 23:12). The Word of God is an extension of Christ and His life (John 1:1) and those who embrace the Scriptures as such find the very person of Jesus.

Chapter 35

THE LAW FULFILLED

Jesus said He came to fulfill, not abolish the Law at the Sermon on the Mount so that a new relationship with God could be born. The Pharisees asked Him a question by trying to tempt Him in Matthew 22:36, *"Teacher, which is the great commandment in the Law?"* Jesus went on to quote Deuteronomy 6:5 (love the Lord with all your heart) and Leviticus 19:18 (love your neighbor as yourself) and then made the following statement in Verse 40, *"On these two commandments depend the whole Law and the Prophets."* These two principles point directly to and fulfill the Old Testament revelation of God.

God's Presence

When Moses came down off the mountain with the two tablets in Exodus 32, he observed the people, led by his brother Aaron, worshiping a golden calf. Although every one of the two million or three million people were eyewitnesses of God's miraculous deliverance from Egypt through the Red Sea, they were not willing to wait the forty days while Moses was on the mountain with God. They were still insecure about God's love. The miraculous demonstration of God's love toward the people was not enough to get them to recognize His personal love. It would take the appearance of the Divine Son to manifest His personal love to the world.

In Exodus 33, God told Moses to lead the people toward the promised land, but His Presence would not go with them because of their obstinance. Instead, an angel would lead them and drive out their enemies in the promised land. This distressed the people greatly; to please God, they put off their outward adornments (jewelry) as a sign of remorse. God promised Moses that His Presence would go with them in the form of the pillar of cloud by day and fire by night and would be with them throughout their time in the wilderness. It would take this physical manifestation of God's Presence to confirm His love. Without any vision of God, the people would be unrestrained (Proverbs 29:18).

HUSBAND AND WIFE

Paul defines for us the intended relationship that wife should have with husband and husband with wife in Ephesians 5. Verse 22 tells us that wives should submit to husbands as the head of the family. He is speaking about respect; the wife needs to respect the husband. On the other hand, husbands should love wives as Christ loves His church (Verses 28-29). What we have here is a picture of the difference between the old and new covenants. The emphasis of the old covenant believer is reverence of God and honoring others while the new covenant is all about love.

When you look deeply into Old Testament Scripture, you will see that the critical aspect of the peoples' relationship with God is the fear (*yare* - reverence, respect, honor) of the Lord. In Psalm 15, David asks the question, *who may abide in Your tent? Who may dwell on Your holy hill?* In Verse 4, this one, *honors those who fear the Lord.* This reverence and respect of the Lord is the avenue into His wisdom (Psalm 111:10, Proverbs 9:10, Job 28:28). The new covenant is all about the husband, the bridegroom, Jesus loving the wife, the bride, His church.

In Deuteronomy 6:4-5, *Hear, O Israel! The Lord is our God, the Lord is one! You shall love the Lord your God with all your heart and with all your soul and with all your might.* These Verses are foundational of the old covenant as the "creed of the Jews," the beginning of the "Shema," morning, and evening prayers. The Hebrew word translated one is *echad* and means not only one, but also unified. It speaks to the fact that Yahweh Elohim is not just the only true God, but He is unified as the trinity, to be revealed at the appearance of Jesus, the Messiah in the new covenant. Every Hebrew letter has a numeric value and the value of *echad* is thirteen. This is significant when you consider that *mashiach*, the Hebrew word for messiah and symbolic of the new covenant, has a value of 358 while the Hebrew word for Moses is *mosheh* (representing the old covenant) and its value is 345. The difference in the new covenant compared to the old is *echad*, one God, expressed in the command to love God. The new covenant *agape* love of God has not only visited man, but also indwells him.

Love Does No Wrong

In Galatians 5:14, Paul says, *For the whole Law is fulfilled in one word, in the statement, "YOU SHALL LOVE YOUR NEIGHBOR AS YOURSELF."* Some scholars suggest that the ten commandments can be segregated into two categories, the first five related to the love of God while the other five deal with the love of neighbor. This is consistent with the passage in Romans 13:8-10 in which Paul states that loving neighbor fulfills the Law, and he identifies the last five commandments as being *summed up in this saying, "YOU SHALL LOVE YOUR NEIGHBOR AS YOURSELF"*. He concludes in Verse 10, *Love does no wrong to a neighbor; therefore, love is the fulfillment of the law*. Love of God and neighbor completes the old covenant and becomes the foundation for the new covenant.

For the Law was given through Moses; grace and truth were realized [came into existence] *through Jesus Christ* (John 1:17). The person and work of Jesus Christ (Colossians 2:9) realizes the fullness of our relationship with God, grace defining His work and connects us to truth. Jesus did for us what we could not do for ourselves, the very definition of grace and He embodies the truth (John 14:6). The believer's faith in who Jesus is (*"Thou art the Christ"*) and that He accomplished full forgiveness of sin (1 Peter 2:24) motivates each one by God's *agape* love (2 Corinthians 5:14).

Royal Law

This kind of love, *agape* love starts with God. In 1 John 4:19, *We love, because He first loved us*. To know God is to know Him by His love. Everything that we learn about God is to bring us to His love. In 1 Timothy 1:5, *But the goal* [objective] *of our instruction is love from a pure heart and a good conscience and a sincere* [non-hypocritical] *faith*. James refers to this love as the royal (regal) law (James 2:8) and says that it should be applied without partiality, or one transgresses the law of Moses. In Leviticus 19:34, *The stranger who resides with you shall be to you* **as the native among you, and you shall love him as yourself,** *for you were aliens in the land of Egypt; I am the Lord your God*. The neighbor is anyone near you, no matter what culture, background, outward appearance, or belief system he may have. To love the stranger in this way is not a natural thing but requires a supernatural love to fulfill. The new covenant is the environment where God's love has been unshackled to operate without restriction.

Let all that you do be done in love (1 Corinthians 16:14).

Chapter 36

THE TRANSFORMATION OF SAUL TO PAUL

Jesus came to us two thousand years ago to introduce a new covenant, one that would solve the deficiency that the Law of Moses did not address. I am referring to the reliance on man to keep the Law. A good case study dealing with the transition from the old covenant to the new covenant is the process of Saul of Tarsus becoming the Apostle Paul. Looking at his life before and after his day of salvation through his own writings enlightens us in the conversion he faced.

Saul of Tarsus was raised the son of a Pharisee and followed in his father's footsteps, moving to Jerusalem as a young teenager to study the Law under Gamaliel. As a committed Jew, he grew up to be an esteemed Pharisee and was a leader against the Christian movement taking place after Pentecost. In fact, he was on his way to Damascus to arrest Christians for trial, *still breathing threats and murder against the disciples of the Lord.* It was with this mindset that Jesus visited him, blinding him, knocking him off his horse, and speaking with him directly. When Saul understood that he was facing the Lord and His name was Jesus of Nazareth, it became the most profound moment of his life.

Jesus told him that God was

"*rescuing you from the Jewish people and from the Gentiles, to whom I am sending you,* **to open their eyes so that they may turn from darkness to light and from the dominion of Satan to God**, *that they may receive forgiveness of sins and an inheritance*" (Acts 26:17-18). And in Acts 22:14-15, "*The God of our fathers has appointed you* **to know His will and to see the Righteous One and to hear an utterance from His mouth**. *For you will be a witness for Him to all men of what you have seen and heard.*"

It would be this personal experience with the Risen Lord that would strengthen him to be willing to suffer for this divine purpose.

THE SON REVEALED IN PAUL

For I would have you know, brethren, that the gospel which was preached by me is **not according to man**. *For I neither received it from man, nor was I taught it, but I received it through a revelation of Jesus Christ. For you have heard of my former manner of life in Judaism, how I used to persecute the church of God beyond measure and tried to destroy it; and I was advancing in Judaism beyond many of my contemporaries among my countrymen, being more extremely zealous for my ancestral traditions. But when God, who had set me apart even from my mother's womb and called me through His grace, was pleased* **to reveal His Son in me so that I might preach Him among the Gentiles**, *I did not immediately consult with flesh and blood, nor did I go up to Jerusalem to those who were apostles before me; but I went away to Arabia and returned once more to Damascus.* **Galatians 1:11-17**

In this passage, Paul is giving us insight into the transformation that needed to take place in Saul of Tarsus. The importance of Paul's "*revelation of Jesus Christ*" was the signature moment of Paul's ministry. It is important to understand that this revelation came directly from

God and not through a rabbi or some other spiritual leader even though he had been an enemy as a persecutor of the church. He also states that he recognized that his calling from God had been from the beginning, from his mother's womb so it was not anything he had accomplished. The revelation that accompanied his salvation experience would become a progressive revelation of the Son and he purposed to fulfill his commission as the apostle to the Gentiles after a visit to Arabia, some suggesting it was to visit Sinai to reexamine his spiritual roots. After returning to Damascus, he spent three years ministering there before going to Jerusalem to meet the other apostles.

In 1 Corinthians 15:6-8, Paul tells us that at least five hundred others saw the Risen Christ, including James, the half-brother of Jesus. In Verses 9-10, the experience humbled Paul, testifying that he was *"not fit to be called an apostle"* and then acknowledged that his ability to fulfill his ministry was only because of God's grace, namely His favor and empowerment. It was this reality that enabled him to devote himself completely to the divine task.

The Torah and the Temple

Paul identifies the impartation of God's life in him as necessary to His ministry to the Gentiles. Saul of Tarsus was a scholar of the Law of Moses, so he needed to understand this new life in the context of the Old Testament. The Jewish concept of religious life revolved around two foundations, the Torah and the temple. The Torah or Law of Moses established the ground rules for worship while the temple served as the center of religious and social life within the Jewish family. So that these pillars would become negotiable, God was making Himself real in Paul's life like few Old Testament leaders would experience. The fact that the gospel is not according to man (Galatians 1:11) fulfills itself in the new relationship with God, that believers are the temple, and the life of Jesus Christ received by faith fulfills the Torah.

Paul testified throughout his letters and ministry that Christianity was not a new religious system with seismic differences from Judaism, but its completion. This is clear in light of the fact that he never denied his Jewish faith but embraced it as a critical part of his new-found spiritual life. He writes in Ephesians 2:20 that Christianity is built on the foundation of the apostles (New Testament) and prophets (Old Testament).

Ultimately, Paul instructed his Jewish heritage that,

> *For I testify about them that they have a zeal for God, but not in accordance with knowledge. For not knowing about God's righteousness and seeking to establish their own,* **they did not subject themselves to the righteousness of God**. *For Christ is the end of the law for righteousness to everyone who believes.*
> **Romans 10:2-4**

When the believer connects with God on the basis of faith in Jesus as Messiah, he receives and becomes subject to His righteousness. This is the end (completion) of the law! In Verse 10, *for with the heart a person believes, resulting in righteousness, and with the mouth he confesses, resulting in salvation*. When the heart is truly engaged in faith, God's righteousness is the result.

Chapter 37

TWO GOATS

The most holy day of the year for the Jew is Yom Kippur, the Day of Atonement. It occurs amid a ten-day period of introspection and repentance. We find the description of its religious requirements in Leviticus 16. One aspect of this celebration is the role played by two goats.

Atonement

*"He shall take from the congregation of the sons of Israel two male goats for a sin offering and one ram for a burnt offering. "Then Aaron shall offer the bull for the sin offering, which is for himself, that he may make atonement for himself and for his household. "He shall take the two goats and present them before the Lord at the doorway of the tent of meeting. "Aaron shall cast lots for the two goats, one lot for the Lord and the other lot for the scapegoat [**azazel** - **goat of departure**]. "Then Aaron shall offer the goat on which the lot for the Lord fell and make it a sin offering. "But the goat on which the lot for the scapegoat fell shall be presented alive before the Lord, to make atonement upon it, to send it into the wilderness as the scapegoat."* **Leviticus 16:5-10**

There is great significance in the roles that the two goats play. One goat was the sin offering to the Lord, for the people. The High Priest would sprinkle the blood on the mercy seat (the lid that covers the Ark of the Covenant). The other was to be the scapegoat, *presented alive before the Lord, to make atonement upon it, to send it into the wilderness as the scapegoat.* God was separating the sins of the people from them *as far as the east is from the west* (Psalm 103:12). *The goat shall bear on itself all their iniquities* **to a solitary land;** *and he shall release the goat in the wilderness* (Leviticus 16:22). Wilderness is a type of the world system and signifies the separation of the believer from worldly influences.

Abraham and his Two Sons

This metaphor appears earlier in the Bible story, in relation to the father of our faith, Abraham. You see, Abraham had two sons, one referred to as the son of the bondwoman and the other, the son of the free woman (Galatians 4:30). Their origins also determined their futures. One was destined to be the sin offering while the other had his future tied to the scapegoat.

In Genesis 22, God told Abraham to offer his son, Isaac as a burnt offering to the Lord. It was a test. Abraham passed the test when he raised the knife to kill his son according to God's command. We know at the end of the story, that the angel of the Lord (could be a Christophany) stopped Abraham and instead provided a ram for the offering. Abraham was willing to follow through because he *considered that God is able to raise people even from the dead* (Hebrews 11:19). God promised blessings to Abraham through his seed and, according to Romans 4:21, he was *fully assured that what God had promised, He was able also to perform.*

Hagar and Ishmael

In Genesis 21, God told Abraham to honor his wife Sarah's wishes to remove the son of the bondwoman from the house and he did that with some hesitancy. In Verse 12, God said, *"Do not be distressed because of the lad and your maid; whatever Sarah tells you, listen to her, for **through Isaac your descendants shall be named**"*. Abraham took his first son and Hagar into the wilderness, providing only bread and water and left them to their own abilities to survive. In Verse 14, *And she departed [with her son] and wandered about in the wilderness of Beersheba.*

The Apostle Paul provides more insight into the relationship between the two sons with reference to their mothers in Galatians 4:21-31. In Verses 24-26, he identifies that the two mothers represent two covenants. Hagar represents Mount Sinai and *corresponds to the present Jerusalem* (old covenant) while Sarah, the mother of Isaac, the child of promise speaks to *the Jerusalem above is free; she is our mother* (new covenant). Paul's conclusion in Verse 31 is *So then, brethren, we are not children of a bondwoman, but of the free woman.* The sin offering represented by the first goat ties the new covenant believer to Calvary and the perfect sin offering of our Savior. Our life in Christ acknowledges our death on that same cross. In Galatians 2:20, *I have been crucified with Christ; and it is no longer I who live, but Christ lives in me; and the life which I now live in the flesh I live by faith in the Son of God, who loved me and gave Himself up for me.*

JESUS OR BARABBAS

There is a third appearance of the two-goat metaphor, found in the New Testament. In Mark 15:7-15, the Jews were given a choice by Pilate to release a prisoner condemned to death and they had two choices: a man named Barabbas or Jesus, "King of the Jews". It is interesting to note that Barabbas is an Aramaic name and is the combination of two words, *bar* meaning "son of" and *abba* meaning "father." Barabbas is the son of his father, the son of the world. We all know that the people wanted Jesus to be crucified, so much so that they were willing to release a robber and murderer. Not understanding the ramifications of their choice, they discarded the first goat and endorsed the second to go back to the wilderness with all his sins on him.

The Perfect Offering

Hebrews 9 addresses the implications of the offerings by the Old Testament priests, that they were not perfect since they did not remove the sin from the conscience. On the other hand, Christ's offering is perfect because of His precious blood, much more valuable than any animal sacrifice. Therefore, *how much more will the blood of Christ, who through the eternal Spirit offered Himself without blemish to God,* ***cleanse your conscience from dead works to serve the living God****?* (Verse 14) The perfect offering is one that cleanses the conscience, having removed sin's effects from each who believes to serve the living God. As the perfect offering, Jesus, the first goat is our answer to everything that separates us from our God while the second goat, our sin nature, should be relegated to the wilderness. *For he who lacks these things is shortsighted, even to blindness, and has forgotten that he was cleansed from his old sins* (2 Peter 1:9).

Chapter 38

BETWEEN HIS FIRST & SECOND COMINGS

Prophecy of a coming Messiah fills the Old Testament, much of it misunderstood by the Jew since the fullness of its understanding is seen through the lens of the New Testament. The greatest example of this misunderstanding may be Isaiah 53. Until the Jew sees Jesus as the object of this chapter, he continues living under a veil (2 Corinthians 3:14-16). The typical Jew of 2021 expects Messiah to be a coming king, taking charge of government and establishing His kingdom. Yet multiple prophecies of Messiah refer to Him as a suffering servant, particularly through Isaiah. Some Jews expect two different Messiahs, one like David (fulfilled in the Kingdom age) and another like Joseph, one who will be rejected.

Some verses/passages speak of both comings, including Isaiah 61:1-2, partially quoted by Jesus Himself in Luke 4:18-19. He was telling the Jews of Nazareth that He was fulfilling His first coming in their midst ("*Today this Scripture has been fulfilled in your hearing*"), but they did not accept Him at His word, and instead, they tried to kill Him. In Isaiah 61:1, *The Spirit of the Lord God is upon me, because* **the Lord has anointed me** *to bring good news to the afflicted.* He purposely left off the reference to His second coming in Verse 2, *the day of vengeance of our God.* Jesus Christ was telling them that He would be the Lord's anointed in both appearances, with the full authority of His Father to complete His work as the ordained Messiah and mediator of the new covenant. Scripture does not clearly spell out the conditions of the new covenant in the church age, but there are two passages that can give us some real definition.

Grace is our Instructor

In Titus 2:11-14, Paul speaks of both comings of Messiah beginning in Verse 11, *For the grace of God has appeared, bringing salvation to all men*. When Jesus came to earth two thousand years ago, He brought the grace of God with Him, it was part of His nature. In John 1:14, *And the Word became flesh, and dwelt among us, and we saw His glory, glory as of the only begotten from the Father, full of grace and truth*. This grace, manifested in His glory, defines the new covenant age of the church. Salvation is always a work of God and not men and must be a free gift (Ephesians 2:8-9).

Titus 2:13 encourages us to look forward to *the blessed hope and the appearing of the glory of our great God and Savior, Christ Jesus*, His second coming. In the meantime, Paul writes in Verse 12: *instructing us to deny ungodliness and worldly desires and to live sensibly, righteously, and godly in the present age*. It is the grace of God and not the Law that is the new covenant believer's instructor or trainer and this instruction points him directly to Calvary's cross, where he learns that the godly life is the by-product of self-denial and taking up his cross each day (Luke 9:23). In Luke 9:24, *"For whoever wishes to save his life will lose it, but whoever loses his life for My sake, he is the one who will save it."* It is the work of His cross that redeems the believer from every lawless deed (Titus 2:14) and allows him to experience salvation by Christ's life.

Mount Sinai

When you examine the delivering of the Law of Moses from Mount Sinai by Moses to the Jews, you will notice that in Exodus 32,

Moses smashed the two tablets of stone upon viewing the people, led by Aaron, worshiping the golden calf. It was not until Exodus 34 that God called Moses back to Sinai to receive the tablets again, which he did. What these events symbolize are the two comings of Messiah, the first one characterized by the rejection of Jesus by the Jews, *He came to His own, and those who were His own did not receive Him* (John 1:11). The church age is the period found between the two comings; between chapters 32 and 34 is chapter 33 and it gives a glimpse into the nature and dynamics of this period as defined by the grace of God.

> *Thus, the Lord used to speak to Moses's face to face, just as a man speaks to his friend. When Moses returned to the camp, his servant Joshua, the son of Nun, a young man, would not depart from the tent. Then Moses said to the Lord, "See You say to me, 'Bring up this people!' But You Yourself have not let me know whom You will send with me. Moreover, You have said, 'I have known you by name, and you have also found favor in My sight.' "Now therefore, I pray You, if I have found favor in Your sight, let me know Your ways that I may know You, so that I may find favor in Your sight. Consider too, that this nation is Your people." And He said, "My presence shall go with you, and I will give you rest." Then he said to Him, "If Your presence does not go with us, do not lead us up from here. "For how then can it be known that I have found favor in Your sight, I and Your people? Is it not by Your going with us, so that we, I and Your people, may be distinguished from all the other people who are upon the face of the earth?" The Lord said to Moses, "I will also do this thing of which you have spoken; for you have found favor in My sight and I have known you by name." Then Moses said, "I pray You, show me Your glory!" And He said, "I Myself will make all My goodness pass before you and will proclaim the name of the Lord before you; and I will be gracious to whom I will be gracious and will show compassion on whom I will show compassion." But He said, "You cannot see My face, for no man can see Me and live!" Then the Lord said, "Behold, there is a place by Me, and you shall stand there on the rock; and it will come about, while My glory is passing by, that I will put you in the*

cleft of the rock and cover you with My hand until I have passed by. **Exodus 33:11-22**

"My Presence Shall Go with You"

Having acknowledged that the Jews were a stubborn, rebellious people (Verse 3), God was threatening to send an angel instead of Himself to lead the people into the promised land against natives occupying the land, but later relinquished and instead He promised Moses that *"My presence shall go with you, and I will give you rest."* In this conversation, Moses acknowledges that His relationship with the Lord is unique, special, *face to face, just as man speaks to his friend* (see also Numbers 12:8), since *Moses was very humble, more than any man who was on the face of the earth* (Numbers 12:3). Just as Jesus humbled Himself to be obedient, even to death on a cross (Philippians 2:8), Moses needed humbling to be the mediator of the old covenant.

Moses recognized the grace of God on his behalf as he acknowledged the favor of the Lord and asked Him *"let me know Your ways that I may know You"* (Verse 13). The Apostle Paul understood that the only avenue to truly know God was to recognize that his natural strengths, gifts, and accomplishments were of no value *in view of the surpassing value of knowing Christ Jesus my Lord, for whom I have suffered the loss of all things and count them but rubbish so that I may gain Christ* (Philippians 3:8). Paul was referring to the cross as the means of going beyond the limitations of self to find an experiential knowledge of God. Moses had spent forty years in the wilderness until he would be ready to lead the people as God was leading him and he was now counting on God's grace to lead them.

God's Glory to be Seen

Moses also asked that the Lord would *"show me Your glory"* and His answer was that all the Lord's goodness would pass before him, revealing his grace and compassion. Before raising Lazarus in John

11, Jesus said to Martha, *"Did I not say to you that if you believe, you will see the glory of God?"* He was identifying that His miracles were a manifestation of God's glory, revealing His grace and mercy to multitudes and faith would be the vantage point by which believers would see. Paul wrote about this glory in 2 Corinthians 4:6 when he wrote, *For God, who said, "Light shall shine out of darkness," is the One who has shone in our hearts to give the Light of the knowledge of the glory of God in the face of Christ*. The Messiah's first coming would reveal God's glory and define the entire church age through His face, His presence. In Jesus's prayer to His Father in John 17, Jesus would give His glory, given by His Father to His disciples, *that they may be one, just as we are one* (Verse 22).

The Apostle Paul uses the term "in Him" or "in Christ" more than one hundred times in his letters to define the new covenant relationship believers have with God through Jesus Christ. It is the place where he is perfected in his position as a child of God and an identity into which he grows. In Exodus 33:21-22 above, the Lord identifies it as *a place by Me* and "*I will put you in the cleft of the rock*". The cleft speaks of a crevice in a rock, large enough for people to hide in or take shelter in and the rock is a clear reference to Christ (1 Corinthians 10:4). "In Christ" is our place of shelter, sealed in Him with the Holy Spirit of promise (Ephesians 1:13). "In Christ," on the other side of the cross, affords the believer not only protection, but also a perfect position where he can experience true intimacy with God through Christ.

Conclusion

Although the Old Testament saints did not clearly see the church age, God always intended it and revealed within the Scripture writings to those who would desire to truly know the Father, only possible through the Son, the Messiah. Knowing God in this way cannot happen through a religious expression, but will only take place through an intimacy, a spiritual relationship with Jesus Christ (*the king has brought me into his chamber* – Song 1:4). In 2 Corinthians 3:17-18, *Now the Lord is the Spirit, and where the Spirit of the Lord is, there is liberty. But we all, with unveiled face, beholding as in a mirror the glory of the Lord, are being transformed into the same image from glory to glory* [ever-increasing glory], *just as from the Lord, the Spirit.* Beholding the Messiah's glory in the details of life produces a transformation in ever-increasing measure so that the believer can more clearly reflect His glory.

Chapter 39

UPPER ROOM

Two important New Testament events occurred in an upper room. Most Christians are aware of the first one: the Last Supper. The second one took place after Jesus's ascension in Acts 1: the 10-day period waiting for the coming of the Holy Spirit. A look at these two events may give us special insight into the introduction of the new covenant as manifested at Pentecost in Acts 2. The upper rooms where these events happened were in many homes a room in the upper part of the house, used to receive company, hold feasts, and retire for meditation and prayer.

In Luke 22:11-12, Jesus instructs His disciples where they would celebrate the Passover meal. He told them that the owner of the house would *"show you a large, furnished upper room; prepare it there."* It was in this place that Jesus celebrated His last Passover until His Second Coming, alluding to the new covenant promised to Israel and the house of Judah in Jeremiah 31:31-34. The account then tells us that Jesus broke the matzah bread and proclaimed that it was His body *"given for you, do this in remembrance of Me."* In a few hours, that body would be offered as the Passover lamb.

The New Covenant in My Blood

After eating the Passover meal, He took the cup of wine and said, *"This cup which is poured out for you is the new covenant in My blood."* This wine signified His precious blood, which would be shed for the remission of sins in establishing the new covenant. There is only one reference directly to the new covenant in the Old Testament and that is in Jeremiah 31. The disciples thought that this covenant as promised to the house of Israel and house of Judah would be happening soon. No one understood that this new covenant would also establish a new relationship with God through the recognition of Jesus as Messiah, namely Christianity and the church age. That revelation would begin to take place in the next upper room.

In Acts 1:9-11, the disciples watched the ascension of Jesus. It was an incredibly powerful moment for each of them but left them all with many questions. What now? What do we do until He comes back?

Introducing the Holy Spirit

*Then they returned to Jerusalem from the mount called Olivet, which is near Jerusalem, a Sabbath day's journey away. When they had entered the city, they went up to the upper room where they were staying; that is, Peter and John and James and Andrew, Philip and Thomas, Bartholomew and Matthew, James the son of Alphaeus, and Simon the Zealot, and Judas the son of James. These all **with one mind** were **continually devoting themselves to prayer**, along with the women, and Mary the mother of Jesus, and with His brothers. At this time Peter stood up in the midst of the brethren (a gathering of about one hundred and twenty persons was there together), and said, "Brethren, the Scripture had to be fulfilled [Psalm 41:9], which the Holy Spirit foretold by the mouth of David concerning Judas, who became a guide to those who arrested Jesus.* **Acts 1:12-16**

There were about 120 disciples in that upper room, and they were *with one mind* and *devoting themselves to prayer*. Peter takes the lead by showing the others that Judas Iscariot's betrayal was not by accident, but in fulfillment of the Scriptures. He references that the Holy Spirit foretold it by David's Psalm 41. Since they had already received the Holy Spirit from the Risen Lord in John 20:22, they were now beginning to learn how to operate under His guidance and leading and experiencing His awe. The full empowerment of the Spirit would take place at Pentecost. This was similar to the response of the disciples to Pentecost in Acts 2:42-43 and 46-47,

> *They were continually devoting themselves to the apostles' teaching and to fellowship, to the breaking of bread and to prayer. Everyone kept feeling a sense of awe; and many wonders and signs were taking place through the apostles.* In Verses 46-47: *Day by day continuing with one mind in the temple, and breaking bread from house to house, they were taking their meals together with gladness and sincerity of heart, praising God and having favor with all the people.*

THE SPIRIT AND THE UPPER ROOM

One cannot understate the significance of the upper room. This room was reserved for special occasions, including meditation and prayer. In the new covenant, the believers' connection to the Holy Spirit is in the upper room. There is a spiritual war going on. In Galatians 5:16-17, *But I say, walk by the Spirit, and you will not carry out the desire of the flesh. For the flesh sets its desire against the Spirit, and the Spirit against the flesh; for these are in opposition to one another, so that you may not do the things that you please.* We learn how to walk by the Holy Spirit in the upper room, where the Spirit of the Lord is, where there is liberty (2 Corinthians 3:17). In the upper room, the flesh has no power.

The Bible teaches that man is trichotomous, meaning he consists of three elements: body, soul, and spirit. Each of these elements speaks to various sources of life. The Greek word for body is *bios* where we get the word biology. The physical body is the center of *bios* life. *Pseuche* is Greek for soul, the immaterial part of man that includes the mind, heart, emotions, and the seat of personality. This Greek word is the source of the English word psychology. For the natural (unregenerate) man, the life of the body and soul exist on the bottom floor of the house.

LIFE IN THE SPIRIT

The Greek word for spirit is *pneuma* where we get the English word pneumatic. *Pneuma* can be translated not only spirit, but also wind or breath. In Proverbs 20:27, the Scripture says, *The spirit of man is the lamp of the Lord, searching all the innermost parts of his being.* The human spirit is the part of man that connects with the Holy Spirit. In Romans 8:16, *The Spirit Himself testifies with our spirit that we are children of God.* The Holy Spirit resides in the upper room, and it is there the believer experiences His presence, just like the disciples. Access to the upper room is available to all who believe that Jesus is God and that He has paid the price for man's salvation. In John 3:8, "*The wind blows where it wishes and you hear the sound of it, but do not know where it comes from and where it is going; so is everyone who is born of the Spirit.*" Guidance by the Holy Spirit is always by faith.

Realizing the new covenant can only take place in the upper room. Fulfilling the new covenant utilizing old covenant dynamics does not work. In Matthew 9:17, Jesus taught, "*Nor do people put new wine into old wineskins; otherwise, the wineskins burst, and the wine pours out and the wineskins are ruined; but they put new wine into fresh wineskins, and both are preserved.*" The wine, symbolic of the new covenant, requires a new wineskin as presented in Hebrews 8:10-12. A New Testament believer living under the old covenant standards and its consequences will not be successful.

HIS UPPER CHAMBERS

Life in the upper room is best described by Jesus in John 6:63-65,

"It is the Spirit who gives life; the flesh profits nothing; the words that I have spoken to you are spirit and are life. But there are some of you who do not believe." For Jesus knew from the beginning who they were who did not believe, and who it was that would betray Him. And He was saying, "For this reason I have said to you, that no one can come to Me unless it has been granted him from the Father."

When the believer decides that he is willing to set aside the *bios* life and the *pseuche* life for the life of the *pneuma*, he moves to the upper room where the presence of God resides, and it is there he experiences *fullness of joy* (Psalm 16:11).

The Lord God of hosts, the One who touches the land so that it melts, and all those who dwell in it mourn, and all of it rises up like the Nile and subsides like the Nile of Egypt; **The One who builds His upper chambers in the heavens** *and has founded His vaulted dome over the earth, He who calls for the waters of the sea and pours them out on the face of the earth, the Lord is His name.* **Amos 9:5-6**

Chapter 40

LEARNING HOW TO FOLLOW

The story of the Bible is the history of God leading His people through the wilderness. The clearest illustration of this appears in the books of Moses and the records of the Hebrew nation and their road to the promised land. It proved to each of God's people that He would be their leader in the wilderness through Moses, as Psalm 77:20 says, *You led Your people like a flock by the hand of Moses and Aaron.*

Once God brought His people through the Red Sea and guided them to Mount Sinai, He defined for them a new relationship with Him through the Torah, His laws. Paul tells us in Galatians 3:23-24 that, *we were kept in custody under the law,* the law becoming a tutor (one who leads children) to lead us to Christ. God's plan was that He would be with them, His presence going before them as a pillar of cloud by day and fire by night. His presence would reside in the middle of all religious activities as the Ark of the Covenant to remind them of His holiness. The Father was guiding His people through the wilderness to find His Son. He was teaching them how to follow.

While the craftsmen constructed the tabernacle and all its elements, Moses would move his tent outside the camp as the tent of meeting where Moses would meet with God, evidenced by the pillar of cloud (Exodus 33:7-9). The people would spend more than a year in this place, getting oriented to this new way of experiencing God. Moses asked God not to lead them anywhere unless His presence went with them (Verse 15). God acknowledged that He would honor Moses' request in Verse 17: *The Lord said to Moses, "I will also do this thing of which you have spoken; for you have found favor in My sight and I have known you by name."*

Then in Numbers 10:11-12, the cloud left Sinai *in the second year, in the second month*, heading to Kadesh-Barnea (interpreted "a holy place in the desert"). It turned out to be a regular stopping point as the people wandered in the wilderness before entering the promised land. It also was from this place that Moses would send spies into the promised land in Numbers 13. God wanted them to **immediately** *go in and possess the land which the Lord swore to give to your fathers* and their descendants (Deuteronomy 1:8). That is not what happened.

Two Conclusions

God instructed Moses to choose twelve men who would sneak into the promised land to, *See what the land is like, and whether the people who live in it are strong or weak, whether they are few or many* (Numbers 13:18). In Verses 27-29, ten of them reported that the land was truly fruitful, but the people living in the land were too strong for them to overcome. These ten spoke for the masses. The other two had a different take. They told Moses, *"We should by all means go up and take possession of it, for we will surely overcome it"* (Verse 30). These two recognized that the people were not limited by their own ability, that the Lord would be the difference. Caleb & Joshua testimonies were not enough to sway the people and the nation ended up wandering in the wilderness for another 38 years.

What caused this difference in conclusions? It had to do with the relationship that each had to God. It is one thing to follow, it is another thing to trust in the leader. In Numbers 14:24, *"But My servant Caleb,* **because he has had a different spirit and has followed Me fully**, *I will bring into the land which he entered, and his descendants shall take possession of it."* God was promising Caleb that he and his descendants would enjoy the fruit of the promised land, unlike those who could not trust Him. In addition, God chose Joshua to succeed Moses in leading the people into the new land because he was *a man in whom is the Spirit* (Numbers 27:18), one who could be trusted because the Holy Spirit was leading him. According to Joshua 14:8, he says, *"I followed the Lord my God fully."*

THE SPIRIT OF CHRIST

If we are to fully follow God, we must believe in and trust in the One in whom we follow. Jesus left us with the Holy Spirit, the Spirit of Truth Who will guide us into all the truth. The Spirit is also known as the Spirit of Christ in Romans 8:9 and 1 Peter 1:11. Without faith, it is impossible to please God. Without faith in Who Jesus is, we become no more than people wandering in the wilderness, just like the nation of Israel. Moses was a great man of faith and Hebrews 11:27 tells us, *By faith he left Egypt, not fearing the wrath of the king; for he endured, as seeing Him who is unseen.* As God led Moses saw Jesus!

> *For all who are being led by the Spirit of God, these are sons of God. For you have not received a spirit of slavery leading to fear again, but you have received a spirit of adoption as sons by which we cry out, "Abba! Father!" The Spirit Himself testifies with our spirit that we are children of God.* **Romans 8:14-16**

The leading of the Holy Spirit produces maturity, sons rather than just children. This happens when we see our heavenly Father as *"Abba,"* Daddy and then our relationship with Him becomes personal and not abstract. It produces an assurance, a confidence that we truly are His children, part of His royal family. We are then able to trust Him no matter where He leads us.

Chapter 41

LORD OF ALL

"Once there was a boy... who listened to an old man. And, thus, began to learn about The Precious Present. 'It is a present because it is a gift,' the contented man explained. And it is called The Precious Present because it is the best present of all. When the boy asked why, the old man explained. 'It is the best present a person can receive because anyone who receives such a gift is happy forever.' 'Wow!' the little boy exclaimed. 'I hope someone gives me The Precious Present. Maybe I will get it for Christmas.'"

These are the first few sentences of a book written by Spencer Johnson entitled "The Precious Present." It is the story about a boy's enlightenment that such a gift exists and then his pursuit of it, without knowing what it was. It is a delightful read, and I will not expose the entire venture, but I will tell you that in the end, the boy found out that The Precious Present is not a thing, but a reality. Between the past and the future resides the present, the immediate moment we are living in. The boy spent each present moment trying to find this precious present that was staring him in the face. Do we do the same thing, chasing after something we already have?

The Greatness of the Cross

We cannot overstate the greatness of what Jesus Christ accomplished for each one who believes! In our acceptance and understanding of what it really means, we join the journey of this boy in finding out that the reality of our faith in what Jesus did gives greatness to our present moments. His accomplishment means that the pursuit of something already provided should not preoccupy the present moments. When Jesus said *"It is finished"* on the cross, He was confirming that His sacrifice, His blood was sufficient to satisfy the Father's justice. As a result, the believer no longer needs to perform for God's acceptance; faith guarantees it.

Just as Jesus died on a cross between two thieves, in the same way the present sits between two thieves, the past and the future. The past is trying to steal our present by the things done in the past and the unknown of the future can keep us in fear or bondage. Since the finished work of Christ has addressed both the past and the future, the present has no remorse.

The Great I Am

When Moses asked God His name in Exodus 3:13-14, *"God said to Moses, '**I AM WHO I AM**'; and He said, 'Thus you shall say to the sons of Israel, '**I AM** has sent me to you.'"* The Hebrew word *"hayah"* translated "I Am" is hard to translate since the ancient Hebrew has no present tense, but scholars suggest a good translation may be "the Lord [Yah – short for Yahweh] is the Lord." Hebrews 11:6 may give us insight when it says, *"And without faith it is impossible to please Him, for he who comes to God **must believe that He is** and that He is a rewarder of those who seek Him."* John 8:58 has another clue when Jesus says, *"before Abraham was, **I am**."* In each case, the Scripture was referring to the Lord in the present tense, the God of the present moment, as He has always been and will always be. In Revelation 1:8, Jesus says, *"'am the Alpha and the Omega,' says the Lord God, '**who is** and who was and who is to come, the Almighty'"*. Before Jesus was, **He is**.

Be Muzzled

On that day, when evening came, He said to them, "Let us go over to the other side." Leaving the crowd, they took Him along with them in the boat, just as He was; and other boats were with Him. And there arose a fierce gale of wind, and the waves were breaking over the boat so much that the boat was already filling up. Jesus Himself was in the stern, asleep on the cushion; and they woke Him and said to Him, "Teacher, do You not care that we are perishing?" And He got up and rebuked the wind and said to the sea, "Hush, be still [be muzzled]." And the wind died down and it became perfectly calm. And He said to them, "Why are you afraid? Do you still have no faith?" They became very much afraid and said to one another, "Who then is this, that even the wind and the sea obey Him?" **Mark 4:35-41**

In the above passage, Jesus is asleep in the boat with the disciples in the midst of a major storm. It had to be major since these storms were common to Galilean fishermen and yet they were afraid of perishing. Upon the realization that the situation was serious, the disciples woke Jesus up and accused Him of not caring that they might die; they only took notice of Jesus when the crisis was at hand. It is like us. Jesus is in our boat, but we only wake Him up when the serious storm arrives. After solving the immediate need with a miracle, Jesus identified His disciples' problem as a lack of faith. He demonstrated His deity by getting the weather to obey Him. Jesus was teaching the twelve that He had the ability to do the impossible. The fact is, once we believe that He is and that He is a rewarder of those who seek Him, we can believe that nothing is impossible with God. Jesus is Lord of all and becomes our Lord in the present moment through our faith in His Lordship.

Joined to the Lord

Paul teaches us that one's relationship to the Law of Moses can undermine his relationship to Jesus as Lord. In Romans 7:1-6, Paul uses the legal relationship of husband and wife to illustrate that the one married to the Law of Moses must die to that Law to be joined to Christ. In Verses 4-6:

> *Therefore, my brethren, you also were made to die to the Law through the body of Christ,* ***so that you might be joined to another****, to Him who was raised from the dead, in order that we might bear fruit for God. For while we were in the flesh, the sinful passions, which were aroused by the Law, were at work in the members of our body to bear fruit for death. But now we have been released from the Law, having died to that by which we were bound, so that we serve in newness of the Spirit and not in oldness of the letter.* **Romans 7:4-6**

It means that allowing the requirements of the Law to dictate one's relationship with God will *bear fruit for death*. When the believer dies to the letter of the law defined by the Torah and recognizes Jesus as the fulfillment of that law (Matthew 5:17), he enters into a spiritual relationship to Jesus as Lord, defined by *newness of the [Holy] Spirit*.

In John's Gospel, seven statements that Jesus made help define His Lordship. He said, "*I am the bread of life*" (John 6:35), "*I am the Light of the world*" (John 8:12), "*I am the door*" (John 10:9), "*I am the good shepherd*" (John 10:11), "*I am the resurrection and the life*" (John 11:25), "*I am the way and the truth and the life*" (John 14:6), and "*I am the vine*" (John 15:1). These seven "I am" statements speak about the diverse ways that He becomes Lord in a believer's life. They are eternal truths experienced in the present.

CRUCIFIED WITH CHRIST

The apostle summarizes this new relationship with the Lord in Galatians 2:19-21 when he says,

> *For through the Law, I died to the Law, so that I might live to God.* **I have been crucified** [perfect passive indicative] **with Christ**; *and it is no longer I who live, but Christ lives in me; and the life which I now live in the flesh I live by faith in the Son of God, who loved me and gave Himself up for me. I do not nullify the grace of God, for if righteousness comes through the Law, then Christ died needlessly.*

Each believer experiences the Lordship of Christ when he lives *by faith in the Son of God,* by acknowledging the reality that he has been *crucified with Christ.* The perfect tense means that it is a divine reality that has future results, and the passive voice indicates that the believer is receiving the action of being crucified, along with Christ.

In that day, "A vineyard of wine, sing of it! "I, the Lord, am its keeper; **I water it every moment***. so that no one will damage it, I guard it night and day."* (Isaiah 27:2-3). The reference here is to Israel, but it speaks to every new covenant believer as well. The Lord is not only our sustainer, but also our protector, every precious moment.

Chapter 42

THE BLESSINGS OF ABRAHAM

> *Now the Lord said to Abram, "Go forth from your country, and from your relatives and from your father's house, to the land which I will show you; And I will make you a great nation, and I will bless you, and make your name great; and so you shall be a blessing; And I will bless those who bless you, and the one who curses you I will curse.* **And in you all the families of the earth will be blessed."** **Genesis 12:1-3**

Over two thousand years before the Messiah would come to the earth as a man, God made some incredible promises to a man from a pagan part of the world who would be willing to obey *by going out to a place which he was to receive for an inheritance; and he went out, not knowing where he was going* (Hebrews 11:8). Simply on the basis of this kind of faith, God made promises to Abram, then changed his name to Abraham, that not only was he to receive the blessing, but that through him *"all the families of the earth will be blessed!"* God also promised that Abraham and Sarah would have a child when it was an impossibility by sight since Sarah was elderly and baron. This kind of faith places its total confidence in God's ability and trustworthiness, recognizing the greatness of God in light of man's shortcomings. As

Abraham considered his life as he was elderly, he recognized that *the Lord had blessed Abraham in every way* (Genesis 24:1). But how would *all the families of the earth* be blessed through the faith of a single man?

The Apostle Paul gives us an answer to this question in his letter to the Galatians in chapter 3. His argument to the church at Galatia is that our connection to the blessings that God promised to Abraham would not be through keeping the Law (of Moses), but through the Messiah and one's faith in those promises. He was stating, through the inspiration of the Holy Spirit, that through our confidence in what Jesus Christ had accomplished, we could receive the inheritance of these blessings. But how? Paul further explains this promise in Romans 4.

Righteousness of Faith

*For the promise to Abraham or to his descendants that he would be heir of the world was not through the Law, but **through the righteousness of faith**. For if those who are of the Law are heirs, faith is made void and the promise is nullified; for the Law brings about wrath, but where there is no law, there also is no violation. For this reason, it is by faith, in order that it may be in accordance with grace, **so that the promise will be guaranteed to all the descendants, not only to those who are of the Law, but also to those who are of the faith of Abraham**, who is the father of us all.* **Romans 4:13-16**

Paul states that it is through the righteousness of faith! Righteousness (e.g., justification) does not come to us through the works of the law, but always it is by faith alone in what God does (Romans 3: 20-21). This means that man cannot attain God's righteousness on the basis of enough works or the right kind of works, but through the agency of grace alone, meaning God's free gift (Ephesians 2:8-9). In fact, Paul tells us in Romans 11:6 that, *but if it is by grace, it is no longer on the basis of works, otherwise grace is no longer grace.* What a relief! This means that the blessings of God intended for *all families of the earth* are not dependent on human ability or effort. The Old Testament saints who operated by faith and considered *the children of the promise* (Romans 9:8) were also to be recipients of these blessings. Abraham's faith becomes the foundation of faith for the Jew and the Christian alike. It is no wonder that the location of Solomon's temple would be the very site of Abraham's willingness to sacrifice the promised child, Isaac in Genesis 22. Hebrews 11:19 tells us, *He considered that God is able to raise people even from the dead*, that God would have to raise Isaac from the dead since he was the avenue through which the blessings of God are realized, and God cannot lie.

When God introduced the new covenant as the Jews were being prepared for captivity in Babylon, He promised both the Northern (House of Israel) and Southern (House of Judah) Kingdoms to be recipients of this everlasting covenant. The Lord Jesus Christ (Messiah) is the mediator of this covenant, so its fulfillment takes place at a future time on behalf of the Jews. The Messiah takes up His throne during the Millennial Kingdom. Yet the fact that this new covenant promise was repeated to the Hebrew Christians tells us that it defines the Christian and his relationship to God.

Christ's Blood

*how much more will the blood of Christ, who through the eternal Spirit offered Himself without blemish to God, cleanse your conscience from **dead works** to serve the living God? For this reason,* **He is the mediator of a new covenant**, *so that, since a death has taken place for the redemption of the transgressions that were committed under the first covenant, those who have been called may receive the promise of the eternal inheritance.* **Hebrews 9:14-15**

The sacrificial offering of Christ's blood on the cross would be the spiritual provision for the believer's service to God. To fully appreciate this new relationship with his God, the spiritual man must recognize that the Messiah's blood has cleansed his conscience from dead works, meaning works like those commanded by the old covenant that can never provide freedom from the bondage of the covenant itself (Galatians 5:1). In fact, *you were called to freedom, brethren; only do not turn your freedom into an opportunity for the flesh* (e.g., dead works), *but* **through love serve one another** (Galatians 5:13).

Role of Works

Was not Abraham our father justified by works when he offered up Isaac his son on the altar? You see that **faith was working with his works,** *and as a result of the works,* **faith was perfected.** **James 2:21-22**

To complete this consideration of dead works, James tells us when our works line up with God's will, as was the case with Abraham's willingness to sacrifice Isaac in Genesis 22, then our faith and our works are working together, complementing each other with God's will and the result is the completion, fulfillment, perfection of our faith. This Greek word *"teleios"* can have the meaning of "being fully developed" or "being carried to the end." In either case, it brings us back to finding its ultimate conclusion and therefore brings us to serving one another in love.

Blessings of Abraham Found in the New Covenant

The blessings that God promised to Abraham that he would be a blessing to *all the families of the earth* are fulfilled in the new covenant, particularly the church age. Just as Abraham was blessed in every way by the end of his life, so the believer is promised *every spiritual blessing* in Christ (Ephesians 1:3). Since anyone who believes in the person and work of Christ receives the gospel, yet the entire world (see John 3:16) is the intended recipient. These spiritual blessings provide the enrichment of life that every believer seeks and referenced by Peter in 2 Peter 1:3, *seeing that His divine power has granted to us everything pertaining to life and godliness, through the true knowledge of Him who called us by His own glory and excellence.* These spiritual blessings are not measured in a material way as some merchants of spiritual blessings and those preaching the prosperity message might claim, that somehow God is interested in prospering every believer with material blessings.

The conclusion we can make from consideration of the blessings of Abraham is that the greatest blessings God has prepared for His people since He promised them to Abraham and his descendants are also meant for new covenant believers, which includes believers in the church age as well as the Millennial Kingdom and that these blessings are spiritual, meaning they have eternal value. When a Christian ministry promises someone blessings of God to those who will invest a certain amount or purchase a particular product, beware! An open, honest, and transparent relationship with God through King Jesus provides the real blessings. Jesus warned us all that, "*Truly I say to you, unless you are converted and become like children, you will not enter the kingdom of heaven. Whoever then humbles himself as this child, he is the greatest in the kingdom of heaven*" (Matthew 18:3-4).

Like so many Biblical principles that are the inverse from what the world values, the greatest in the kingdom is also a child in his/her heart. As Paul states in 1 Corinthians 1:27-28,

> *but God has chosen the foolish things of the world to shame the wise, and God has chosen the weak things of the world to shame the things which are strong, and the base things of the world and the despised God has chosen, the things that are not, so that He may nullify the things that are.*

The deepest relation with God and His real blessings is a paradox! The methods of the world and even the religious mind will never understand.

Chapter 43

THE EIGHTH DAY

Numbers have important meanings in Scripture. For example, the number four represents the world (four corners), five speaks about grace, six is the number for man, and seven references perfection or completion. But what about the number eight?

The number eight is incredibly significant such that it is used seventy-three times in the Bible. It is the symbol of resurrection and regeneration. In Bible numerology, eight means **new beginning**; it denotes "a new order or creation, and man's true 'born again' event when he is **resurrected from the dead into eternal life**." The first historic reference is to Noah and his family as *eight persons were brought safely through the water* (1 Peter 3:20). Those eight persons experienced a true new beginning once the flood receded. God also instituted a sign of the covenant He was making with Abraham in Genesis 17:12, that each child is circumcised on the eighth day. This covenant with Abraham represented a new relationship with God.

Above and Beyond the Seventh Day

The Hebrew word *shemoneh* is translated eight or eighth and is most likely derived from the root word meaning plumpness, as if a surplus above the "perfect" seven. Of course, the first mention of seven appears in Genesis 1 with the creation story, in reference to seven days as a week. Metaphorically, the eighth day takes us above and beyond the seventh day, the day of rest.

Two other Old Testament references to the number eight include 1 Samuel 17:12-14 indicating King David as the youngest of eight children, the eighth child and the one who would become known as *a man after My* [God's] *heart.* In 2 Chronicles 34:1-3, Josiah, one of only three good kings, became king when he was eight years old. In Verse 3, Scripture says, *For* **in the eighth year** *of his reign while he was still a youth, he began to seek the God of his father David.* A new beginning took place in Josiah's heart in his eighth year. It says he began to purge the images of other gods from Judah and Jerusalem. Both David and Josiah changed the course of history.

THE GREAT DAY OF THE FEAST

In Leviticus 23:33-36, the Lord institutes the Feast of Tabernacles (Sukkot) celebrated for seven days in fabricated booths as a reminder of the nation's exodus from Egypt. In Verse 36, *For seven days you shall present an offering by fire to the Lord.* **On the eighth day** *you shall have a holy convocation and present an offering by fire to the Lord; it is an assembly. You shall do no laborious work.* This eight day of Sukkot is also known as Shemini Atzeret and is a separate—yet connected—holy day devoted to the spiritual aspects of the festival of Sukkot. Part of its duality as a holy day is that it is simultaneously considered to be both connected to Sukkot and a separate festival in its own right. It is also referred to as *the great day of the feast.* John's gospel cites a particular event that occurred on that day in John 7:37-39:

> *Now on the last day,* **the great day of the feast***, Jesus stood and cried out, saying, "If anyone is thirsty, let him come to Me and drink. He who believes in Me, as the Scripture said, 'From his innermost being will flow rivers of living water."* **But this He spoke of the Spirit***, whom those who believed in Him were to receive; for the Spirit was not yet given, because Jesus was not yet glorified.*

This connection between the eighth day and the Holy Spirit is significant.

Anointing

A Hebrew word closely related to *shemoneh* is *shemen* and translated "anointing" in the King James version. In Isaiah 61:1, *The Spirit of the Lord God is upon me, because* **the Lord has anointed me** *to bring good news to the afflicted; He has sent me to bind up the brokenhearted, to proclaim liberty to captives and freedom to prisoners.* This is a clear reference to Jesus as Messiah and quoted by Him in Luke 4:18 fulfilled *in their hearing* (Verse 21). The Holy Spirit is the source of His anointing and will become that for the new covenant believer as well at Pentecost.

It is commonly accepted that God gave the Law to Moses on the Feast of Shavuot, otherwise known as Pentecost. This means that the old covenant and the new covenant recognize the same birthday, some 1,680 years apart. When the Holy Spirit came upon believers in Jesus as Messiah in Acts 2, it was the completion of the old work and the new beginning of a better covenant (Hebrews 8:6). Like Shemini Atzeret, it is connected to the old covenant, yet it is its own separate celebration, bringing in an anointing to the believer by the Holy Spirit not experienced by Old Testament believers. This eight day is really a brand-new week in God's sovereign plan to take us to the Second Coming of Messiah.

Messiah Fulfills the Seven Jewish Festivals

One last point is important to consider. The two comings of Messiah prophetically fulfill the seven major Jewish festivals, the ones occurring in the spring pointing to His first coming and the last three, which all happen in the fall, point to His second coming. Specifically, Rosh Hashanah is also the Feast of Trumpets and fulfilled by the rapture of the church, Yom Kippur (the Day of Atonement) looks to the Great Tribulation, and Sukkot, the Feast of Tribulation is a picture of the Kingdom age. If those connections are real, then the eighth day of Sukkot brings us to the end of human history and the new beginning is eternity, itself, a higher quality of life. Amen!

Chapter 44

THE MANTLE OF THE LORD

Elijah the Tishbite is one of the most notable and accomplished prophets of the Old Testament. He appears on the scene from nowhere in 1 Kings 17 to be a severe thorn in the side of King Ahab & Queen Jezebel of the Northern Kingdom and their introduction of Baal worship. Elijah was at the center of God's display of power in opposing the prophets of Baal on Mount Carmel in 1 Kings 18. During his public ministry, he found Elisha, the son of Shaphat while Elisha was plowing and *threw his mantle on him* (1 Kings 19:19). What was the significance of Elijah's mantle?

The Hebrew word for mantle is *adderet* meaning a sheepskin cloak or robe, but also has reference to glory. It was some form of outerwear in the physical realm, but it signified the glory of Elijah's ministry, the anointing that God had placed on Elijah. God used Elijah to confront not only Ahab, but also his son, King Ahaziah and King Jehoram, Ahab's son-in-law. Through Elijah, the Lord would continually press these evil kings to remind them of His ultimate authority and power. Elisha understood by this display of Elijah's mantle that he was promoted to take Elijah's place, to take his mantle. Elisha began by having a ministry to Elijah.

Chariots of Fire

Now fifty men of the sons of the prophets went and stood opposite them at a distance, while the two of them stood by the Jordan. **Elijah took his mantle** *and folded it together and struck the waters, and they were divided here and there, so that the two of them crossed over on dry ground. When they had crossed over, Elijah said to Elisha, "Ask what I shall do for you before I am taken from you." And Elisha said,* **"Please, let a double portion of your spirit be upon me.**" *He said, "You have asked a hard thing. Nevertheless, if you see me when I am taken from you, it shall be so for you; but if not, it shall not be so." As they were going along and talking, behold, there appeared a chariot of fire and horses of fire which separated the two of them. And Elijah went up by a whirlwind to heaven. Elisha saw it and cried out, "My father, my father, the chariots of Israel and its horsemen!" And he saw Elijah no more. Then he took hold of his own clothes and tore them in two pieces.* **He also took up the mantle of Elijah that fell from him** *and returned and stood by the bank of the Jordan. He took the mantle of Elijah that fell from him and struck the waters and said, "Where is the Lord, the God of Elijah?" And when he also had struck the waters, they were divided here and there; and Elisha crossed over.* **2 Kings 2:7-14**

In this passage, Elijah's earthly ministry ends as a chariot of fire takes him up to heaven. The power of Elijah's mantle is also on display as God divides Jordan's waters to allow its crossing. Before Elijah takes his chariot ride, Elisha asks him for a *double portion of your spirit be upon me*. The proof that the mantle still had its power manifests itself when Elisha uses it to cross over the Jordan again. As it turns out, Elisha would be responsible for twice as multiple miracles as Elijah to fulfill Elisha's request.

The Power of the Holy Spirit

We have a similar event take place with larger ramifications in Acts The Risen Lord has spent 40 days ministering to His disciples and all that remains is His final words and then His ascension. He tells those in His presence, *"but you will receive power when the Holy Spirit has come upon you; and you shall be My witnesses both in Jerusalem, and in all Judea and Samaria, and even to the remotest part of the earth"* (Verse 8). The commissioning of those who would take Jesus's place required the Holy Spirit, the Spirit of God's power to fulfill. Just like Elisha needed Elijah's mantle to complete his ministry, so the disciples needed the mantle of the Lord, His Holy Spirit, the Spirit of Christ (Romans 8:9).

Just as Elisha watched Elijah raised up in the chariot of fire, the disciples watched as Jesus was lifted up *and a cloud received Him out of their sight* (Verse 9). And just as Elisha received a double portion of Elijah's spirit, the disciples were promised that *he who believes in Me, the works that I do, he will do also;* **and greater works than these he will do**, *because I go to the Father* (John 14:12). Jesus also told them that it was necessary that He should go away so that the Holy Spirit would come upon them (John 16:7). The disciples of Jesus, not only the ones who walked with Him, would receive the extraordinary ability of the Holy Spirit to accomplish more than what Jesus did while walking the earth two thousand years ago.

In Acts 19:11-12, *God was performing extraordinary miracles by the hands of Paul, so that handkerchiefs or aprons were even carried from his body to the sick, and the diseases left them, and the evil spirits went out.* Consider how much more God can accomplish with multiple disciples like Paul, equipped with God's Spirit since the ascension of Christ. And this ability of God, the Mantle of the Lord resides in each one of us who believe!

Chapter 45

FROM RELIGIOUS TO SPIRITUAL

As a new believer, I tried my best to live up to the standards of God and what I thought He expected of me. Like Paul confessed in Romans 7, I learned that it was not possible to always do the things I have to do and to stop doing the things I should not. We all must go through this process to find the real life in God, where we are no longer putting any confidence in the flesh (Philippians 3:3).

Some think there is little difference between being religious and being spiritual, yet to God it is the difference between bondage and freedom, between law and grace (Galatians 5:1-4). The religious man preoccupies himself with the "letter of the law" while the spiritual man walks by the leading of the Holy Spirit and the "spirit of the law." The religious man tries to please God through human effort, a "good showing in the flesh," while the spiritual man is resting in his faith in God, knowing that there is nothing he can do to make God love him more. The principle of the temple illustrates the transition from the religious life to the spiritual life.

WE ARE THE TEMPLE

At Mount Sinai, God introduced the concept of the temple to the people of Israel in the form of a tabernacle, a temporary structure where the people would meet God and fulfill the requirements of the Law of Moses throughout the wilderness. Later, Solomon constructed his Temple in Jerusalem as a permanent dwelling for God. Zerubbabel and others rebuilt this temple and then later, after its destruction a second time, under King Herod.

In John 2, Jesus entered the temple and began turning over the tables of the money changers, exposing their unfair treatment of visitors by extorting excessive payments for animal sacrifices and the exchange of foreign currencies for the temple tax. Many religious people were profiting from the poor in the temple. Jesus's anger demonstrates just how important it is to have a cleansed temple.

Later in the chapter, Jesus identified the temple as His body rather than that large structure in Jerusalem where religious people met. In John 4, He spoke to the Samaritan woman about worship no longer needing to take place in any particular location, but the Father requires the proper heart that motivates worship (John 4:20-24). These passages reveal a change in the meaning and role of the temple in the new covenant. In 1 Corinthians 6:19, our bodies and not any physical structure are now the temple of God.

CLEANSING THE TEMPLE

The old covenant temple was a grandiose place of splendor and awe where the believer visited to fulfill his religious duties and to receive all necessary teaching. In this way, he could go there to be religious while maintaining his personal life separate from the religious. It reminds me of the view of the Emerald City that Dorothy and her friends had with all its magnificence and associated expectations. It was a wonderful place to visit, with the hope of receiving everything they needed to defeat the evil witch, but in the end, it was not home.

The new covenant temple goes with us wherever we go because it is us! God wants to make His home in us.

Many times, the avenue from religious to spiritual requires a refiner's fire (Malachi 3:2-3). God promises to *purify the sons of Levi and refine them like gold and silver.* Consider this story:

A woman went to see a silversmith in action. The silversmith explained that he had to put the silver in the hottest part of the flame to burn away the impurities. The woman asked if it was necessary for the silversmith to be always present. *"Absolutely,"* he answered. *"If the silver remains on the fire for a moment too long, it could be destroyed."* The woman asked, *"How do you know when the silver is refined?"* The silversmith answered, *"That's easy. When I can see my image in it."* This story illustrates that this work of God in each of us is so that the reflection of Christ would be visible to others.

Choosing That Which is Profitable

In 1 Corinthians 6:19-20, Paul tells the believer that he no longer belongs to himself, but he now belongs to God because he has been bought with a price. It means that the spiritual man no longer has a personal life, and he can now begin to recognize God's work within, as He rebuilds the temple. The religious man compartmentalizes his life to fulfill his religious requirements while maintaining his own personal life. The spiritual man recognizes he is now a work of God, a transformation rather than conformed by human effort. In Verse 12, Paul says, *All things are lawful for me, but not all things are profitable. All things are lawful for me, but I will not be mastered by anything.* In God's economy, I can choose to do anything, but I choose the things that are beneficial for me, the things that will not control me and cause me to sacrifice my liberty, my right to choose good.

The transition from religious to spiritual is the process of embracing the reality that we are the temple and Jesus will cleanse us from all unrighteousness. The night before His crucifixion, Jesus took time to demonstrate this principle to His disciples when He washed their feet (John 13). Peter had a tough time with it until Jesus explained that *"If*

I do not wash you, you have no part with Me." Spirituality happens when we let Jesus do His work in us.

The new covenant believer has the option of choosing a program of works, religious rites, or other human efforts to find and please God or he can decide to surrender to the will of God and His Word. One exalts himself because of performance while the other recognizes the transcendency of the work of God and allows Him to do what He wishes to conform each to the image of Christ (Romans 8:29). In Romans 7:24-25, *Wretched man that I am! Who will set me free from the body of this death? Thanks be to God through Jesus Christ our Lord! So then, on the one hand I myself with my mind am serving the law of God, but on the other, with my flesh the law of sin.*

Chapter 46

THE HEART OF THE MATTER

In 1 Samuel 16, God commands Samuel to go to the house of Jesse in Bethlehem to find a new king who would replace the rejected King Saul. Upon entering the house, Samuel was looking at Jesse's sons and wondering, *Surely the Lord's anointed is before Him.* The Lord corrected Samuel in Verse 7 by saying, *"Do not look at his appearance or at the height of his stature, because I have rejected him; for God sees not as man sees, for man looks at the outward appearance,* **but the Lord looks at the heart**". The wickedness of the heart is not always visible from the outside. Jesus illustrated this point with the Pharisees in Matthew 23:25-26 when He said, *"Woe to you, scribes and Pharisees, hypocrites! For you clean the outside of the cup and of the dish, but inside they are full of robbery and self-indulgence. You blind Pharisee, first clean the inside of the cup and of the dish, so that the outside of it may become clean also."* God is interested most in the condition of the heart.

God favored David because he was a man after God's heart, *who will do all My will* (Acts 13:22). The heart is the place where man's value judgments are determined, where man determines his priorities. Jesus said, *"For where your treasure is, there your heart will be also"* (Luke 12:34). The problem that man has is that his heart is "*desperately wicked* " in its unregenerate form and needs the work of a righteous God to test his heart and mind (Psalm 7:9). With all the corruption that one faces living in a fallen world and under the influence of fallen angel (Satan), man needs the spiritual guidance of the Lord of Righteousness. A conscious decision of the heart to recognize the authority of God and His Word and a willingness to obey puts the believer in line to receive the best of His bounty.

A Spiritual Man

For he is not a Jew who is one outwardly, nor is circumcision that which is outward in the flesh. But he is a Jew who is one inwardly; **and circumcision is that which is of the heart***, by the Spirit, not by the letter; and his praise is not from men, but from God.* **Romans 2:28-29**

When the heart is open to God, man invites Him in to accomplish what the man is not capable of doing. The spiritual man, whether Jew or Christian has allowed the Holy Spirit to circumcise his heart, a removal of excess skin that is symbolic of eliminating the excesses of life that only produce a compromised relationship with Him. These excesses may take on the form of too much of this or too many of that; to be filled with the Spirit is to be free of excesses (Ephesians 5:18). The son became a prodigal when he left his home of order and moderation for loose living.

Walking by the Spirit and not the letter (i.e., living under rules and regulations without the heart behind them) defines the one who is pleasing God and not man. Paul says in Philippians 3:3 that the true circumcision are those who *worship in the Spirit of God and glory in Christ Jesus and put no confidence in the flesh.*

The Power of Sin

The heart is also the place where the believer gains victory over the power of sin. The writer of Psalm 119 understood this well when he wrote verse 11, *Your word I have treasured in my heart, that I may not sin against You.* The believer wrestles with the power of the sin nature; the Word of God, treasured (placed in high esteem) in the heart provides the avenue to victory. Paul explains in 2 Timothy 3:16 that, *All Scripture is inspired by God and profitable for teaching, for reproof, for correction, for training in righteousness.* The authority of God's Word delivers the believer from all his carnal battles. In Psalm 24, King David asks the questions, *Who may ascend into the hill of the Lord? And who may stand in His holy place?* He is asking who has conquered his own fallenness. His answer in Verse 4 is, *He who has clean hands and a pure heart, who has not lifted up his soul to falsehood and has not sworn deceitfully.* Since his heart is continuously under the authority of the Word of God, God is consistently convicting David to let that authority deliver David's heart.

It is Time to Risk it All

What God wants from His people is an honest, transparent relationship in which there are no secrets. Jesus declared in the Sermon on the Mount, *"Blessed are the pure in heart, for they shall see God."* This purity of heart includes the sense not only of clean, but also genuine, real, not phony or hypocritical. The one who approaches God on the basis of transparency is the one who trusts God to his own hurt; he is risking it all. But is not that exactly what God asks of the one whom He invites into His sanctuary. Placing one's confidence completely in the Person and work of Jesus Christ is to deny that any reliance on personal ability or performance makes any difference with God. David understood this reality when he said in Psalm 27:4, *One thing I have asked from the Lord, that I shall seek: that I may dwell in the house of the Lord all the days of my life, to behold the beauty of the Lord and to meditate in His temple.*

God is looking for anyone willing to make that kind of commitment to Him. In fact, in 2 Chronicles 16:9, *For the eyes of the Lord move to and fro throughout the earth* **that He may strongly support those whose heart is completely His**. This kind of relationship with Him requires the whole heart, not holding back out of fear or feelings of unworthiness. The measure of a godly man is in his confidence in Who God is and what He has accomplished to man's benefit.

The heart of the matter is a matter of the heart.

www.ingramcontent.com/pod-product-compliance
Lightning Source LLC
LaVergne TN
LVHW091542070526
838199LV00002B/162